Project Management Success with CMMI®

Project Management Success with CMMI®

Seven CMMI Process Areas

James Persse

PRENTICE
HALL

Upper Saddle River, NJ • Boston • Indianapolis • San Francisco
New York • Toronto • Montreal • London • Munich • Paris • Madrid
Capetown • Sydney • Tokyo • Singapore • Mexico City

Many of the designations used by manufacturers and sellers to distinguish their products are claimed as trademarks. Where those designations appear in this book, and the publisher was aware of a trademark claim, the designations have been printed with initial capital letters or in all capitals.

The author and publisher have taken care in the preparation of this book, but make no expressed or implied warranty of any kind and assume no responsibility for errors or omissions. No liability is assumed for incidental or consequential damages in connection with or arising out of the use of the information or programs contained herein.

The publisher offers excellent discounts on this book when ordered in quantity for bulk purchases or special sales, which may include electronic versions and/or custom covers and content particular to your business, training goals, marketing focus, and branding interests. For more information, please contact:

U. S. Corporate and Government Sales
(800) 382-3419
corpsales@pearsontechgroup.com

For sales outside the United States, please contact:

International Sales
international@pearsoned.com

This Book Is Safari Enabled

The Safari® Enabled icon on the cover of your favorite technology book means the book is available through Safari Bookshelf. When you buy this book, you get free access to the online edition for 45 days.

Safari Bookshelf is an electronic reference library that lets you easily search thousands of technical books, find code samples, download chapters, and access technical information whenever and wherever you need it.

To gain 45-day Safari Enabled access to this book:

- Go to http://www.prenhallprofessional.com/safarienabled
- Complete the brief registration form
- Enter the coupon code 8UD6-PP2E-31M6-ZLDY-5XB3

If you have difficulty registering on Safari Bookshelf or accessing the online edition, please e-mail customer-service@safaribooksonline.com.

Visit us on the Web: www.prenhallprofessional.com

Library of Congress Cataloging-in-Publication Data

Persse, James R.
  Project management success with CMMI : seven CMMI process areas / James Persse.
      p. cm.
  Includes index.
  ISBN 978-0-13-233305-4 (hardcover : alk. paper) 1. Project management. 2. Capability maturity model (Computer software) 3. Computer systems. I. Title.
  T56.8.P48 2007
  658.4′04—dc22

                                                          2007014367

ISBN-13: 978-0-13-233305-4
ISBN-10:   0-13-233305-8
Text printed in the United States on recycled paper at Courier in Westford, Massachusetts.
First printing, June 2007

For John Patrick, Thomas, and Maggie Persse

Contents

Preface

This book is intended to help shed some practical light on how companies can use process to help promote and achieve project management success. The term *project management success* can, of course, mean many different things. The definition will vary from company to company, and this can be particularly true for technology companies. The nature of their work, their industrial focus, their size, the makeup of different customer bases—all of these contribute to how a project is viewed, managed, and in the end deemed successful. And so this book will begin with a look at what the domains of project management typically entail, what performance factors are typically pursued, and what measures (or perceptions) usually shape the picture of success.

But first, I offer a few quick words about the process center of this book, the Capability Maturity Model Integration (CMMI), and about the book itself.

The Purpose of This Book

This book explains how the Capability Maturity Model Integration, specifically CMMI-DEV, version 1.2, can be used to foster project management success in technology development shops. More specifically, I discuss how the seven Process Areas defined for Maturity Level 2 particularly address the needs of project management in shops large and small.

This book—and I have kept its focus condensed to the realm of project management—is not intended as a full-bore explanation of all 22 Process Areas in CMMI. Nor is it positioned as a tome on process improvement or what might be called the art of project management. This book takes a practical approach to the business and operational needs of project management, illustrates these against the recommendations contained under CMMI Maturity Level 2, and then describes ways and methods of realizing these recommendations in your organization.

If you read through this book carefully, I hope that in the end you'll be able to better appreciate four factors relevant to CMMI, process improvement, and project management:

1. The general requirements for project management success
2. The general scope and purpose of CMMI
3. The structure, use, and benefits to be derived from CMMI Maturity Level 2
4. The complementary relationship that can exist between CMMI and project management bodies of knowledge such as the Project Management Body of Knowledge (PMBOK) by the Project Management Institute (PMI).

The Audience for This Book

This book has been designed for two distinct but related audiences: project managers and process managers. Both of these groups should find value in the ways that CMMI can contribute to the management of technology projects and connect with specific project management disciplines, as well as how it can support environments in which these disciplines have not yet been introduced.

Project Managers

If you are a project manager, you may come to this book with a Project Management Professional (PMP) certification or you may not. You may be certified by the American Management Association (AMA). You might have no formal credentials but possess solid management and organizational skills. You might work in a formalized environment—one supported by long-standing methods and practices. Or you might operate in a more freeform culture, one with a get-up-and-go approach to doing business. Whatever the situation, project managers remain the driving force behind the coordinated execution of project work in any enterprise, so this book is written especially to address the issues that surround that mission.

The intention of the book is to introduce you to what might be new techniques and management strategies founded in CMMI, not as a total or complete project management solution, but rather as a foundation for growing a capable and effective project management program that can help you better achieve your tactical goals and objectives.

Process Managers

This book is also intended for process managers. In the technology industries, the term *process manager* has been floating around more and more lately (and that's a positive thing), but unlike project managers, process managers' roles and requirements have yet to be solidly defined. They can vary widely from shop to shop. However, the generic function should be recognized. The process manager is the person in an organization who manages that organization's process program and is generally responsible for the way it is implemented, measured, and maintained. And while there is a PMP designation for project managers, there is no similar designation for process managers. You might assign to the position a Six Sigma black belt, an ISO auditor, or a CMMI lead appraiser, but those are all individual designations. Whoever takes on the role takes on an important responsibility. Process managers serve at the strategic level of operations; the programs they maintain define how their organizations work. And so this book should be of interest to process managers, particularly with regard to their role in supporting project development and management activities.

The methods and process disciplines we discuss in this book, based on CMMI (and related from time to time to the PMI's PMBOK), can be shaped and tailored to form an evolving process program, or they can be borrowed and trimmed to extend existing process programs. An appreciation for how CMMI can contribute to project management success, within a PMBOK environment or even as a PMBOK alternative, will serve process managers well.

How This Book Is Organized

This book is organized into three general sections.

In the first two chapters, we look at the overall structure of CMMI, explore its focus and purpose, and discuss how one slice of the model—the view from Maturity Level 2—can be used to augment successful project management in a technology shop. We also begin to relate the seven Process Areas typically found at Level 2 to the Knowledge Areas and Process Groups of the PMI's PMBOK.

Then, in Chapters 3 through 9, we discuss the Specific Goals and Specific Practices of the following seven Process Areas with a view toward implementation for project control:

- Project Planning
- Project Monitoring & Control
- Requirements Management
- Configuration Management
- Supplier Agreement Management
- Measurement & Analysis
- Process & Product Quality Assurance

In Chapter 10, we look at the Generic Goals and Generic Practices designed to support these Level 2 Process Areas.

Finally, in Chapter 11, we discuss how to integrate the functions and operations of Maturity Level 2 into a well-founded project management program, one based on the principles of process improvement, one built to coexist within the framework of the PMBOK, or one that can be used by project managers outside of, or as an alternative to, the PMBOK.

Let's begin with an overview of process itself and the case that can be built about the relationship between process and project management success.

Acknowledgments

I'd like to thank the following for their help in the realization of this work: Linda Fernandez, whose early reviews and comments strengthened the recommendations in each chapter; West Wicker, who suggested the original idea to me; and Edgar Ulmer, Fritz Lang, Linda Wertmuller, and James Whale, for providing general guidance.

I'd also like to express thanks to the various corporate officers and IT professionals who allowed me to quote their views in this book.

About the Author

James Persse has 18 years of experience providing process improvement design and consulting services to both large and small technology organizations. His specialties include CMMI, ISO 9001:2000, Six Sigma, and ITIL. He holds a doctoral degree in Information Technology Management with an emphasis in process improvement.

He has worked with a diverse client base that includes T-Mobile USA, Athena Technologies, the U.S. Department of Defense, Celerity Technical Services, Pitney Bowes International, MCI, BellSouth Science and Technologies, and Palmetto GBA.

He is the author of the following books:

- *Process Improvement Essentials: CMMI, ISO 9001, Six Sigma* (O'Reilly Media, 2006)
- *Implementing the Capability Maturity Model* (John Wiley and Sons, 2001)
- *Bit × Bit: Topics in Technology Management* (Little Hill, 2000)

Dr. Persse can be reached at jpersse@AltairSol.com or jrp@persse.com.

Chapter 1

Introduction

When designed properly, process programs can drive the business forward by operationalizing the mission and goals of the organization. It can serve to articulate—through structured expectations—the organization's goals, placing importance on processes that help the organization achieve these goals.
John Cline, CEO of eTrials, Inc.
Data management for clinical drug trials

A few years back I was consulting with a company called Impetus[1] in a northwest suburb of Atlanta. Impetus produced asset management software for manufacturers in capital-intensive industries: oil refineries, power plants, pulp and paper mills, and so on. I was brought in to help establish a process management program based on CMMI. The company was having a hard time getting its software releases out the door on time and intact. As a consequence, its market position was suffering. Management thought the introduction of internal workflow controls might help. CMMI looked like it might hold some keys.

When I came into the company, the first two operational areas I began to look at were Project Planning and Project Monitoring & Control, two

---

1. The case studies presented in this chapter are accurate; names of companies and people have been changed.

1

core CMMI Process Areas. I figured that whatever the release problems might be, they would probably at least evidence themselves in one of these two realms.

As part of my initial investigation, I interviewed the software group's project managers, including a bright, energetic guy named Brick Weathers. Brick had been with the company about three years and was managing the 5.5 release, one of the releases that appeared to be going well. I thought if I could find out what his secret was, maybe we could institutionalize that for the other teams.

Brick did not hesitate to tell me what his secret was—once I confirmed that I'd keep the source confidential. Right off the bat, he admitted it was not an intuitive aptitude for dealing with people. And it was not a heightened attention to administrative detail. Here was his secret to success:

> Always maintain three versions of the project schedule.
>
> Make sure the one you give to management says everything's on track. Make sure the one you give to your project team says everything's off track, so pick up the pace. And the third one, well, make sure that one's real because that's the one you manage by.

So that was Brick's methodology for managing project schedules. However, it was not one I was going to propose we set up as company policy.

As it turned out, the 5.5 release was in just as much trouble as all the others. Brick's approach simply forestalled attention to the release until it had reached a crisis pitch. Then his team got every resource the company could muster.

In fact, that was the way everyone at Impetus managed projects. Brick's secret actually had been institutionalized; it was just a secret institutionalization. The philosophy was this: Avoid pressure, negotiation, and accountability by avoiding the spotlight; then once the whole company was in the same boat as you, plea for patriotic support.

Another case comes to mind. Two years ago I was contracted by a commercial software development shop called SoftMil. SoftMil was owned by a much larger corporation called SystemAmerica (SA), which dealt a lot with U.S. Department of Defense agencies. SA wanted SoftMil to achieve CMMI Maturity Level 3 so that SA could bid on lucrative defense contracts. My job was to get the program in place, exercise it across a series of internal projects, and then arrange for a formal company-wide appraisal.

Beginning pretty much from scratch, we were able to build the program over a series of months, and a pretty good program at that. But when it came time to begin using it, I began to get conflicting messages from the project management office. This office was directed by a fellow named Mike McScottle, a guy with "PMP" stamped prominently on his business card. Mike administered the assignment of project managers and facilitated that reporting chain up through executive management. The point of contention was that Mike's project managers were not deploying the process program to new projects. I went to see him about this. Had we misdesigned things? No. Were the right assets not ready? No. Well, then what?

Mike said it was simply a timing issue. He explained that he assigned particular project managers to particular customer projects with the right personality mix in mind, with sensitivity to the project manager's individual approach. To mess with that now by introducing new methods and procedures would jeopardize project equilibrium. He wanted to wait for the right time to roll the program out, a time when the right "client-culture mix" came along.

Now, I am not sure I know exactly what a client-culture mix is, but at the time it didn't sound like "we'll do it" to me. Needless to say, the Level 3 program stalled in the hands of people who did not want to learn it or use it. Last I heard, SoftMil had abandoned its process initiative altogether and the company, having lost most of its project business, supported itself mainly through staff augmentation. SA shifted its CMMI directive to another internal division.

In the field of technology development, an organization's ability to successfully manage its project work is an indication of its overall ability to successfully manage itself. Today we have the skilled resources and tools we need to develop and deploy the most sophisticated of technology systems. Technical innovation and complexity are no longer the impediments to achievement they once were. More and more, the emerging differentiator is management: management at the strategic level, at the program level, and perhaps most essentially, at the project level.

When you look at it in a pure light, almost all organizational success comes from project success—because almost all organizational work is organized into project initiatives. That's true for just about all of corporate America, not just technology shops. But this trait has a tendency to carry more and more weight in technology shops because today's technology projects carry the full weight of the business mission on their shoulders.

And so it's important today for technology shops to embrace the proper form and function of project management, to view it as an essential component to a responsive and accountable management program, and to ensure that competent project management skills and practices are in place in the shop.

That brings us to the topic of process. The terms *process, process improvement*, and *process management* are being tossed around a lot these days in discussions of management and organizational efficiencies. But many times the rhetoric has little push behind it. Many of the executives and managers I know have an intuitive appreciation for process and its relationship to sound operations, but their practical understandings—and often their practical experiences—bring out concerns of overhead, inflexibility, and uncertain investment. Process seems by default to be heavy to them. That's an improper perception, and it's one I deal with continually in my practice as a process consultant.

The important point is that process does not have to be heavy, and it does not have to stiffen an organization. It need not require a large investment (although it will require some kind of investment), and it need not add a layer of overhead to a company's layout.

That's what process does not have to be. What it should be is a carrier of corporate values.

Project Management as Value Management

Look at any successful company and you'll see a distinct, discrete, and tangible corporate culture. Many companies that fail, that fade from the market scene, do so because they were not able to determine who they were within that market; they could not solidify an image of what they were focused on or what they brought to the table. Successful companies invariably achieve identity, focus, and purpose—big success or small success.

Culture is a strong force in any company. It may be the strongest force. It's the shape of the organization, the conduct and habits of its people. It's the way we do things around here. But it is also pretty much invisible. You always feel culture, but you don't always see it. Process can be seen as a very real and visible extension of culture. It is culture on paper. It is culture you can see, manage, measure, bend, and improve.

The view that culture is itself process is not a common one, even among process people. But it is true. Culture is a pattern for behavior; it governs action, it directs energies, it carries the unspoken rules of the workplace. When you create a well-designed process program to manage certain aspects of your operations, all those things should hold true as well. Process needs to mirror the culture because the ultimate goal of any process is to promote the culture, to help it succeed.

I don't think any experienced, considerate manager would negate the value of culture within an organization. They might wish to *change* some aspects of it, but I doubt they'd want it removed altogether. Culture is generally viewed as a positive force.[2] Yet many of those same managers flinch at the idea of process. I think they would flinch less if they simply equated process with cultural value.

Any process is a carrier of value. Here's a quick example. Every morning I drive to the office. I leave at a regular time. I follow a regular route. I follow this process because it has been shown over time to get me to work in a pretty efficient way by minimizing congestion, stoplights, and so on. That reflects what's valuable to me: I want to get to the office at a certain time every morning; I don't like idling on busy thoroughfares. Someone else with different values might take a different route. For example, a person might take a longer way, following the school bus because his or her daughter is on board.

The same approach should be evident in a project planning process or a requirements management process or a status reporting process. The steps in those processes should promote activities that are beneficial to

---

2. Except, of course, in highly dysfunctional organizations, where negative cultures can corrode even the most talented and dynamic of groups.

the mission of the organization. They should help realize organizational value. Process for the sake of process is no good to anyone. Process linked to cultural value is usually good for everyone.

Recently I was speaking with John Cline, the founder and CEO of eTrials, Inc. eTrials builds and markets products and services that help pharmaceutical companies manage the mountains of data that must be collected, analyzed, and interpreted during clinical drug trials.

Like most entrepreneurs, John started eTrials on a run-and-gun basis, doing everything and anything he could to keep the company growing and viable. Not surprisingly, in those early days eTrials had little use for formal process. But within a few years the company assumed a firm spot in its marketplace. Growth continued, and John was able to take the company public. Over time, process became more and more important to eTrials. When I spoke with him, he reinforced this idea of process as a carrier of culture. In his words:

> When designed properly, process programs can drive the business forward by operationalizing the mission and goals of the organization. It can serve to articulate—through structured expectations—the organization's goals, placing importance on processes that help the organization achieve these goals.

The phrase I like in that comment is "structured expectations." That's a great way to define what process can be. It's a way to formally define what is expected in terms of activity, communications, and output—expectations that reflect standards for quality, performance, and accountability. Because eTrials serves a heavily regulated industry, it developed an innate appreciation for process—and not process conducted solely to exert control over employees. John notes that that approach "has the potential to minimize creativity and individual initiative, which is never good for an organization." That's a tip I'd like to share with everyone thinking about embarking on a process program of any kind. For eTrials, process has become a way to promote and protect not only its own missions but also those of its pharmaceutical clients and industry regulatory bodies.

Everything we have mentioned to this point complements the realm of project management. Project management shares this trait with process management: Its job is to fulfill the mission of the organization. Well-functioning project management will reflect the culture just as process management does. Those elements of project work being managed are those things that the company holds important. In some shops, budget might take precedence over schedule. In others, resource levels might be the key focus. For others, it might be scope. And so, while project management should be recognized as an independent discipline in the fields of management science and organizational design, it should not operate as an independent discipline.

Some disciplines need to operate independently of the organizational mission. Accountants are bound to use generally accepted accounting principles whether the company is crazy about them or not. Rocket scientists honor Galilean trajectory curves no matter what the culture at large thinks about Galileo. But that's not true when it comes to project management. Project management that is not anchored in corporate values or to the corporate mission becomes management by personal preference. Whatever it is that's important to the individual project manager—scope, schedule, cash—will receive the bulk of management energy. That's fine as long as the project manager happens to be in sync with corporate goals; but happenstance is no way to run a business.

That's why project management and process (both process management and process improvement) have a true affinity for each other. When you link project management to a process program born out of the organization's culture, you end with a view of project management as value management. Through established policies, procedures, and workflows, project management helps the organization reach success according to the organization's own definition. And that may well be the best kind of project management program to have.

Visible Management through Process

The theme of this book is that technology shops will be able to plan and run development projects more effectively when they base their approach to project management in process. That approach works best when supported by three tactics.

1. Process should be shaped to promote corporate values.
2. Process should be only as heavy as it needs to be—and often enough that is light.
3. Process should be shaped to make progress visible.

We've already touched on points 1 and 2. Now let's take a quick look at point 3.

Brick Weathers at Impetus was what I call a black-box project manager. He preferred to work on the inside, keeping the details out of sight of anybody who might make independent decisions or draw independent conclusions from the data. He operated on the "Trust me, I know what's best" principle. Maybe he believed that really was the way to manage. Maybe he did it because his managers provided no other options. Whatever the reason, there are plenty more project managers out there just like Brick. They feel that any other approach constitutes micromanagement and so should be avoided. They believe that successful project management begins and ends with talented project managers.

That brings us to a subtheme of this book. In the following chapters, we'll look at how process can aid project management. More specifically, we'll look at how the Capability Maturity Model, the well-known process improvement framework from the Software Engineering Institute, can be used to build an effective project management program. And on top of that, we'll look at how project management standards such as the Project Management Body of Knowledge (PMBOK) from the Project Management Institute (PMI) can find full and powerful expression in programs based on CMMI. The purpose of the PMI's PMBOK is to prepare project managers to manage with eyes wide open, with an understanding of a project's dimensions, dynamics, tethers, and interactions. Because the PMBOK can prepare a project manager to manage to professional standards, that helps create a talented individual. Given the choice between a reckless company staffed by reckless project managers and a reckless company staffed by conscientious PMPs, I'd take the latter every time.

But even the best of project managers, the most talented, the most gifted, will stumble without organizational support. And I don't mean the kind of support that says, if you fall, we'll pick you up. I mean the kind designed to prevent falls. Project management, like any other kind of management, operates best when it operates from a framework. Sales management uses territories, quotas, contact sheets, and call reports. Human resource management uses regulations, policies, reviews, and assessments. The common trait here is visibility. Sales do not happen inside a black box. Human resource management is not a company secret. The procedures these managers follow allow each to operate in a visible way, a way that allows for accountability, measurement, and when needed, course correction. That's the value of process with regard to project management. Even the most knowledgeable PMP may find it hard to manage in an unordered environment. Maybe that's why many project managers go "underground." But it should not be that way.

Process is a tool that can be used to bring visibility to project management activities. It can be used both to light the way and to illuminate the current position. This concept of visibility is important in any development shop, in any operational environment. eTrials uses process to bring visibility to each of its key operating areas. Here's John Cline again:

> Data and ensuring its integrity is the most important artifact of our software and services. We have policies, procedures and technology to assist us in managing customer data: who uses and accesses it. The quality assurance team, in working with the organization, ensures that our standard operating procedures (SOPs) meet regulatory requirements and that our employees fully understand our policies surrounding clinical data use and access. In addition, we employ technology to manage and audit our data use. It's a permission-and-role-based system that is fully auditable.

One of the main missions of project management is to keep project activities moving within a set of predefined bounds. Another is to communicate to others how this mission is going. With process—with structured expectations in place to support these two—activities and status become visible. They become visible through recognized plans, reporting forms, measurements, progress analyses, milestone meetings, and so on.

A good process, for whatever purpose you have in mind, is typically defined using the information shown in Table 1–1.

Notice the bent toward visibility here. Use is stated. Responsibility is defined. Explicit conditions are described. Work products are specified. Measures are stated. All of these elements provide two things to a project initiative.

1. They standardize project externals. That is, they identify tangibles that should appear at certain points in project progress.
2. They establish a threshold of acceptable performance.

Through this approach, project management based in process makes progress visible. It takes the practice out of the black box, and safely out of the black box, by using an alternative methodology that should prove more conducive to management, more open to analysis and input, and more amenable to predictable outcomes. In short, one better oriented to success.

Table 1–1: *The Structure of a Well-Designed Process*

Purpose	*The objective of the process*
Actors	The roles needed to perform the activities of the process
Entry criteria	Conditions that need to be in place before the process activities can begin
Inputs	Documents or products that need to be in place or referenced before the process activities can begin
Steps	The step-by-step sequence of the process
Output	Documents or products to be produced by process activities
Exit criteria	The condition(s) that will exist once the process is completed
Measures	Any measures that need to be collected once the process is completed

Here's another case story from an e-company. A Web-based discount brokerage was having an internal performance problem.[3] The company's software projects were routinely running six to eight weeks over schedule. That drag was causing delays in product and service rollouts and was showing up as a distinct marker on the company's bottom line. To address this problem, and in conjunction with the company's overall focus on quality, the company set into place a process improvement program based on CMMI. It took a few operating quarters to get the program in place. The managers targeted CMMI Maturity Level 2 as their goal and worked on seven distinct areas of technology development, including project planning and project tracking.

Here's what they found. After the project teams had adapted to the new procedures and were operating comfortably with them, schedule slippage began to shrink. After three months in the new paradigm, most schedules averaged less than two weeks behind schedule. The problem didn't go away, but the situation had dramatically improved. And best of all, company teams have been able to sustain this efficiency increase over time, meaning that their new processes really do help project management performance.

The full title of this book is *Project Management Success with CMMI®: Seven CMMI Process Areas*. These seven process areas, often associated with CMMI Maturity Level 2, represent a particular slice of CMMI. It centers on seven areas that invariably play a part in project success: planning, tracking, managing requirements, managing configuration, managing suppliers, measuring progress, and auditing for quality control. For each of these areas, CMMI defines a set of goals that can be achieved by implementing a set of specific practices, practices that have been proven to work well over time in technology industries.

That's what we'll be looking at in this book—how you can interpret the practices described for CMMI Maturity Level 2 in such a way that you can then create processes to support them for your shop. Processes shaped to reflect what's valuable and important to your shop. Processes designed with the right degree of weight and flexibility.

---

3. This case study comes from the course material "Introduction to CMMI" by the Software Engineering Institute (2007). Visit www.sei.cmu.edu/products/courses/ for more information about courses.

Processes shaped to make tracking project progress open, visible, and accountable.

In the next chapter, we'll begin to assimilate the framework provided by the Capability Maturity Model with the traditional expectations of project management.

Chapter 2

Project Management Success through Process

A large technology company with over $500 million in annual revenues can't afford to underestimate the value of project management. Because we maintain our position in the marketplace by continually deploying enhanced document management solutions, we rely on the ability of product and project management to successfully usher these new tools to our industry partners. Through the use of our CMMI and Six Sigma programs we've been able to support that mission with a process foundation that promotes consistency, repeatability, and ongoing improvement.

Charlie Soong, Director of Quality Improvement for BSC-MS
Global leader in data-stream management

The aim of this book is to illustrate the relationship that can be forged between CMMI for Development, version 1.2, and an organization's project management needs. As we'll see in the following sections, CMMI is a process improvement framework that consists of 22 Process

Areas. Each Process Area contains a set of goals and practices targeted to a specific management or development need.

Although you can deploy CMMI-DEV in any number of environments—wherever you are building a product or a service—this book focuses on using CMMI for technology development: in software shops, systems shops, hardware engineering contexts, and so on.

Within this focus, three general audiences may find this subject of particular, applicable value.

1. *Project managers trained as PMPs*[1] may wonder how a framework like CMMI compares to or can integrate with the Project Management Institute's PMBOK.

2. *Project managers without PMP certification* may be interested in learning how a popular process model like CMMI may be able to promote and further the mission of their project management offices.

3. *Process managers working to implement process programs* in their organizations might want to better understand how CMMI can be shaped to support specific project goals and objectives.

This book will address each of these three audience groups and their related issues. To begin this exploration, let's start with a brief overview of CMMI.

The Capability Maturity Model—A Process Improvement Framework

The Capability Maturity Model has been around for just over 20 years. It is a process improvement framework governed by the Software Engineering Institute (SEI), a federally funded research organization chartered by the U.S. Congress and supported by both the U.S. Department of Defense and Carnegie Mellon University. Carnegie Mellon houses the SEI headquarters at its campus in Pittsburgh.

---

1. Or any of the other well-known project management certifications, such as those from the American Management Association.

Two quick points here.

1. Being around for 20 years, CMMI has had time to prove its value. Organizations that have adopted it have been able to realize distinct and tangible benefits. CMMI has helped to streamline costs, improve timelines, reduce rework and defect rates, and demonstrably improve quality.

2. Because the U.S. government sponsors the SEI, the work that supports CMMI is in the public domain. It is free to anyone who would like to work with it. This includes the CMMI specification itself plus a wealth of implementation and support materials, cost/benefit analyses, and tips and techniques for CMMI success. You can access (and download) all this material by visiting the SEI Web site at www.sei.cmu.edu.

CMMI Is Not a Process Program

People sometimes casually refer to CMMI as a process program. That's fine from an informal standpoint, but that's really not what CMMI is. CMMI is a process improvement framework. It is a collection of performance targets and activity recommendations you can use as the basis for establishing your own process program. And it provides you with additional elements to embed improvement actions into your program as well.

If you are familiar with the PMBOK, you understand the intention of a framework. The ten Knowledge Areas in the PMBOK present management considerations and techniques around which you can frame a particular project management program. The same is true with CMMI (and for this reason, as we'll see later, CMMI and the PMBOK tend to integrate well).

A Framework of Integrated Constellations

The SEI shaped CMMI as a process improvement framework to address a broad range of application environments. In doing so, SEI created three different and distinct CMMIs.

1. CMMI for Development (CMMI-DEV) is a model designed for process management and improvement in development shops.

2. CMMI for Acquisition (CMMI-ACQ) is a process model designed for use in shops that must initiate and manage the acquisition of products and services.

3. CMMI for Services (CMMI-SVC) is a model structured to help organizations deploy and manage services.

All three of these models share much in common: several core Process Areas, Generic Goals and Generic Practices, common terminology, common descriptive and implementation approaches, and common methods of appraisal. And of course, each of the three features its own particular set of unique Process Areas, goals, and practices.

CMMI-DEV, CMMI-ACQ, and CMMI-SVC are called *constellations*. You can imagine them as revolving around the foundation of the CMMI model, as extending from that model perhaps like the separate arms of a spiral galaxy.

For the purposes of this book, we will focus only on CMMI for Development. In terms of a technology organization's project management needs, CMMI-DEV presents the most relevance.

Disciplines Covered by CMMI-DEV

If you approached the content of CMMI-DEV from the standpoint of pure process improvement, you could probably apply its principles successfully in any development environment, whether you were making satellite controllers, garage door openers, or shoelaces. From a practical standpoint, however, CMMI-DEV has something of a finer focus. It has been shaped for use chiefly in technology development shops. Within this domain, CMMI addresses four technology disciplines:

1. Software Engineering

2. Hardware Engineering

3. Systems Engineering

4. Integrated Process and Product Development (IPPD)

Software Engineering naturally deals with the design and implementation of software systems. Likewise, Hardware Engineering deals with the design and manufacture of hardware components and systems. Systems Engineering deals with the design and integration of disparate operational systems. And Integrated Process and Product Development tends to combine the previous three. IPPD deals with complex or large projects, projects that require the integration, coordination, and collaboration of separate and/or specialized teams.

As a single integrated framework, CMMI-DEV supports all four of these disciplines. In most cases, it provides amplifications and extensions that highlight particular ways to address each discipline. In the case of IPPD, CMMI-DEV provides goals and practices that directly address the extended needs of this discipline.

CMMI-DEV for Process Improvement

The official CMMI-DEV publication is *CMMI for Development, Version 1.2* (Technical Report CMU/SEI 2006-TR-008). CMMI can be used to develop products more efficiently and to improve the processes by which we plan, manage, and control that development. To me, the single term *process improvement* covers both of those objectives in a classical sense.

Reading through the CMMI specification reveals that it is an organized collection of proven industry practices. (Sometimes they are called *best practices*, but *proven* or *dependable* might be more accurate terms.) These practices are not what I would call innovative, earth-shattering, or eye-opening. And I think as you read through them you'll agree. For the most part, they are based in common sense. They encompass the things we know we probably should do as technology professionals, but without a formalized approach, these things all too often can slip through the cracks.

These practices have been culled from observations of successful technology shops and from the lessons provided by such quality pioneers as Crosby, Juran, and Baldridge. The basic assumption in place here is that process works. Successful technology shops, when you examine them, can demonstrate the ability to meet a set of very specific targets. Schedule objectives, budget objectives, and quality objectives tend to be managed with a high degree of control and predictability.

Coincidentally (or correlatively), these shops also tend to embrace process. Their preferred way of doing business is to provide their people with a structured environment, one that promotes planning, consistency, and feedback—and standards to follow in support of each of these. When you observe a shop with such high capability, you'll find that it is also more often than not process mature. Its capability not only is embedded in its process maturity but also springs from it. You'll find that in shops like these, predictability is high because folks know how things will get done. And when predictability is high, risk is reduced (Figure 2–1)—the risk of going over schedule, of exceeding budget, of encountering quality problems. Process is a way to promote consistency and predictability. When these two factors are in place within a technology shop, elements of risk begin to taper off over time. Project management success depends on controlling risk, and process is one way to promote that.

That's the idea of process improvement. Create a path to consistency. And that's the guiding idea behind CMMI.

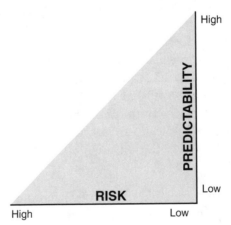

Figure 2–1: *The relationship between risk and predictability*

To enhance predictability and promote consistency requires some type of process, be it heavy or light, common or proprietary. The central idea behind all process improvement models, frameworks, or approaches is the same.

1. Set a path in place.
2. Follow the path.
3. Evaluate its effectiveness.
4. Refine it where it can be improved.
5. Follow it again.

The path is your process program. For any program, you create the right mix of procedures, templates, forms, and guidelines that your people can use to work in consistent, predictable ways. Through its collection of proven practices, CMMI can be used as the foundation for developing a process program.

You follow the path by using your program, by putting its elements through full cycles of implementation. Through this full use, you begin to learn which elements perform well and which elements can be improved or refined. You then work to make the program better.

You repeat this cycle of use and evaluation. Repetition—conscious and informed repetition—is the key to improvement over time.

The broader concept of professional project management can't help but embrace the philosophy presented here. In the absence of such a way, a cleared and directed path, all you are left with is individual ability. People are on their own. From my experience, many technology shops seem resigned to such a situation. (The companies I mentioned in Chapter 1, Impetus and SoftMil, certainly were.) They believe that good project management can come only from good project managers, or rather from talented individuals who have taken on project management duties.

What's missing from this view is the organizational obligation to provide its people—whether strong, average, or novice—with the tools they need to succeed. This is all that a process program based in CMMI really is. It's a set of tools provided by the organization that reflects organizational values to be used to help achieve organizational objectives. When an organization foregoes this responsibility and places the future of a project solely in the hands of one person, or a team of persons, it has in effect walked away from the project. It has outsourced it, even if that outsourcing is internal.

Intuitively, most technology shops do realize this. But to embrace the concept effectively, that process works and that capable organizations are those that work to improve their processes, two commitments are required:

1. A commitment to process
2. A commitment to time

Let's discuss these commitments further.

A Commitment to Process

This is not news. Since the time of the pyramids and the lighthouse at Rhodes, project management has been a discipline of process. That doesn't change just because the domain changes. Whether the focus is on construction or on technology development, a process should be followed to carry the work from concept to completion.

I don't want to appear to be knocking the value of individual talent as I discuss the link between project management success and process. Talent, initiative, experience, and judgment are highly desirable traits in the people who work with you. By all means, seek out and cultivate those qualities. Process is not a substitute for people, but it does serve as a mechanism to focus and direct people's energies along common lines, toward coordinated targets. And good people may not perform to their potential in the absence of process.

In fact, process and people are codependent qualities on the triangle of organizational design (Figure 2–2). Organizational dynamics—and therefore organizational effectiveness—spring from three separate but equal qualities: process, people, and technology.

You can plainly see the value of process as a complement to talent when you look at obviously successful companies such as Coca-Cola or

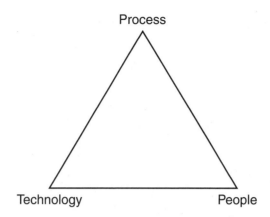

Figure 2–2: *The triangle of organizational design*

Kentucky Fried Chicken. If you buy a Coke at a market in Beijing, it has the same fizz as one you would buy in Santa Fe. KFC tastes the same in Paris, France, or Paris, Texas. Quality, consistency, and control are essential to these two organizations. And so Coca-Cola and KFC invest heavily in process.

Technology shops can benefit the same way from their own process programs. In order to realize these benefits, however, organizations must make a firm commitment to developing their processes, training their people in how to use them, and then exercising the processes to their fullest ability. This level of commitment is not particular to CMMI. If you were to rigorously employ elements of the PMBOK (or ISO 9001:2000 or Information Technology Infrastructure Library [ITIL] or Six Sigma), you would need to make the same level of commitment. Adopting process is a way to change how your organization approaches, manages, and measures its work and its performance. It applies basic business principles to technology development, an arena in corporate America that has often been left to devise its own management principles.

It's important here to discuss the size of the commitment required.

Your process program does not have to be a feat of engineering marvel. It does not have to be broad in scope, a machine turning gears in all corners of the organization. Process does not have to be heavy. In fact, from what I have seen, the better process programs are those that start off small, using light processes to address specific areas of work. These kinds of programs tend to stick more quickly in a shop, to more easily integrate with current habits. Once the light elements are firmly in place, you can then expand them as needed.

So, when it comes to process and its relation to your project management needs, size the commitment to the size of your needs.

A Commitment to Time

Your commitment to process will not realize its full benefits without a commitment to using the program over time. This is an essential and integral element to process success. You may be able to develop your process program fairly quickly. You may be able to roll it out to appropriate groups quickly. You may be able to get senior management to make a firm commitment to the program's use. But even with all this done, the real job is just beginning.

Process success takes time. The key to realizing an effective process program is to use it over time, to observe where it performs well, to note where it could be better, to refine and shape it as needed so that more and more, little by little, it takes on the desired qualities of efficiency and effectiveness. Today, with the benefits and value of process assuming a prominent place in the technology marketplace, many organizations are stepping up to make a commitment to process. But sometimes they do so without fully appreciating the required commitment to time. New programs, fresh out of the gate, may not show instant benefits. They may even cause a certain degree of disruption to status quo work streams. But given the right amount of time—enough time to put the program through a series of cycles and exercise its different parts—you'll find that the program begins to unify the shop, that it adds stability to the workplace, that it fosters consistency, and that standards for quality and performance become, more and more, automatic considerations across your different work teams.

Together, a commitment to process and a commitment to time, to the extended use of process, will help you realize the full value of your mission to heighten project management success for your shop.

With this said, let's now look at the content of the CMMI model, specifically, at the 22 Process Areas that make up CMMI-DEV.

CMMI-DEV Process Areas

As we noted earlier in this chapter, the core or common CMMI model consists of several Process Areas. Revolving around this core, sharing it, are what the SEI calls CMMI constellations. There are currently three constellations: CMMI for Development (the focus of this book), CMMI for Acquisition, and CMMI for Services (Figure 2–3). While sharing the core components, each constellation features its own specialized Process Areas.

CMMI-DEV consists of 22 Process Areas designed to enhance technology development (Figure 2–4). Of these, 16 are based in the core model,

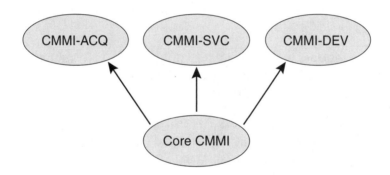

Figure 2–3: *The constellations of CMMI*

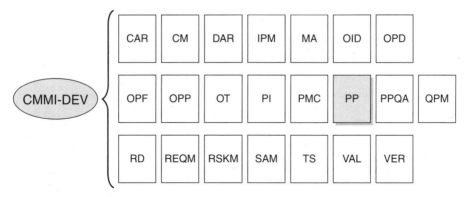

Figure 2–4: *CMMI for Development as a collection of Process Areas*

and 6 address specific needs of technology development. Under CMMI, a Process Area is a collection of one or more Specific Goals. Reach the goals and you've satisfied the intention of the Process Area. Each Specific Goal is a collection of Specific Practices. The practices are actions you can take to reach the goals.

Each Process Area is a model element focused on a particular and related set of development objectives, supported by one or more Specific Goals (Figure 2–5). When the Specific Goals of a Process Area are achieved, the Process Area is said to be satisfied.

Each Specific Goal consists of two or more Specific Practices (Figure 2–6). While Specific Goals are usually strategic in nature, Specific Practices are almost always tactical. They describe concrete activities that can be implemented in order to help achieve the related Specific Goal. All Specific Practices should be accounted for in order to achieve the Specific Goal.

For organizations with special or unique needs or environments, CMMI allows the adoption and use of valid alternative practices as substitutes for its defined ones.

To help institutionalize Process Area activity within an organization, CMMI provides a set of Generic Goals and Generic Practices that apply in common ways to each Process Area.

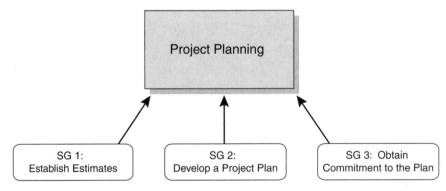

Figure 2–5: *Each Process Area is a collection of recommended goals*

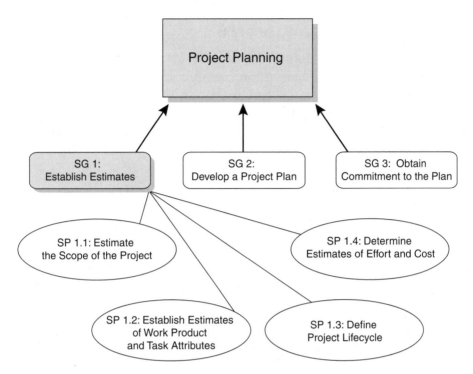

Figure 2–6: *Each Specific Goal is realized by accomplishing a set of recommended practices*

A good way to organize the Process Areas is by category. The 22 Process Areas of CMMI-DEV can be arranged into four categories. This is not a mandatory grouping; it's simply a convenient way to think about and relate different Process Areas to each other. The four categories are:

1. Project Management
2. Process Management
3. Engineering
4. Support

In the following sections, we'll take a quick look at each of the Process Areas in each of these categories.

Project Management Process Areas

Six Process Areas are defined to directly address various levels of project management needs within an organization. Some call for a more progressive level of process execution than others. But all deal with the same major target: to guide how projects are planned, monitored, controlled, and measured. Here are the six Process Areas for the Project Management category:

1. Project Planning
2. Project Monitoring & Control
3. Risk Management
4. Supplier Agreement Management
5. Integrated Project Management
6. Quantitative Project Management

Let's take a quick look at them now.

Project Planning

Project Planning (PP) describes practices that address establishing the estimates and plans that will be used to shape and manage the project. Three goals are described for this Process Area:

SG 1: Establish Estimates

SG 2: Develop a Project Plan

SG 3: Obtain Commitment to the Plan

The first goal is to calculate estimates of the scope, effort, and cost of the project. Second is to establish the project plan, including such elements as the budgets, schedule, resources, skill sets, risks, data management, and stakeholder involvement. The third goal is to review the plan (or the collected plans) and then approve and commit to it. (This Process Area is part of Maturity Level 2 and is discussed in more detail in Chapter 3.)

Project Monitoring & Control

Project Monitoring & Control (PMC) is the natural extension of Project Planning. Here you track the progress of the project against what you described in the plan. There are two goals defined for this Process Area:

SG 1: Monitor Project Against Plan

SG 2: Manage Corrective Action to Closure

The first goal is to monitor the progress of the project against the plan. This includes such activities as keeping an eye on plan parameters (budget, schedule, and so on), monitoring data management, and conducting periodic progress and milestone reviews. The second goal is to identify risks and issues as they arise, address them as needed, and then track actions against them to closure. (This Process Area is part of Maturity Level 2 and is discussed in more detail in Chapter 4.)

Risk Management

The focus of Risk Management (RSKM) extends from Project Planning and Project Monitoring & Control and complements their focus on issue management. Three goals are defined for this Process Area:

SG 1: Prepare for Risk Management

SG 2: Identify and Analyze Risks

SG 3: Mitigate Risks

The first goal is to prepare for risk management. This involves setting up a risk management capability in the organization: establishing a risk management strategy, categorizing typical and known risks, prioritizing them, and setting thresholds for when risk mitigation actions should be set into motion. The second goal is to identify and analyze risks as they emerge. This includes documenting the risks, assessing their impacts, and prioritizing them for potential action. The third goal is to mitigate risks. This includes developing risk mitigation plans and then implementing those plans to minimize risk impacts.

Supplier Agreement Management

Supplier Agreement Management (SAM) addresses how a project team can establish supplier agreements and then coordinate work with suppliers to ensure productive integration. Two goals are in place for SAM:

SG 1: Establish Supplier Agreements

SG 2: Satisfy Supplier Agreements

The first goal is to establish supplier agreements (or contracts) according to the types of acquisitions made and the field of vendors qualified to supply the range of required products. The second goal is to satisfy the agreements by making informed purchases, monitoring the creation and delivery of the product, and then integrating the product into your development efforts. (This Process Area is part of Maturity Level 2 and is discussed in more detail in Chapter 7.)

Integrated Project Management

Integrated Project Management (IPM) is a progressive Process Area that adds enhanced capabilities to the other project management Process Areas. The following goals are attached to IPM:

SG 1: Compose the Defined Process

SG 2: Collaborate and Coordinate with Relevant Stakeholders

SG 3: Apply IPPD Principles (for those using IPPD)

SG1 and SG2 are the main goals. The first is to manage the project using selected organizational processes. This includes tailoring the organizational processes to project needs, creating the right work environments, establishing appropriate plans, and managing against these plans. The second goal places special emphasis on collaborating and coordinating with relevant stakeholders. This includes managing stakeholder involvement, managing dependencies among and across teams, and resolving any coordination issues that might arise.

A third goal is also defined for IPM if your organization is involved in Integrated Process and Product Development. This third goal is to apply IPPD management principles to the project. These principles include establishing a shared vision for the project, creating integrated teams, distributing work responsibilities, and ensuring collaboration and coordination among individual teams.

Quantitative Project Management

The sixth Process Area under Project Management is Quantitative Project Management (QPM). QPM is often called a high-maturity Process Area because it requires a level of sophistication and capability that usually comes only with shops that have been dedicated to process improvement for quite a while. The assumption with QPM is that the organization's processes have become so stable and predictable that they can now be managed quantitatively, using statistical projections.

Two goals are set in place for QPM:

SG 1: Manage the Project Quantitatively

SG 2: Analyze Subprocess Performance

First is to manage the project quantitatively by establishing performance objectives, composing the defined processes based on these objectives, and then managing process performance to remain in line with the objectives. The second goal is to add to quantitative management capability by measuring selected subprocess performance and analyzing the results.

Process Management Process Areas

As we mentioned earlier, CMMI-DEV is a process improvement framework. It provides a structure on which you can build your own process program. That being the case, the model provides five Process Areas that support the framework's focus on process integration and product improvement:

1. Organizational Process Definition
2. Organizational Process Focus
3. Organizational Training
4. Organizational Process Performance
5. Organizational Innovation & Deployment

The following subsections briefly describe these Process Areas.

Organizational Process Definition

Organizational Process Definition (OPD) has two goals:

SG 1: Establish Organizational Process Assets

SG 2: Enable IPPD Management (for shops doing IPPD)

The main goal is for the organization to establish a standardized set of processes that teams within the organization can access and shape to manage their work. This includes creating a process library housing such assets as the standard processes, development lifecycles, tailoring guidelines, environmental standards, and a measurement repository.

If your organization is involved in Integrated Process and Product Development, you can apply a second goal to OPD. This second goal asks you to enable IPPD management. That includes establishing mechanisms to empower teams, setting up rules for coordination and collaboration, and ensuring that home office and field team responsibilities are properly balanced.

Organizational Process Focus

Organizational Process Focus (OPF) deals with the organization's strategic vision for process improvement. Three goals are assigned to this Process Area:

SG 1: Determine Process Improvement Opportunities

SG 2: Plan and Implement Process Improvements

SG 3: Deploy Organizational Process Assets and Incorporate Lessons Learned

First is to determine the process improvement opportunities the organization will focus on. This includes determining improvement needs, assessing against those needs, and then selecting improvement targets. The second goal is to plan and implement process improvements by establishing process action plans and implementing those plans over time. The third goal is to deploy the new process assets into the organization. This includes implementing the assets, monitoring use and adoption, and noting any potential for refinement.

Organizational Training

Organizational Training (OT) deals with setting up a training capability within the shop. Two goals are defined for OT:

SG 1: Establish an Organizational Training Capability

SG 2: Provide Necessary Training

The first goal is to establish a training capability by understanding training needs, determining training courses, establishing a tactical training plan, and then developing the resources and materials needed to deliver the courses. The second goal is to follow through on this capability by delivering the needed courses, establishing training records, and collecting feedback on training effectiveness.

Organizational Process Performance

Organizational Process Performance (OPP) is another Process Area often associated with high-maturity shops. One goal is defined for OPP:

SG 1: Establish Performance Baselines and Models

What this means is to create statistical descriptions of how processes will perform when they are called into play for a given project. This typically involves establishing measuring mechanisms and performance objectives and then using these two to determine performance baselines and performance models. The intention here is clean and obvious, but the organization must have accumulated a solid enough base of data to ensure that the models and baseline are statistically reliable. And that of course takes time and dedication.

Organizational Innovation & Deployment

Organizational Innovation & Deployment (OID) describes goals and practices designed to manage the development and rollout of new processes into an organization. This Process Area has two goals:

SG 1: Select Improvements

SG 2: Deploy Improvements

The first goal directs the shop to systematically determine which improvements it wishes to deploy. This includes analyzing improvement opportunities and proposals, analyzing potential innovations, piloting selected improvements, and then choosing the promising ones for deployment. The second goal is to systematically deploy the improvements into the organization. This includes planning the deployment, managing the deployment against the plan, and measuring improvement results.

Engineering Process Areas

CMMI-DEV describes six Process Areas that deal with the engineering aspects of development. Together with Supplier Agreement Management (discussed under Project Management Process Areas), five of these (Requirements Management being a core Process Area common to all constellations) make up what is original and specific to CMMI-DEV. Other CMMI models, such as CMMI-ACQ and CMMI-SVC, share the same core components found under the Project Management, Process Management, and Support Process Areas. But the six Engineering Process Areas listed here are unique to CMMI-DEV:

1. Requirements Management
2. Requirements Development
3. Technical Solution
4. Product Integration
5. Verification
6. Validation

They describe how development components are specified, designed, assembled, verified, and validated. Let's take a further look at each of them.

Requirements Development

The focus of Requirements Development (RD) is to develop, analyze, and validate the requirements needed to develop a product or service. Three goals are defined for RD:

SG 1: Develop Customer Requirements

SG 2: Develop Product Requirements

SG 3: Analyze and Validate Requirements

The first goal is to develop customer requirements by eliciting business needs and then establishing the customer requirements from those. The second goal is to develop the product requirements based on the customer requirements. This includes establishing product component requirements and then allocating them to appropriate system components, including interfaces. The third goal is to analyze and validate the sets of requirements to ensure completeness and sufficiency to the business needs and to confirm proper scope in terms of expectations and resources.

Requirements Management

Within Requirements Management (REQM), there is a single goal:

SG 1: Manage Requirements

Requirements Management has an integral and iterative association with Requirements Development. The purpose of REQM is to help control the scope of the project that you establish using RD. This is typically accomplished by understanding and committing to the requirements, managing any changes to the requirements, establishing requirements traceability, and then working to maintain synchronicity between the requirements and the project work products. (This Process Area is part of Maturity Level 2 and is discussed in more detail in Chapter 5.)

Technical Solution

Technical Solution (TS) is geared toward taking the developed requirements and establishing from them workable designs that can be implemented into appropriate solutions. TS has three goals assigned to it:

SG 1: Select Product Component Solutions
SG 2: Develop the Design
SG 3: Implement the Product Design

The first goal is to select appropriate product component solutions. This involves examining and evaluating potential alternatives and then choosing the best one. The second goal is to develop the design. This includes the pro forma design, any interfaces needed for the design, and a technical data package to support the design. The third goal is to implement the design: realizing the solution and then supporting it with appropriate documentation.

Product Integration

The focus of Product Integration (PI) is to provide for an orderly manner in which to assemble product components into an integrated whole ready for delivery to the customer. Three goals are defined for PI:

SG 1: Prepare for Product Integration

SG 2: Ensure Interface Compatibility

SG 3: Assemble Product Components and Deliver the Product

The first goal is to prepare for product integration by defining the integration sequence, establishing the integration environment, and creating integration procedures and criteria. The second goal is to ensure interface compatibility. This typically involves validating the completeness of the interface descriptions and then managing these through the integration process. The third goal is to assemble the product and deliver it to the customer. This includes making sure the product components are ready for integration, integrating them according to procedures, validating the success of the integration, and then packaging the product for delivery.

Verification

The Verification (VER) Process Area deals with making sure that the product (or product component) matches the requirements specified for its design. Three goals are applied here:

SG 1: Prepare for Verification

SG 2: Perform Peer Reviews

SG 3: Verify Selected Work Products

The first goal is to prepare for verification. This is typically done by identifying the work products to be verified, establishing an appropriate verification environment, and defining verification procedures and criteria. The second goal is to perform peer reviews on selected work products. To do this you prepare to hold the reviews, conduct them as planned, and then analyze and assess the data and comments that come out of the review. The third goal is to verify the work products by conducting verification sessions as intended and then analyzing the results.

Validation

The Validation (VAL) Process Area deals with making sure that the product (or product component) operates properly in its intended environment. Two goals apply to this Process Area:

SG 1: Prepare for Validation

SG 2: Validate Product or Product Components

The first goal is to prepare for validation by selecting the products to be validated, establishing an appropriate validation environment, and then developing validation procedures and criteria. The second goal is to conduct validation activities using the environment, procedures, and criteria and then to analyze the results that emerge.

Support Process Areas

Five Process Areas are described for the Support category. These Process Areas describe a set of practices—some fundamental, some progressive—that can be set into place to support the procedures and activities found in the Project Management, Process Management, and Engineering realms. The following Process Areas provide a set of operational goals to be shared across projects at play within an organization:

1. Configuration Management
2. Measurement & Analysis
3. Process & Product Quality Assurance
4. Decision Analysis & Resolution
5. Causal Analysis & Resolution

We'll look at each of these briefly.

Configuration Management

Configuration Management (CM) is focused on protecting the integrity of work products developed across the life of a project. This Process Area has three goals:

SG 1: Establish Baselines

SG 2: Track and Control Changes

SG 3: Establish Integrity

The first goal is to establish work product baselines. This includes establishing some form of configuration management system, identifying work items to control through the system, and then releasing baselines from the system. The second goal is to protect versions of the work products by tracking and controlling changes to these products. The third goal is to establish integrity by periodically confirming that the contents of the configuration management system truly represent the state and version of the associated work products. (This Process Area is part of Maturity Level 2 and is discussed in more detail in Chapter 6.)

Measurement & Analysis

Measurement & Analysis (MA) is concerned with collecting the kinds of performance and use data that can help indicate the success and effectiveness of your management and process capabilities. Two goals are defined for MA:

SG 1: Align Measurement & Analysis Activities

SG 2: Provide Measurement Results

The first goal is to align MA activities with the business needs of the organization. This involves defining measurement objectives, determining specific measures to address those objectives, specifying collection and storage procedures, and specifying analysis procedures. The second goal extends the first. It is to provide measurement results by collecting the data as planned, analyzing it, storing it for future reference, and communicating the results to relevant parties. (This Process Area is part of Maturity Level 2 and is discussed in more detail in Chapter 8.)

Process & Product Quality Assurance

Process & Product Quality Assurance (PPQA) can be seen as the audit arm of a process program. PPQA is designed to provide management with the objective oversight needed to evaluate the effectiveness and proliferation of the process program across projects as well as across the organization. Two goals are described here:

SG 1: Objectively Evaluate Processes and Work Products

SG 2: Provide Objective Insight

The first goal is to evaluate program use by periodically auditing process use and work product development. The second goal is to provide objective insight by resolving noncompliance issues and establishing appropriate compliance records. (This Process Area is part of Maturity Level 2 and is discussed in more detail in Chapter 9.)

Decision Analysis & Resolution

Decision Analysis & Resolution (DAR) is set into place to provide guidance for the organization when it needs to make certain decisions of particular or important weight. One goal is defined for this process:

SG 1: Evaluate Alternatives

This typically includes such activities as establishing formal decision-making guidelines, defining evaluation criteria and thresholds, identifying potential decision alternatives, evaluating them against one another, and selecting the best option open to the organization.

Causal Analysis & Resolution

Causal Analysis & Resolution (CAR) is set into place to help an organization address the root causes of performance and management deficiencies. Two goals are defined for CAR:

SG 1: Determine Causes of Defects

SG 2: Address Causes of Defects

The first goal is to determine the causes of defects. This includes selecting the right sets of defect data to analyze and then analyzing this data to precisely determine the cause or causes of the defects. The second goal extends from the first one: to address the causes of defects. Action proposals to remove the defects are implemented, the results of the fixes are evaluated for effectiveness, and performance data is recorded for future reference.

Institutionalizing Process Areas with Generic Goals

Each of the 22 Process Areas described under CMMI-DEV has a specific focus that helps you manage certain aspects of the development lifecycle. The idea is that, for each Process Area you implement, you will introduce a series of sound practices that not only will make your work more controllable and accountable but also will give you a foundation you can use to forge continuous improvements. The first part of that intention—implementing sound practices—is the straightforward part. The part about instituting a foundation for improvement requires some additional help, and that's where CMMI's Generic Goals come into play.

The Generic Goals are a common set of goals and practices that can be applied to all Process Areas within CMMI. They are not specific to a Process Area's focus; they are—as the name implies—generic. The purpose of the Generic Goals is to provide you with an improvement path that begins with basic recommendations and then grows in sophistication to promote more advanced and progressive recommendations. These recommendations all deal with the organization's implementation of its processes. They work to help an organization institutionalize its process program. When a process has become institutionalized, it has become ingrained in the way the organization conducts its business; it has become part of the way of doing business. In order for process programs to flourish and evolve, they need to become institutionalized.

CMMI has five Generic Goals, GG 1 through GG 5. While you can look at each Process Area as existing pretty much as a stand-alone, independent entity, that is not so with the Generic Goals. The higher Generic

Goals always build on top of the lower ones. For instance, GG 2 adds on to GG 1; GG 4 is an accumulation of GG 1, GG 2, and GG 3. Through this building up over time, institutionalization moves deeper and deeper into the organizational culture.

Let's take a quick look at the five Generic Goals of CMMI.

GG 1: Achieve Specific Goals

GG 1 is in place to help less mature organizations begin to embrace the Specific Goals and Specific Practices described for each Process Area. The aim here is to be concerned just with building a process (or a set of processes) that provides for the realization of the goals and practices in the Process Areas you are focusing on. To do this, you usually make sure that your processes help produce the right kinds of input products in order to produce the right kinds of output products. This approach is called a *performed process*. It is a process designed to perform the basic work described for a particular Process Area. (GG 1 applies to the focus of this book. We discuss this Generic Goal in more depth in Chapter 10.)

GG 2: Institutionalize a Managed Process

GG 2 is often cited as "the big GG" because of its scope. GG 2 recommends a series of ten practices to help manage the use of your processes across your project teams and, if desired, throughout your organization. With GG 2, you institutionalize a managed process, and you do this by taking your performed process and wrapping it in a broad set of support activities. These include policy endorsement, planning of process activities, resource allocation, responsibility assignment, training, data management, stakeholder involvement, monitoring and control, objective evaluation, and communication with senior management. With GG 2, you set into place the practices that make performing the process an integral part of doing the business of your development shop. And that's the key to making institutionalization work. (GG 2 applies to the focus of this book. We discuss this Generic Goal in more depth in Chapter 10.)

GG 3: Institutionalize a Defined Process

With GG 3, the organization makes a significant move up the scale of maturity and capability. The managed process you implemented with GG 2 is now institutionalized as a defined process. A defined process is one that has shown its efficacy, proven its value, and become standardized for the whole organization. A defined process is supported at the enterprise level by organizational repositories, tailoring guidelines, and the collection of improvement data.

GG 4: Institutionalize a Quantitatively Managed Process

GG 4 represents another big move forward in both maturity and capability, often a big move forward in time, too. With GG 4, you take your defined processes and add to them the ability to manage quantitatively. In other words, you can now apply statistical analyses to predict how your processes will perform when deployed in given environments for given efforts. Naturally, to manage them quantitatively, your processes must exhibit a high degree of control. They must be exceedingly reliable and predictable. That's why it takes time to institutionalize a quantitatively managed process. You need the time to work your processes and refine them so they are very much under control, and then you need the time to collect enough performance data so you can apply dependable statistical analyses to them.

GG 5: Institutionalize an Optimizing Process

The last Generic Goal, GG 5, instructs you to take your quantitatively managed process and institutionalize it as an optimizing process. Notice the form of the adjective *optimizing*: The process is ongoing, in a state without an end. At this point in its maturity and capability, an organization's processes are so integral to how it produces product that its real focus turns away from product to process. A proven process—one eminently controllable and predictable—will comfortably guarantee the production of a predictable product, one whose performance, quality, and suitability for purpose can all be statistically anticipated. This being the case, the organization's chief impetus is to become a process refinement shop, a shop that is continually bettering its processes through incremental, measurable improvement and innovation.

Two Ways to Implement CMMI

As we have seen so far, CMMI is a collection of Process Areas—22 of them in all. Each Process Area is supported by one or more Specific Goals, and each Specific Goal can be attained by following the Specific Practices recommended for that goal. To help institutionalize use of the Process Areas in an organization, CMMI also describes a series of Generic Goals. There are five Generic Goals in the model, and each has it own Generic Practices associated with it.

So that's 22 Process Areas, 50 Specific Goals, 173 Specific Practices. Add to that 5 Generic Goals and 17 Generic Practices and you have quite a process improvement model on hand. But you don't have to implement all of CMMI to reap benefits from the model. In fact, CMMI was designed with scalability in mind. You can implement those portions of the model that suit the needs of your organization. That might be a single Process Area, or it might be a selected group of Process Areas. From an official viewpoint, the Software Engineering Institute recognizes two ways to implement CMMI. One is called the Continuous Representation, and the other is called the Staged Representation. With each approach, you implement only portions of the model until (if you so choose), after following a committed path of improvement, you can implement everything.

Let's take a look at each approach.

The Continuous Representation

The Continuous Representation can be thought of as a Process Area–by–Process Area implementation of CMMI. You select which Process Areas you want to implement based on specific needs within your organization, and you implement just those. It's the à la carte approach to CMMI. It's a way to direct process improvement along very specific lines.

For example, if your technology shop manages its internal resources very well but has some problems with the vendors you are obligated to outsource work to, then you might adopt Supplier Agreement Management. This Process Area sets forth practices for establishing vendor agreements, defining performance standards, and monitoring vendor activity.

A different shop might have a different problem: Close and casual relationships with its customers may be introducing a stream of undocumented requirements changes. This shop might elect to implement two Process Areas to deal with this situation. Requirements Management can be used to manage requirements input and traceability. Configuration Management can be used to implement protective forms of change control and baseline management.

In each case, the adoption of Process Areas is up to the organization. With the Continuous Representation, you fix the path of process improvement.

Under CMMI, the Continuous Representation is built to measure improvement along a six-tier capability scale. Each Process Area you work with can be advanced at its own capability rate. The assumption is that the higher up the scale you move, the more capable you have become with each Process Area.

The scale of Capability Levels is as follows:

> 0 = Incomplete
>
> 1 = Performed
>
> 2 = Managed
>
> 3 = Defined
>
> 4 = Quantitatively Managed
>
> 5 = Optimizing

Incomplete

At Capability Level 0, although the Process Area may be partially in line with CMMI, it is not yet in full compliance. You may be following some of the Specific Goals and Practices or some of the Generic Goals and Practices, but not in a way that completely addresses the recommendations. It's an incomplete—perhaps a very elemental—approach to Process Area adoption.

Performed

At Capability Level 1, the organization begins to consciously work toward the Specific Goals described for each Process Area it has adopted. It typically does this by following the Specific Practices recommended for each Specific Goal (of course, alternative practices of equal validity are allowed as substitutes when needed).

This is important to understand because all other Capability Levels build from this point. At Capability Level 1, you adopt all of the Specific Goals and Practices for the Process Area, and you'll continue to embrace these as you advance in capability over time.

Under the Continuous Representation, advancing in Capability Levels is achieved by adopting sequential Generic Goals. So here at Level 1, in addition to working to achieve the Specific Goals and Practices as described for the Process Area, you'll adopt Generic Goal 1 and its single Generic Practice.

Managed

At Capability Level 2, you take the performed process you established at Level 1 and develop it into a managed process. This is done by adding Generic Goal 2 to the Process Area. GG 2 features ten Generic Practices that augment your processes with the kind of supports that help institutionalize them in the organization. You now begin to support the Process Areas with corporate policies, planned activities, applied resources, assigned responsibility, training, data management, stakeholder involvement, objective evaluations, monitoring and control, and communications with senior management.

In short, your process program has now taken on an increased level of sophistication. You've begun to ingrain it as a normal part of the way you do business.

Defined

At Capability Level 3, the use of your Process Areas has matured to the point where the organization can now standardize on them. It can adopt them for organization-wide use. Here you take the managed processes you had at Level 2 and develop them into a defined process. You do this by implementing Generic Goal 3 and the two Generic Practices associated with it. This move puts the organization at large into full-blown process improvement mode. The whole organization is now focused on the proper use, maintenance, and growth of the process program and its components.

Quantitatively Managed

Capability Level 4 is considered a level of high capability, so high in fact that many development shops might have no need to reach this tier. The concept at Level 4 is that your defined processes have become so stable, controllable, and predictable that you are now able to manage their performance using statistical and analytic techniques. You establish a quantitatively managed process by adopting Generic Goal 4 and its two Generic Practices.

It takes time (sometimes a lot of time) to reach Capability Level 4, for two reasons. First, it takes time to develop processes that are so stable they can be quantitatively managed. And second, it takes time to accumulate the wealth of performance data needed as a basis for managing quantitatively. But for those who achieve this level of control, the benefits are heightened capabilities in planning, management, and quality delivery.

Optimizing

The Continuous Representation reaches its apex at Capability Level 5, the optimizing level. Here the organization adopts Generic Goal 5 and its two Generic Practices for all its implemented Process Areas. At this level, the organization is realizing a systematic culture of continuous improvement, innovation, and defect prevention across its whole process program.

That's a quick look at the Continuous Representation. Let's summarize a few of the key points. The Continuous Representation:

- Allows you to implement any Process Area you wish, in any order or group
- Measures improvement on a six-tier capability scale, from 0 to 5
- Rates individual Process Areas in terms of Capability Level
- Recognizes advancements in capability by the addition of sequential Generic Goals

Now let's look briefly at the Staged Representation.

The Staged Representation

The alternative to the Continuous Representation is the Staged Representation. The Staged Representation takes a different view on process improvement, one that is born out of the original version of CMM, back when there was only one way to implement the model. This view is one of prescribed process improvement. With the Staged Representation, CMMI gives you a predefined process improvement prescription, a set path to follow on your process improvement journey. This is not an à la carte approach in the way that Continuous Representation is; it's more of a prix fixe approach. The menu is set.

While the Continuous Representation focuses on evolving capability, the Staged Representation focuses on evolving maturity. The Staged Representation measures organizational maturity along a five-tier scale, from Maturity Level 1 through Maturity Level 5. The organization does not have a choice about which Process Areas to adopt. At each level, it adopts the prescribed set of Process Areas defined in CMMI. Maturity is advanced by adopting additional Process Areas and Generic Goals.

For example, if an organization had an objective to reach Maturity Level 2, it would adopt the seven Process Areas prescribed for Level 2 along with Generic Goals 1 and 2. Subsequently, if the organizational objective were to reach Maturity Level 3, it would adopt the additional 11 (or so) Process Areas prescribed for Level 3 along with Generic Goal 3 as well.

The scale of Maturity Levels of the Staged Representation is as follows:

> 1 = Initial
> 2 = Managed
> 3 = Defined
> 4 = Quantitatively Managed
> 5 = Optimizing

Notice that this scale shares much of the same structure as the six-tier scale of Capability Levels for the Continuous Representation. In fact,

Levels 2 through 5 share the same names and really the same intentions for improvement. Aside from the view of which Process Areas to implement, the big difference between Continuous and Staged has to do with the adoption and use of the Generic Goals.

The Continuous Representation is pretty much based on the Generic Goals. For each Process Area you implement, you advance in capability (up to Capability Level 5) by adding more Generic Goals. At Level 0, you've added none. By Level 5, all are in place.

This is different with the Staged Representation. With the Staged Representation, only Generic Goals 2 and 3 apply. You implement Generic Goal 2 (and by implication Generic Goal 1) and its practices when you are forming your Maturity Level 2 program. You add Generic Goal 3 and its practices when you are forming your Level 3 program.

Maturity Levels 4 and 5 do not require the addition of new Generic Goals. This is because at each advancing Maturity Level you are required to implement a set of Process Areas, and the form, function, and practices of these Process Areas replicate in many places those of the Generic Goals 4 and 5. For the sake of parsimony, the requirement to adopt them has been relieved.

Following is a brief description of each Maturity Level in the Staged Representation.

Initial

At Maturity Level 1, an organization or project team is at the initial stage. It has no formalized process management program in place. It may be performing some sound practices, and it may be reaching some business-worthy goals, but it lacks consistency and predictability. Work is typically performed in an ad hoc manner and is heavily dependent on the individual talents and motivations of people within the organization. The mission in shops like this is simply to get the work done, and to get it done any way that works. Sound levels of accountability, efficiencies, and improvement are more often than not noticeably lacking.

Managed

When an organization moves to Maturity Level 2, it establishes a process program designed to be consciously managed from the center of its project teams. Here the foundation is laid not only for process-based management but for process improvement as well.

The following seven Process Areas are implemented at Maturity Level 2: Requirements Management, Project Planning, Project Monitoring & Control, Configuration Management, Measurement & Analysis, Process & Product Quality Assurance, and Supplier Agreement Management. The recommended Generic Practices of Generic Goal 2 are also implemented.

The focus at Maturity Level 2 is on two key factors. The first is project management—effectively planning, managing, and controlling project components. The second is process management—implementing a program to ensure that the established processes are being honored within a project team or company at large.

Defined

At Maturity Level 3, the organization has learned enough from its project-centered process management efforts that it can now establish enterprise-wide standards for process use across a full range of developmental and managerial areas. To further this mission, the organization augments its Level 2 program with a host of new Process Areas, including Requirements Development, Technical Solution, Product Integration, Risk Management, Decision Analysis & Resolution, Verification, Validation, Integrated Project Management, Organizational Process Focus, Organizational Process Definition, and Organizational Training. The organization also implements Generic Goal 3.

The move to Maturity Level 3 is substantial. At Maturity Level 3, the organization has a broad and robust process management and improvement program in place that reaches into the areas of project management, engineering, process management, and support.

Quantitatively Managed

As with Capability Level 4, at Maturity Level 4 the organization begins to shape its process and management programs through the use of empirical measurements, statistical techniques, and quantitative analysis. Just as moving from Maturity Level 2 to Level 3 signifies a major step forward in the commitment to process improvement, the move to Level 4 marks another major advancement. Organizational processes here have become highly controlled; their performance can be predicted. Data takes on a new degree of importance. Management decisions become in large part data-driven. At Maturity Level 4, the organization implements two new Process Areas, Organizational Process Performance and Quantitative Project Management. As mentioned earlier, no new Generic Goals are required at Level 4. The functionality included in Generic Goal 4 is present in the two new Process Areas.

Optimizing

The highest Maturity Level is Level 5, Optimizing. Optimizing is an ongoing process of continuous innovation, improvement, and refinement. Here the organization adopts two final Process Areas: Organizational Innovation & Deployment and Causal Analysis & Resolution. (Again, no new Generic Goals are required at Level 5. All functionality has now been accounted for.) At this point, the organization has entered a level of maturity in which the full enterprise is focused on continuous process and product improvement.

That's a quick look at the Staged Representation. Let's summarize a few key points. The Staged Representation:

- Allows you to follow a fixed, predefined path of process implementation and improvement
- Measures improvement on a five-tier maturity scale, from 1 to 5
- Rates organizational performance in terms of Maturity Level
- Augments advancements in maturity through the use of Generic Goals 2 and 3

A Note on the Any-Way-You-Want Way

We've just looked at the two official ways to implement CMMI, the Continuous Representation and the Staged Representation. I call these two official because these are the only two modes of implementation recognized by the SEI for Standard CMMI Appraisal Method for Process Improvement (SCAMPI) appraisals, the official way to recognize CMMI achievements. If your shop wishes to eventually be appraised, it will want to adopt CMMI using the Continuous or the Staged approach. However, there is a third approach, one that the SEI itself endorses, which I call the any-way-you-want approach. You use the goals and practices of CMMI any way you want, taking its recommendations and lessons and using them to make your shop better. It is process improvement solely for the sake of process improvement, and that may be the best way of all to work toward making your shop more operationally effective.

CMMI and Project Management

So far, we have outlined, in broad strokes, some general characteristics and traits of CMMI-DEV.

- It is one of three CMMI constellations from the SEI.
- It is a framework you can use to build a process improvement and production management program.
- It consists of 22 Process Areas.
- The Process Areas can be grouped into four categories: Project Management, Process Management, Engineering, and Support.
- Each Process Area consists of one or more Specific Goals; each Specific Goal consists of two or more Specific Practices.

- You can implement CMMI-DEV by using the Continuous Representation (freeform) or the Staged Representation (fixed-form).
- Success with CMMI (as is true with any improvement program) takes a commitment to process and a commitment to time.

With that overview in place, we can now extend our discussion of CMMI and its relevance to project management success.

Project Management Success with CMMI

The title of this book is *Project Management Success with CMMI®*, but there is probably no universal definition of what project management success really means. A classic or ultimate definition might read something like this:

> The product (or service) was delivered on time, within budget, in a way that met the expectations of the customer, while furthering the business mission of the organization.

Four conditions are contained in that definition, and they are the ones we most often think of when we consider whether or not a certain effort was successful.

1. Did we deliver on time?
2. Did we deliver within budget?
3. Does the product do what it's supposed to do?
4. Did we realize a positive return on investment?

More often than not, however, not all those conditions are met, or they are met with varying degrees of certitude. In some shops, a project might run 20% over schedule and 12% over budget and still be considered a success. In a different organization, say, one with a different customer base, those same numbers might indicate a seriously compromised effort.

Success is a judgment shaped by the people who are impacted by an effort. If things are perceived to have gone well, the concept of success might be easily applied. But because it can be based on perceptions, the definition itself can shift in the eyes of the person doing the viewing. A project that the customer considers a success might be thought by senior management to have been a dismal failure. A project manager might consider a project a success while the customers feel they were put through the wringer.

As we'll see in this book, one of the keys to fostering project management success is to define up front what success will mean for the project. This definition is cooperatively defined—by you, senior management, and your customer. We'll see later that the recommendations and activities contained in our slice of CMMI directly support this idea.

But the real aim of this book is not so much focused on arriving at the finish line of success. It is more concerned with preparing for success. The finish line itself may be something we—as project managers and technology managers—cannot always draw a tape across. After all, we live in the real world, and more than that, we live in the sometimes unreal world of business. Customers change their minds. Funding gets pulled. Market conditions change. Executive strategies shift. A lot of what can ultimately contribute to project success is very often out of our control. The best we can do (and this is not a compromise; it's an appropriate assumption of responsibility) is to prepare our shops to be successful, to set into place the right kinds of controls and oversight mechanisms so that we can influence those success elements that fall within our domains.

What are those elements? What things contribute to budget, schedule, customer, and business success? If you happen to be a project manager, you'll probably know them from rote experience. If you are familiar with PMI standards, you'll recognize them from the PMBOK. They are not proprietary, nor are they secrets.

These elements are what I call *externalized organizational capabilities*. They have been developed by the organization to guide and support the people who must manage and execute project work. Often these capabilities are expressed as operational standards. In process-centric shops, they'll turn up as parts of a process or procedure. In fact, the theme of this book is that these capabilities *should* become part of a project management process program. They address the core concerns that govern the raison d'être for the discipline of project management. They are the guidelines and policies you need to (among other things):

- Define the mission and goals of the project
- Estimate the work of the project
- Create a plan for the project
- Assign resources
- Establish budgets
- Schedule tasks
- Allocate work responsibility
- Monitor and report on progress
- Review and assess key work products
- Control key work products
- Track milestones
- Manage change
- Communicate with relevant internal and external parties
- Measure quality
- Evaluate project effectiveness

Those are pure project management concerns, pure in the sense that they apply just as well to bridges or shoelaces as they do to technology development. And that's a good place to start when you wish to establish a project management program in your technology shop.

The advantage of CMMI is that the seven Process Areas described for Maturity Level 2 deliver these capabilities to you in a proven framework well supported by the industry at large. That's the reason for this book and the reason for its focus.

The Seven Process Areas of Maturity Level 2

Our discussion now leads us to the central theme of this book: You can establish an effective project management program by using a subset of the Process Areas in CMMI, namely, those seven Process Areas described for Maturity Level 2. That's not to say that I am recommending you implement the Staged Representation of the model. You can just as effectively use the Continuous Representation with the same seven Process Areas, developing each at its own pace. The convenient characteristic of Maturity Level 2 is simply that it was designed to introduce project management controls into organizations that may be lacking process exposure or experience. The idea is that the foundation of any process program should probably begin with basic project management capabilities. That's what technology development is all about anyway, so it might as well be set into place at the beginning.

In this book, we'll discuss the following seven Process Areas:

1. Project Planning: estimating, planning, and commitment
2. Project Monitoring & Control: tracking progress, adjusting parameters, and dealing with risk
3. Requirements Management: understanding and controlling scope
4. Configuration Management: managing the evolution of key work products
5. Supplier Agreement Management: coordinating vendors and assessing vendor work
6. Measurement & Analysis: using metrics to quantify progress, efficiency, and quality
7. Process & Product Quality Assurance: monitoring quality and compliance goals

The heart of this book deals with these seven CMMI Process Areas, the ones you'll typically implement when you want to achieve Maturity Level 2.

Level 2 Is the Beginning

The intention of this book is not to deliver a comprehensive tome on project management, process improvement, or CMMI. The intention is to present you with an overview—light enough, I hope, to be both digestible and actionable—that you can use to introduce effective project management processes into your organization. I am not advocating the replacement of standards such as ISO 9001:2000, OPM3, or your own proprietary quality program. I wish to address those shops that have not moved far down the process road.

That being the case, it's important to appreciate the scope of what we encounter at Maturity Level 2.

Maturity Level 2 will in all likelihood not address all of your project management needs. Those needs vary so much between organizations that there is no complete common core set. But you will find that you can use the goals and practices described for Maturity Level 2 to institute an effective process program, one designed to enhance your project management capabilities and one designed to be improved on, expanded, and extended over time. If you come to this book with this beginning step in mind, I think you will find value in what we discuss here.

A Note on CMMI and the PMI's PMBOK

Some people look at process frameworks such as CMMI and at project management standards such as the PMBOK and see two different things. They perhaps think that CMMI is better suited to technical teams, while the PMBOK is the thing for the project management office. They see domain distinctions that they don't want to cloud up with redundancies or conflicting viewpoints.

That's a perception I'd like to clear up.

I work with many project management organizations over the course of a year. And more and more, I see organizations requiring their project managers to carry PMP certification. But the organizations themselves don't always provide an appropriate PMP-like infrastructure. And often, when they do, it's little more than a soft lifecycle standard like Initiation, Planning, Execution/Control, and Closure.

In preparing this book, I revisited the PMBOK with the theory that the focus of it and the recommendations of CMMI Maturity Level 2 would be not only compatible but also complementary. And what I found confirms this. We'll discuss the relationship between the PMBOK and CMMI in some more depth in Chapter 11, but for now let's just take a quick look at a very brief condensation of the major considerations contained within the PMBOK's ten Knowledge Areas and see whether they are accounted for in CMMI (Table 2–1).

Table 2–1: *A Generalized CMMI–PMBOK Mapping*

Focus	PMBOK Knowledge Area	CMMI-DEV Process Area
Integrating mission	Scope Management	Project Planning
Integrating scope	Project Management	Project Planning
Integrating teams	Staffing Management	Project Planning
Defining scope	Scope Management	Requirements Management
Managing scope	Scope Management	Requirements Management
Identifying key work products	Milestone List	Project Planning
Version control of key work products	Baseline Management	Configuration Management
Establishing schedules	Schedule Management	Project Planning
Identifying milestones	Milestone List	Project Planning
Establishing budgets	Cost Management	Project Planning
Monitoring expenditure activities	Project Management	Measurement & Analysis
Establishing quality goals	Quality Baselines	Process & Product Quality Assurance
Monitoring quality goals	Quality Management	Process & Product Quality Assurance
Providing adequate resources	Staffing Management	Project Planning

Continues

Table 2–1: *A Generalized CMMI–PMBOK Mapping (Continued)*

Focus	PMBOK Knowledge Area	CMMI-DEV Process Area
Ensuring communications	Communications Management	Project Monitoring & Control
Managing issues and risks	Risk Management	Project Monitoring & Control
Managing procurement actions	Procurement Management	Supplier Agreement Management
Managing vendor contributions	Procurement Management	Supplier Agreement Management

The answer, obviously, is yes. And that leads us to an obvious conclusion: The CMMI Process Areas we discuss in this book are plug-and-play compatible with the project management viewpoints your PMPs have been trained to consider. The two approaches can integrate seamlessly, supporting one another, with no redundancy, overlap, or conflict of goals.

In the following chapters, we'll look at each of the seven Maturity Level 2 Process Areas in more depth and explore how each, as an element of an ongoing process management and improvement program, can contribute to project management success in your organization.

Chapter 3

Project Planning

We push planning in a big way at Olive. I have seen companies that treat it more as an overhead obligation, something to get through to get to the work. We see it much more as the beginning of the real work, and so we strive to take as much time as we can to plan and we like to involve our clients as much as we can in planning activities. In this industry, it's a well-known maxim that the more time you spend on design, the less time you'll spend on programming. It's the same with projects. Plan them well up front and you'll find that major realignments and unattended misdirections are usually avoided.

Kricket Ichwantoro, President, Olive, LLC
Process improvement consulting organization

The first CMMI Process Area we'll look at is Project Planning. That's a logical place to start given that the focus of this book is on using the seven CMMI Process Areas found at Maturity Level 2 to foster project success. When you look at the discipline of project management, you'll find a solid emphasis on planning, no matter what the industry. Construction projects rely on layers of architectural schematics, military campaigns rely on battle and logistic plans, oceanic excursions rely on navigational plots. They are all forms of project plans, mapping a path to the desired end point based on a set starting point. Narrowing this more to the reach of this book's audience, you'll find that the bodies of knowledge put out by organizations like the Project Management Institute and the American Management Association share this dedication to planning. You may have heard the axiom: If you fail to plan, you plan to fail. There's a lot to that outlook.

Planning is also big in the realm of process improvement. CMMI, as we'll see here, stakes a lot on it. The other major process improvement methodologies do also. Six Sigma, ISO 9001, and ITIL (to name three of the other well-known ones) all base their process and management activities on documented, agreed-upon plans.

In short, the institutions that drive the approaches and philosophies to project management, while differing in many aspects and views, are all in agreement on the value of planning. In this chapter, we'll look at how the Project Planning Process Area can be used to shape and frame a technology project from the outset so that success can be managed and achieved.

The Purpose of Project Planning

The chief purpose of Project Planning under CMMI is to develop an externalized mechanism for managing the project. A couple of key points here. First is the idea of externalization. For a plan to be effective, it can't exist solely in someone's head. It needs to be documented in some form or fashion, externalized, placed out in the open. I'm surprised by how often I run into this issue when I work with development shops. Many people prefer to outline only the thinnest of plans on paper and then rely on their inner visions to carry the bulk of the activities from concept to realization. People usually adopt this approach because they feel it will streamline accountability, shield folks from unnecessary detail, or reduce the amount of points of conflict or contention that might come from a more open approach. Those reasons may be heartfelt, but they are not based in sound business practice. In fact, a good plan, placed in the open early on, will effectively promote accountability, establish necessary detail, and provide a basis for common agreement that will help minimize conflict. Externalization is the key for taking a plan from being a subjective approach to being an objective one.

The second point is that the plan is a management mechanism. Many people I have met can plan very well, but once the project gets going, they never go back to the plan; they manage on the fly. The value of a well-designed plan is its ability to predict action. With the predictions in place, actual project activity can then be compared to what you planned for. When you use the plan as your chief management mechanism, you provide a common referential base all stakeholders can use to acquire a common understanding of status, progress, and issues to be addressed.

That's the strategic purpose of planning. The tactical view is a little more concrete. Under CMMI, the tactical purpose of Project Planning is to establish realistic estimates as the basis for planning, document the path needed to move from objective to realization, and then establish a level of common agreement among relevant parties. Let's take a quick look at each part of the tactical purpose.

Establish Realistic Estimates

Any project, no matter how small it might be, requires the commitment of resources—people, money, tools, facilities. And that cost has to be accounted for in a responsible fashion. Management 101 says that a business should not commit its resources until it has a general idea about what it's committing to. Jumping in blind or with unfounded enthusiasm can lead to more than a few unpleasant situations: wasted spending, diminishing returns on investments, strained customer relationships. So the first consideration that CMMI introduces for Project Planning is estimation. The idea here is both basic and sound. Before you can adequately plan for what you want to build and before you can intelligently decide whether you should build it, you should estimate the commitment required. This could be expressed as time, cost, resources—whatever factors are important to your organization. The estimates you come up with, in order to reflect the true shape of the project, should be based on some kind of manageable formula and should be derived to reflect reality. They should be realistic.

Document a Management Approach for the Project

This second purpose lies at the heart of Project Planning, and that is to document the plan. As we'll see in the next section, a plan (and here we can use the PMBOK's definition) usually consists of a series of components, plans of individual focus that can include the following:

- Project scope management plan
- Schedule management plan
- Cost management plan
- Quality management plan
- Process improvement plan
- Staffing management plan
- Communication management plan
- Risk management plan
- Procurement management plan

For the sake of simplicity at this point, let's describe all these elements as a charter of commitments and a schedule of action (with activities mapped out over time). Taken together, the charter and the schedule constitute the management approach for the project. In a way, you can see them representing a management contract. It details what the team is going to do, when the team will do it, what the team will need in order to do it, and how other people are going to know when it's done. Here the idea of externalization comes to fruition. The plan documents the management approach that will be used to guide the project. This approach is then available to all parties who have a stake in the successful outcome of the project. And that takes us to the third purpose.

Obtain Commitment to the Approach from Relevant Parties

The project plan can serve as a common base of understanding for everyone who has a stake in the project. This includes the project team members, executive management, and customer representatives. Establishing this common understanding—success criteria and acceptance criteria—is important. Before a project begins in earnest, before commitments and expenditures are released into the work stream, the key players should agree to the commitments and resource descriptions contained in the plan. In order for a project to be considered successful when it has been concluded, the folks waiting at the finish line will need to agree that things are indeed good. The best way to ensure this agreement at the finish line is to set it in place at the starting line. Early commitment to the mission, scope, cost, and run of the project aligns all parties to work toward a common goal, one that can readily be acknowledged as successful.

What Is a Plan?

From a practical standpoint, a project plan can be anything you want it to be, as long as it helps you manage the project along common lines of expectations. But under CMMI, and in the realm of disciplines such as the PMBOK, the idea of a plan means something very specific. In my consulting work, I encounter a lot of people who use Microsoft Project as a project management tool, and to many of these people, the schedule that's based in Project is considered to be the plan. From a formal viewpoint, that is only partly right. If you looked at the PMI's PMBOK, you would find a definition of a project plan that includes two major components: the schedule, of course, and a prerequisite, the project charter. The charter is usually formed as a narrative document. Its purpose is to document the mission, goals, and scope of the initiative; to define needed resources; to establish communications and reporting accountability; to document benchmarks and milestones; and to bind all of this into a distinct and autonomous work effort, something with a specific start date and end date.

The schedule, which is most often born out of the charter, provides the work breakdown structure that delineates major and minor tasks and workflows and assigns associated responsibility. Together the charter and the schedule make up the full project plan.

CMMI pretty much shares this view with the PMBOK. It defines the project plan as the chief tool used to manage the project. From the plan, all management activity should spring. Plan adjustments are welcome, but managing outside the plan is frowned upon. The plan does need to encompass a full picture of the project: scope, requirements, objectives, goals, resources, budgets, stakeholders, constraints, risks, and so on.

In the following sections, we'll look at the parts and pieces that CMMI recommends you include in a project plan, and we'll discuss the value that each can bring to your project management efforts.

Project Planning Goals and Practices

CMMI defines three Specific Goals and fourteen Specific Practices for Project Planning. Here is the official specification text for each of these elements.

SG 1   ESTABLISH ESTIMATES
Estimates of project planning parameters are established and maintained.

SP 1.1   ESTIMATE THE SCOPE OF THE PROJECT
Establish a top-level work breakdown structure (WBS) to estimate the scope of the project.

SP 1.2   ESTABLISH ESTIMATES OF WORK PRODUCT AND TASK ATTRIBUTES
Establish and maintain estimates of the attributes of the work products and tasks.

SP 1.3   DEFINE PROJECT LIFECYCLE
Define the project lifecycle phases on which to scope the planning effort.

SP 1.4   DETERMINE ESTIMATES OF EFFORT AND COST
Estimate the project effort and cost for the work products and tasks based on estimation rationale.

SG 2   DEVELOP A PROJECT PLAN
A project plan is established and maintained as the basis for managing the project.

SP 2.1   ESTABLISH THE BUDGET AND SCHEDULE
Establish and maintain the project's budget and schedule.

SP 2.2   IDENTIFY PROJECT RISKS
Identify and analyze project risks.

SP 2.3   PLAN FOR DATA MANAGEMENT
Plan for the management of project data.

SP 2.4   Plan for Project Resources
Plan for necessary resources to perform the project.

SP 2.5   Plan for Needed Knowledge and Skills
Plan for knowledge and skills needed to perform the project.

SP 2.6   Plan Stakeholder Involvement
Plan the involvement of identified stakeholders.

SP 2.7   Establish the Project Plan
Establish and maintain the overall project plan content.

SG 3   Obtain Commitment to the Plan
Commitments to the project plan are established and maintained.

SP 3.1   Review Plans That Affect the Project
Review all plans that affect the project to understand project commitments.

SP 3.2   Reconcile Work and Resource Levels
Reconcile the project plan to reflect available and estimated resources.

SP 3.3   Obtain Plan Commitment
Obtain commitment from relevant stakeholders responsible for performing and supporting plan execution.

Generic Goals and Practices

See Chapter 10 for information about the important Generic Goals and Practices that support project management success for all the Process Areas at Maturity Level 2.

SG 1: Establish Estimates

The responsibility for coming up with project estimates varies from organization to organization. In some large shops I have worked with, the job went to project estimators, people specifically charged with figuring and calculating costs. (This is actually a fairly common role in the more established project management disciplines, such as major construction.) In other shops, the job goes to a certain level of management, the idea being that estimation belongs at the strategic approval level. And in still others, the job is assigned to a project manager who rounds up the facts, data, and assumptions needed to put the required estimates together. Of course, all three of these are valid approaches as long as they are founded on the same assumption: Estimates should be calculated. That is, they should be systematically generated.

I'm sure you've been in organizations that take a different approach. They take the "How long do you think it will take?" approach, along with "What do you feel it will cost?" and "How many do you suppose we'll need?" That's the intuitive approach to estimation, and it's the approach that CMMI would like to see minimized as much as possible. The reasoning is clear. All estimations—no matter how they are achieved—are approximations and so are rarely right on target. The problem with relying solely on intuition or personal experience is that you have no real way to objectify the estimation techniques, so you have no real way to improve or refine them. By using a systematic approach—even if it is a simple formula or a simple method of soliciting expert opinion—you can evaluate the estimate, measure it, and improve it.

Naturally, poor estimates can lead to poor planning. So this first goal of the Project Planning Process Area is to establish estimates that can be generated in a consistent and predictable way, for the duration of a particular project as well as across projects. The subtext that can be understood here is to produce estimates that are logically derived, are realistic given the needs and constraints of the project, and serve as good indicators of the level of commitment required of the organization. It's also important to note that estimates should include the rationale used to derive the numbers, so that estimates can be regenerated when needed. And it's a good rule of thumb to remember that the best estimates usually come from those people who will be required to do the work.

Specific Goal 1, Establish Estimates, introduces practices that prompt us to think through a range of mission, scope, and complexity issues (Figure 3–1) so that we can not only derive viable, practical estimates

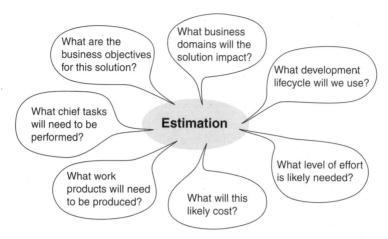

Figure 3–1: *Project estimation as a set of planning considerations*

but also do so in a systematic way, one that can be repeated and thus improved.

Four Specific Practices are defined for this first Project Planning goal. Through these activities you establish a picture of six foundational project elements. The scope of the project is estimated so that you can get a handle on the business mission of the initiative. Major work products that will probably be needed to realize this mission are then tentatively identified. The work tasks necessary to produce these products are likewise identified. The likely lifecycle the project will follow to structure these tasks is then defined. Finally, approximations of the effort and costs (usually expressed in terms of time and money, but you're free to use any denominational units your shop wishes) are derived from the prior four elements.

You'll notice two things here. First, these elements all build on each other; they are all related to each other. And second, once these estimates are in place and approved, you have the base you need to begin planning how you'll manage the project according to these constraints.

Let's look at the four Specific Practices that CMMI recommends to help you achieve the first Specific Goal.

SP 1.1: Estimate the Scope of the Project

Estimating the scope of the project is important because this will give you a feel for the size of the mission you are trying to take on. Sometimes you'll have plenty of information in order to thoroughly understand this scope. You may have a complete customer requirements document. You may be adding to an existing well-documented system. Here the scope is readily available. In other instances, you may have only the thinnest description of what your customer wants. In this case, you'll have to ally with them to discern just what the true scope is likely to be. The other elements you estimate will use this initial positioning as a logical baseline. I have found that whether you understand the scope well or not, you will benefit by taking into consideration three steps that, when taken together, work to give you a true picture of the potential project scope.

1. Understand the business reach.
2. Establish the technical foundation.
3. Evaluate integration considerations.

Let's take a quick look at each.

Understand the Business Reach

It's usually a good idea, even if the project's scope appears to be well defined, to meet with your customers and discuss the business reach of the project, that is, what business functions the system will pull from, manage, and push to. Business users, while quite expert at business and data flows, may not always consider those three areas of technical manipulation. Your discussions might simply confirm what has already been expressed, or they may lead to insights that help you pinpoint the full reach of the solution. The value in this liaison is that very early, you and your customers establish a common understanding of the project's likely business scope.

Establish the Technical Foundation

Understanding the technical foundation that the solution must rest on or work through is another important estimation element. System architectures can have direct and profound influences on the scope and cost of a technology project. As part of understanding scope, it's a good idea to document the foundation that the project—and the project team—will need to live on. Does the foundation already exist within the company? Is it established, proven, and stable? Or is it new, an area the company has had little exposure to or experience with? These considerations will play an important role as you begin to determine such factors as risk, resources, skill sets, and so on.

Evaluate Integration Considerations

Finally, it is helpful to think through any integration considerations that might be in play for the project. Business solutions and systems rarely operate in isolation. Chances are that the scope of your project may reach into realms and domains that you cannot directly control, so you will need to plan for cooperation from these other areas. You may have to pull from other systems, you may have to push to other systems, you may need data storage that is managed by a separate team, you may be required to send reports to specialized organizational units. All of these integration considerations have the potential to impact the scope of the project. By working to identify them—at least as possible connections—early, you will position your understanding of scope to account for the right mix of work tasks, products, and resources.

SP 1.2: Establish Estimates of Work Product and Task Attributes

Once you have a good understanding of the scope of the project, you can take your estimation analysis a step deeper and begin to assess the kinds of work products you'll need to produce within this scope and what tasks might be required to get these products out. All projects have deliverables, small ones and major ones. At this point, the major ones are probably the important ones to consider. Of course, specialized team tasks and activities can be associated with these work products. Taken together, the work products and the associated production tasks take your understanding of the project, and your ability to accurately estimate it, to a finer level of detail.

Two steps are valuable here.

1. Define key deliverables.
2. Identify major production tasks.

A Note on the Order of CMMI Practices

As I discuss the Specific and Generic Practices contained in CMMI at Maturity Level 2, I'll tend to imply an implementation order to them. This order is artificial. It's simply my way of explaining the tips and techniques I've observed for using the practices effectively. And while the practices in the model are themselves numbered, the numbering is not intended to be sequential. You are free to implement the practices in any order you choose, using any relation to others that you find helpful.

Define Key Deliverables

When you plan a project within what I'll call an organized technology shop, you'll find that you can readily identify two types of major deliverables: standard ones and custom ones. The standard deliverables are those work products you automatically produce for your shop, no matter what the scope of the project. They are policy within the shop. For example, a well-run shop will probably always expect that a project plan will be produced for any project that comes in its doors. Likewise, it will probably insist on some form of requirements document, a data and document repository, and perhaps a lessons-learned closing document. One value of a process program is that it helps instantiate these kinds of deliverables across all projects, so they are always included as part of an estimate.

Custom deliverables are those products particular to the needs of the current project. Will your project require a set of custom deliverables? Will it require a particular high-level design? A specific user acceptance test plan? Will you need to create a prototype? Will you need to create specialized, mock-up test data? Will you have to set up a special environment to accommodate unique project characteristics? Thinking through these kinds of custom deliverables will enable you to identify the full set of major products you and your teams will be required to produce.

Identify Major Production Tasks

With an inventory of the work products your project will likely require, you can then estimate the range of activities that will be required to produce each work product. If your project requires a unique set of test data, you might identify the following tasks for your team: specify test data, create test data, and validate test data with the customer. The team needs to accomplish these three tasks to get to the final product. If you need to establish a configuration management plan, you might identify four major tasks: draft the plan, review the plan, revise the plan, and publish the plan. By associating a set of tasks with each major deliverable, you are, in effect, setting into place the beginnings of a work breakdown structure, an ordered set of activities that will result in a detailed project schedule.

SP 1.3: Define Project Lifecycle

The project lifecycle is another important estimation consideration. The lifecycle contains a series of work phases that you'll require the project to pass through. It will also establish an order for the availability of skill sets and resources. In SP 1.2, you identified the work products and the tasks that your project would require of your teams. When you select a lifecycle, you can then integrate the work products and the activities into the defined phases of the lifecycle. You are now a step closer to producing a full and detailed work breakdown structure.

Two steps are handy here.

1. Determine the lifecycle.
2. Map the development phases within the lifecycle.

Determine the Lifecycle

Some technology shops use one and only one lifecycle. It might be one of several approaches: waterfall, modified waterfall, spiral development, Agile, RAD, Xtreme. Others will sanction a choice of lifecycles. In a less desirable turn, some shops leave the decision completely up to the project manager or the lead engineer. The best option aside, the point here is to set the choice of a lifecycle in place early because the one you select will have an impact on the costs and duration of the project.

Your organization may choose to establish a lifecycle selection procedure, or it might define preset criteria for using one lifecycle over another. However you approach it, select and document the lifecycle at this stage of estimation, and then map your development phases to it.

Map the Development Phases

At this point, you have gone through a recommended series of analyses and assessments that will bring you from a general understanding of your project's needs down to a level that encompasses much more detail. Scope should now be much clearer, as should work products and production tasks. The picture won't be perfect, and it's not critical that it be. Rather, you have put into place a set of concrete elements against which you can now apply systematic and realistic estimates.

A last analysis is to use the lifecycle as a base to map the products (milestones) and work tasks across the life of the project. Your picture of the likely shape of the project can be considered complete.

SP 1.4: Determine Estimates of Effort and Cost

Now you can determine the factors that management and your customers probably have the most interest in: how long it will take and how much it will cost. Most people think of this practice in terms of time and money. But effort and cost do not have to be interpreted this way. Your shop might quote cost as total resource hours. Likewise, effort might be calendar days or aggregate team work days. The denomination is not as important as is the documentation of what these numbers are.

This is the culmination of the estimation process. You have quantified the qualitative characteristics of the project. And, if you have followed these practices, you have done so in an organized and systematic manner. You now have at hand what can be seen as an appreciation of the kind of commitment you, your shop, and your customers will need to sign up for in order to successfully take on the project. For this reason, once you have documented the estimates of effort and cost, you should review these with all the impacted parties and seek their approval for moving forward. With this approval, you can now work to establish the driving management tool for the project, the project plan.

SG 2: Develop a Project Plan

Establishing a set of practical and realistic estimates is the first goal of Project Planning. As you exercise the practices recommended for that goal, you will emerge with a good understanding of the size and scope of what you have to build. And with this understanding, you will be able to plan your approach to the project. Of course, you can always begin creating the plan before the estimates are all done, but it should be clear that the detail of the estimates is what gives you the foundation you need to carve out your attack plan. In the absence of the estimates—or at least in the absence of the greater part of the estimation picture—much of your planning may fall back to intelligent guessing or wishful thinking. But with the estimates in place, and with their review and approval by authoritative parties, you can now set the pro forma plan in place.

Earlier in this chapter, I mentioned that many people consider the project schedule to be equal to the project plan. No doubt the schedule is crucial and essential, and it may be the most actively referenced element of a plan, but it is only one part of the plan. I also mentioned the PMI's view of a plan: a collection of plans that can be used to address, among other things, scope, cost, resources, procurement, and communications management. I simplify this view for the purpose of this book by referring to the plans together as the project charter and the ordered, coordinated WBS as the detailed schedule. That's pretty much the view of CMMI, too, although CMMI doesn't organize the plan into those distinct components. It leaves the organization up to you.

A project plan is really a collection of distinct planning elements, each of which contributes to a project's strategic positioning (Figure 3–2).

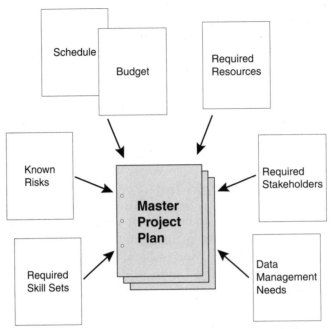

Figure 3–2: *Planning as a series of integrated plans*

The project plan you document might be one big plan or a collection of smaller, integrated plans. What's important is the content addressed under planning considerations. The goal is to develop a comprehensive approach to managing the project once it begins.

The purpose of this second Project Planning goal is to put a plan down on paper, to document the management approach you will take to realize the project's objectives. CMMI defines seven Specific Practices for this goal. If you look at these practices, you can discern an implied table of contents for a project plan. You can see what kinds of essential content CMMI recommends be stated in a plan, no matter what else you might elect to include. The content areas are as follows:

- Budget
- Schedule
- Data management needs

- Resources
- Knowledge and skill sets
- Stakeholder involvement

The Specific Practices describe activities that will help you establish the details that will drive plan creation. Let's take a look at each now.

SP 2.1: Establish the Budget and Schedule

This first practice is considered by many to be the heart of the plan. Here we establish what the effort will cost over its lifecycle (based on the estimates we derived earlier) and what activities mapped out over time will be required to complete the mission. The budget and schedule have particular importance in the realm of project management because these two items control the main commitments of the organization. The budget will be used to manage the financial obligation in terms of cash flow, expenses, cost efficiencies, and profit. The schedule will be used to manage the time obligation. Every company deals with a fixed cache of time, limited by its people and its other commitments. Schedule interruptions or deviations almost always impact the budget. The budget and schedule should be carefully established as interrelated components.

Often I recommend that this be the last practice you undertake before publishing the plan. Many of the other details that follow under this goal have potential to shape both items. However you move to put together the budget and schedule, here are four steps that might help you think through them.

1. Establish the cost factor.
2. Establish the burn rate.
3. Establish key milestones.
4. Establish the WBS baseline.

Establish the Cost Factor

The first consideration is to establish the cost factor or, in other words, to understand or acquire the cost factor. This is naturally related to the budget. Most people think of budgets in terms of dollars—how much money we have allocated to a given effort. But in many shops, project managers don't deal with money issues, which are left to another area of responsibility. The project managers are asked to work with another cost factor. Usually this is something like resource hours or work weeks or staff load. For your project, it's important to establish what cost factor your management wants you to manage by. This will help you then establish such cost measures as burn rate.

Establish the Rate of Consumption

Consumption is an expectation of how project costs should ebb and flow over time. This bears direct relationship to the schedule and to the resources assigned to the project. You can realistically anticipate that the level and intensity of work activity will rise and fall across the various project phases. The goal is to get to the end of the budget at the same time as you've arrived at the end of the project. Without tracking this rate of use, you run the risk of burning up your capital well in advance of the finish line. So, as part of the budget, perhaps as a description of budget expenses laid out over time, set a burn rate in place. You'll find it becomes a valuable item to monitor once the project starts moving.

Establish Key Milestones

The first two considerations above deal with the budget. These next two deal with the schedule. Milestones are critical junctures at which project progress can be ascertained. They typically serve as the foundation of the work breakdown structure. Milestones are usually described in one of two ways: either as the production of a major work product or as a point in the schedule in which certain critical path activities should have been realized. Most often these two are combined. Milestones let you map out checkpoints along the project lifecycle, and they help you establish the work breakdown needed to get to these checkpoints. With the right set of milestones, you have a way to ensure that you won't veer too far off course during the project. They provide smaller goals and objectives; if you manage well against these, the larger goals and objectives should be well protected.

Establish the Schedule Baseline

The WBS can best be managed by capturing it in a detailed schedule that describes the individual activities that will be executed in a particular sequence with identified resources in order to achieve a related set of milestones. Many people develop a schedule using tools like Primavera and Microsoft Project. And many people see the WBS reflected in the schedule as the chief management component of any project plan. It certainly is the one that is most prone to adjustment and change. In fact, its purpose is to be adjusted and changed. The WBS reflects the use of time and resources. The initial version of the WBS—the one that you develop here—should be seen as a starting point. It's a baseline aligned with the budget, the resources, and the milestones. But as we'll see in Chapter 4, Project Monitoring & Control, the WBS contains many planned values that will be continually assessed against what's actually happening, the actuals. One of the main jobs of the project manager is to keep the actual values in sync with the planned values.

SP 2.2: **Identify Project Risks**

This second practice introduces a level of risk management into this Process Area and into Maturity Level 2 as a whole. Identifying project risks is an important management step that reaches across two planes. First is to note any assumptions that the plan is based on. The estimates that you and your team derived earlier and use as the foundation for the plan may have been developed using a set of assumptions. If those assumptions turn out to be unfounded or if their foundations change, the plan itself may need revisiting. Second is to identify known risks. At this stage in the project—and we should be very early in the lifecycle here—you'll probably not be able to identify all the risks that will pop up after the project begins to unfold in earnest. But you may be well aware of some known risks. Soft requirements, potential staff changes, evolving business needs—a host of factors in flux at the start of a project can carry the potential to dramatically affect the project.

The plan you are putting together needs to acknowledge these risks because if one or more of them percolates into a real issue, you and your teams will likely have to adjust the plan or the commitments within the plan to address the issues. Because commitment to the plan by all key stakeholders is such an important trait of smooth project management (see the third goal that follows), you need to give your plan participants all the relevant information that they need to sign up to the plan. This includes the risks.

Here are three quick activities to take into account when you are preparing to identify project risks.

1. Document known risks (and assumptions).
2. Understand constraints.
3. Prepare to track issues.

Document Known Risks

You should document known risks and assumptions in the plan. Often it's helpful to prioritize these items, assign some value to the likelihood of each occurring, describe the potential impact of each, and even assign an owner, a person or persons responsible for keeping an eye on the risk threshold. If you are unaware of any noteworthy risks at this point, it's a good idea to state that in the plan. Once you circulate the plan for review, this placeholder will serve as a visual cue for others to think about this topic and perhaps identify their own sets of risks and important assumptions.

Understand Constraints

It's also a good idea to understand the constraints facing the project at the outset. For example, you may be building a product that absolutely has to be available at a very specific point in time. This schedule is so essential to business objectives that it is to be considered unmovable, so any project or plan adjustments must exclude touching the schedule. This is a constraint. You may be faced with resource constraints or budget constraints or any number of other constraints. It's a good idea to identify and understand these constraints in your plan so that all parties impacted by the constraints know that these drivers must be acknowledged across the life of the project.

Prepare to Track Issues

Once you have identified major assumptions, known risks, and project constraints, you should prepare to track these as a part of ongoing project monitoring and control. There are a number of ways you can do this. You can create an issues tracking log, perhaps something as simple as a spreadsheet, that serves as both a plan reference and a tracking tool. Some shops set up risk management databases and input the set of items during planning for follow-up as the project gets started. Whatever approach you take, the idea is to not simply record risks, assumptions, and constraints for planning purposes only, but to use this information as a foundation for moving forward in project management.

A Note on the Term Plan

The next four practices we look at start with the word *plan*: Plan for Data Management, Plan for Project Resources, Plan for Needed Knowledge and Skills, Plan Stakeholder Involvement. In the realm of CMMI (and most other process and management approaches), to plan means to identify what will be done, when it will occur, and who will do it. And that's what will be needed for these next practices. Your planning will be stronger if you make sure to include the tasks required to fulfill the activity, the schedule for executing the tasks, and an assignment of the resources responsible for carrying out the tasks on time.

SP 2.3: Plan for Data Management

Projects are pretty much data-making machines. You may turn out any number of work products, plans, reports, schedules, issue logs, test cases, memos, and so on. This third practice addresses the importance of managing this data. Implied here is that people will need access to certain data sets in order to do their work, and the data sets produced will need to be protected and controlled in a way that ensures their ongoing integrity. That's why it's important to plan for data management. This practice is actually a complement to the Process Area we'll discuss in Chapter 6, Configuration Management.

I offer two steps to consider here.

1. Account for system and data access.
2. Plan for configuration management.

Account for System and Data Access

Your project plan should identify the kinds of data and system access your people will need in order to begin project work. This is an often overlooked management duty. But because it is essential to uninterrupted progress and usually involves coordination with other organizational groups, it's important that access be described at the most practical level of detail in the plan. This usually involves documenting which team resources will need what level of access into which systems, databases, and information repositories.

Plan for Configuration Management

As just noted, we discuss planning for configuration management in full detail in Chapter 6. The purpose here is for the plan to define where project data will be stored, what types of check-in/check-out procedures might be used, who will have access to which components of data, how data will be backed up and archived, and so on. There are usually two levels of data management. The lighter of the two is version control, which often applies to project management documents such as schedules and activity plans. Change tracking and version numbering are used to keep the latest release of a document available to the teams. Configuration management is the heavier discipline, and it provides for full (usually automated) security around data sets, governing access to the data, the ability to change data, and the authority to distribute data.

SP 2.4: Plan for Project Resources

Your project will require the use of very specific resources within your organization, most notably human resources. Your plan will need to identify the resources you expect from the organization. Of course, resources are not just people. They can also be work areas, computing facilities, tools and equipment, and so on. If you do not establish the need for these up front, you risk running into one of two situations. First, management may not allow you to have the resources if they are seen as excessive, out of scope, or cost-prohibited. Second, even if the resources are allowed, if you have not reserved them through your plan, they may not be available to you when you need them. That's why it's a good idea to play it safe and provide a section in your plan where you identify the kinds of resources you'll require.

There are four steps you should consider taking when building this part of your plan.

1. Plan for team size and roles.
2. Plan for needed facilities.
3. Plan for needed tools.
4. Account for integration requirements.

Plan for Team Size and Roles

Identify the team resources your project will need over its lifecycle. This may not be as specific as citing people's names, but it is important to identify the required job roles, how many people you anticipate needing for each role, at what points in the lifecycle these resources will be used and for how long, and how the size of the team may grow or shrink over the different phases of the project.

Plan for Needed Facilities

Your project may require special facilities—office space, conference rooms, laboratories, access to restricted areas, and so on. If this is the case, you should identify what these facility needs will be. Management and your customers may be unaware of such needs and their potential to influence the project. On top of that, this requirement can often have a significant impact on the budget and the reach of the project within the organization. If this item is omitted from the plan, you may have a hard time recouping it when the need for a special facility presents itself.

Plan for Needed Tools

Aside from special facilities, your project may require the use of specialized or customized tools or access to existing tools within the organization. If you identify these in your plan, you are better assured of gaining access to them when needed. Securing these tools may require something as simple as extending existing license agreements to members of your team. Or it may be more involved, requiring the solicitation and purchase of special tools (compilers, databases, development environments, middleware, and so on) that address custom or proprietary needs for your project.

Account for Integration Requirements

Finally, think of resources in terms of integration requirements. We addressed this briefly earlier in this chapter. Your core project team may not be the only resource you need. You may need the ancillary help of other work groups in your organization. For example, you may need to borrow storage space from a capacity management group. You may need to reserve time with a shared test team. You may have to test functionality by piping data to other systems. All of these are examples of integration resources that you will need to identify, inform, and then use to schedule work. If you identify them in the plan, you will have paved the way for a smooth, coordinated work relationship.

SP 2.5: Plan for Needed Knowledge and Skills

This fifth practice is related to the previous one. SP 5 has to do with the type and level of human resources you'll need on your team. A project team—one involved in technology development—needs people qualified in several realms, with certain abilities, experience, and skills. The focus of these is driven from the nature of the project itself, from what your management and customers want you to develop. This balance of knowledge and skills will impact the cost of the project and may influence such factors as resource availability, so you should work to identify in your plan just what these skills and knowledge sets will likely be.

You should consider three kinds of capabilities:

1. Technical skills
2. Management skills
3. Process skills

Technical Skills

Technology projects require people with specific technical skills. Business analysts, system architects, programmers, quality controllers—each of these is a specialized role that plays a particular function in a development effort. And within each of these disciplines can lie a whole set of specialties. Your project plan should identify just what technical skills will be needed within the project team, when these skills will be required during the lifecycle, and what types of job roles will be needed to apply them.

Management Skills

In addition to technical skills, a development project also requires management skills. The central need here is, obviously enough, a description of the project management skills needed for the project. But there may be other management needs, too. You may need someone with a skill set specifically geared to support requirements management. You may need people who can handle change management and configuration management. Large projects may require dedicated resources to cover customer management, schedule management, and cost management. Each of these need a description of the skill sets required of the role.

Process Skills

If you are going to run your projects under a CMMI program, or even simply use some of the processes recommended in this book, you will need people who are familiar with the processes, who can work under their forms and functions, and who can carry out the proscribed activities. Identifying these process skills in your plan can go a long way toward ensuring that the organization supports and promotes the use of process. If the skills are not readily available, the organization may need to provide a degree of classroom or on-the-job training. If you call attention to this in the plan, the plan participants will be able to prepare in advance to meet the process needs of the project.

SP 2.6: Plan Stakeholder Involvement

If you are familiar with the PMI's PMBOK, you know about the role that a communications plan is intended to play in a project: to keep relevant parties informed as to the project's progress and status through such coordinated means as meetings, reports, and inspections. That idea is carried forward here under CMMI with an extension into active involvement. As usually defined, a stakeholder is any party who either has a direct role in project activities or may be impacted by certain project activities. And because stakeholders may move in and out of a project over time, their travels should be coordinated to ensure timely involvement. That's why CMMI recommends this sixth practice, Plan Stakeholder Involvement. I have found it helpful to plan this involvement with three general stakeholder groups in mind:

1. Involvement of key team members
2. Involvement of senior management
3. Involvement of customer contacts

Involvement of Key Team Members

By key team members, I mean those members of your project team who have major roles to play in the development lifecycle. Your chief architect would be a key team member, as would your lead programmer, configuration manager, senior business analyst, and so on. Some organizations do not consider these folks to be stakeholders per se; they are simply members of the project team. But I think it's helpful to think of them as stakeholders for two reasons. One, it encourages you to plan the points when their key contributions will come into play. And two, it links them to the other two stakeholder groups, management and customers, thereby linking all three into a larger group with shared interests and objectives. Your chief architects have a lot at stake in the project in the same way that your senior management does and your customers do. So if you treat them as stakeholders, their issues, insights, and status needs will tend to be addressed on par with the other two.

Involvement of Senior Management

Planning for the involvement of senior management over the course of the project is necessary because senior management is the most immediate authoritative group that can influence the progress and quality of your project's efforts. By planning to periodically and regularly keep senior management informed, you align them with the current state of the project at specific points in time. This will help keep them abreast of success factors, risks, and issues that need to be addressed. Keeping them out of the loop may result in unpleasant surprises when things require attention; and management may not be so amenable to course corrections when they did not know the project was off course in the first place. An open channel of communication, planned up front, will maintain a symbiosis of expectation and cooperation between management, you and your team, and the project's objectives.

Involvement of Customer Contacts

Senior management may be the most immediate authoritative group hovering in your project's domain, but the customer is probably the most important. Regular, coordinated communication with your customer contacts is essential to smooth project progress. In fact, one of the chief duties of any project manager is to keep the customer informed as to how the project is proceeding. Active involvement on the part of the customer is also desirable. If the customer can participate at certain points in strategic decision making, such as scope meetings, design reviews, and in-process inspections, you'll find that the customer becomes more attuned to the overall needs of the project. They become participants rather than passive observers and so will typically invest greater support and enthusiasm for the details of project success.

SP 2.7: Establish the Project Plan

You have now come to the end of planning considerations, as recommended for this Process Area. You have established a range of estimates for the scope, duration, effort, and cost of the project. You have established a budget and a schedule based on those estimates. You have noted project risks and constraints and defined an approach for data management. You have identified required resources, knowledge, and skills, and you've planned for the involvement of relevant stakeholders.

At this point, the content of your plan should be pretty much complete. You can now integrate all of this information into a consolidated plan, a draft version that you can share with your approver groups to seek their comments, inputs, and ultimately their commitment to the plan.

There are two steps here.

1. Publish a draft of the plan.
2. Announce its publication.

Publish a Draft of the Plan

Your job now is to put the plan together, to integrate all of the information you have collected into a well-organized, readable document. Professional presentation is important here. A plan must not only have sound content but also *look* as though it has sound content. This is an often over-looked characteristic of plan development. But the appearance of your plan, as superficial as that sounds, communicates the level of commitment and thoroughness you have dedicated to it. So work to present a solid first draft. Your approvers will then approach their job of reviewing and approving it with a similar level of commitment and thoroughness.

Announce Its Publication

With the plan components consolidated and the document published, it's a good idea to announce this publication to those parties in your organization who will need to review and approve the plan. Of special concern here is the implication carried by the announcement. The idea is not to communicate that the plan is done and ready to go, although after all the work that went into it that would be an understandable tempta-tion. The idea is rather to communicate that a draft of the plan is now ready and that the plan itself will not be finalized until all relevant par-ties have had a chance to comment on it and provide any input they feel is important to the plan's integrity. This should position your approver audience to read your plan with an openness that will provide for con-structive improvement and will lead to a consensus of commitment.

As we will see in later chapters, the central project plan can be sup-ported by other plans you develop, particularly those to help shape

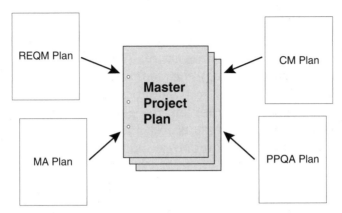

Figure 3–3: *CMMI encourages a set of subplans as a complement to the main project plan*

activities in other Process Areas, such as Requirements Management, Configuration Management, Measurement & Analysis, and Process & Product Quality Assurance (Figure 3–3).

SG 3: Obtain Commitment to the Plan

The idea of commitment is central to the concept of project management success. Commitment implies several environmental characteristics. First is agreement. The major players driving a project forward agree on the attributes of the project, things like scope, cost, and schedule. Next is alignment. The parties are aligned to move in unison in a common direction. And third is cooperation. The parties acknowledge the importance of working together cohesively across the life of the project. Without these characteristics—without a solid commitment from the project players—the project effort remains little more than a series of disconnected initiatives and specialty teams. That's why this final goal for Project Planning is so important.

The project plan you've developed through the practices recommended under the first two goals will serve as the chief management tool for the project. It will be used to monitor and control the scope, cost, and schedule. It also represents what can be considered the acceptable outcome for the effort; it contains the definition of project success. So once the plan is in place, ready to be published and base-lined, it's important to gain the commitment of key players by actively seeking their input and validation (Figure 3–4). Give stake-holders the opportunity to review the plans that affect the project, make suggestions for adjustments and changes, and then—once satis-fied with the final form—commit to working according to its approach and parameters.

CMMI defines three Specific Practices for this third goal. These prac-tices can be seen as specific to Project Planning, but they also have a universal application across the full CMMI framework. The tactic here is to develop a plan, have the affected parties review it and validate that the contents are acceptable, have them commit to the plan (through some form of sign-off or explicit agreement), and then publish the agreed-to plan. The universal value here is that this approach can

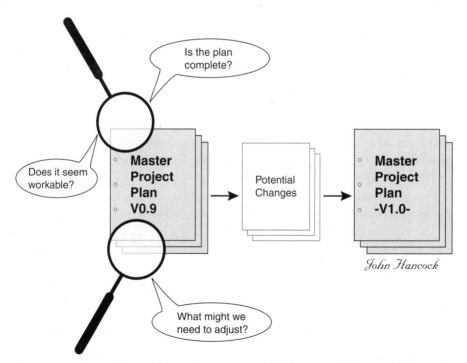

Figure 3–4: *Review and input as an essential element of plan commitment*

be used not only for all plans you establish for your project but also for the major work products and deliverables that emerge. This is a good, straightforward way to establish commitment up front and keep it in place across the life of the project.

Let's look at the three Specific Practices recommended to help you achieve commitment to the project plan.

SP 3.1: Review Plans That Affect the Project

When I talk about the project plan, I tend to use the singular form, as if you have developed one master plan that contains in it everything recommended under CMMI. That may or may not be the case. In some larger tech shops, a project may be managed by a series of separate plans. There might be a schedule, a cost plan, a resource plan, a communications plan, and so on. And it's not uncommon in these large shops to have separate project managers manage these individual plans. In smaller shops, plans tend to be more compact, usually contained in a few integrated documents. Either approach is valid under CMMI. The consideration here is to identify the audiences that may be impacted by any of the plans you have put in place for the project. In all likelihood, the plans will establish some kind of commitment that the members of separate organizational groups must follow through on. So it makes good business sense to give these groups an opportunity to review the plans and comment on their workability as it relates to the project mission.

In general, I have found it helpful to include four audience groups when you are preparing a draft of your plan (or plans) for review and approval:

1. The project team
2. Any potential integrators
3. Senior management
4. Customer stakeholders

Review with the Project Team

The members of your project team—at least the key team members, if the team is unusually large—should have an opportunity to familiarize themselves with the plan prior to having to work it. You'll find that they can provide technical and practical insights that strengthen the overall viability of the plan. Some organizations might want the team members to share in plan approval. Others simply request input and comment. The approach depends on your shop of course, but reviews by the team members still add value under either circumstance.

Review with Potential Integrators

This group is often overlooked when it comes to planning and plan reviews. Potential integrators are those people who may be called on at different points in the project to provide you with ancillary help. They are not core members of the project team, but they play a support role. They may provide you with test data; they may link your work to other systems; they may supply you with certain tools or other resources. Because these integrating groups might be responsible for critical path activities, their review and input into the plan can help ensure both readiness and important availabilities.

Review with Senior Management

Senior management is an obvious target group for plan review and approval. It is senior management after all that will be required to back the major commitments contained in the plan: scope, budget, and schedule. Of course, it's a good idea to seek management input early in the planning stage, and in most cases senior management will seek you out at the start to provide you with general planning boundaries. Once the plan is in place, with all its parts having come together, you'll want management to take a final look at the plan to make sure it reflects the business needs of the organization. In some industries and with some clients, the plan itself can be considered a contract. This being the case, management needs to back the contents of the plan.

Review with Customer Stakeholders

Finally, and perhaps in many ways most importantly, the customer should have the opportunity to review the plan. Depending on the nature and makeup of your plan, it might not be necessary for the customer stakeholders to review all the details you have mapped out, but they will probably want to confirm that you have captured their key concerns. They may want to know that you have captured scope appropriately, that you have mapped out a workable schedule, that the costs match their expectations, that you have a solid status and communication approach. When the customer is comfortable with your plan, you will be well positioned to work together in a synchronized fashion.

SP 3.2: Reconcile Work and Resource Levels

The purpose of the reviews established in the previous practice is to get the kind of feedback you need so that your plan does not remain just your plan but becomes everybody's plan. In this next practice, Reconcile Work and Resource Levels, you balance the scope of work you have mapped out in the plan with the resources you actually have available at hand. Can you do the work with the amount of people, money, and time you have been allotted? That's what you want to validate at this point; that's what you want your reviewers to confirm for you. To do this, you should consider two general activities.

1.   Analyze and integrate feedback.
2.   Balance expectations with capability.

Analyze and Integrate Feedback

One of the surest ways to gain commitment to the plan is to earnestly seek, collect, and integrate feedback from your primary audience groups. Pride of authorship sometimes interferes with this objective. But you'll go a long way toward solid plan investment by all parties if those who will stand by the plan can see their points of interest protected by the plan. During the review sessions, you'll no doubt receive good suggestions, trivial suggestions, large recommendations, and small recommendations. Naturally your judgment and knowledge of the needs of the project will be required to establish the right level of revisions. But if you work to reflect the major needs and concerns of your audiences, they will tend to back the plan with firmer commitment.

Balance Expectations with Capability

Once you have consolidated the recommendations and suggestions for plan revision and integrated the changes into a new version of the plan, you should now review the refreshed plan with your audience groups. What you will have set into place here is a fine-tuned set of expectations, a set that has been shaped to match the capabilities of the organization. Once you confirm that this is a viable and acceptable match, you are ready to seek final approval.

SP 3.3: Obtain Plan Commitment

Project management success cannot be obtained (excluding the miraculous) without an explicit commitment to its success. Commitment often comes in two flavors: implicit and explicit. Implicit commitment ("Sure, go ahead") is the softer of the two and is sometimes the one that people prefer to deliver—implicit commitment can initiate action but leaves little in the way of an audit trail. Explicit commitment is the firmer version. Because by definition it takes a physical form (e.g., a signature, an e-mail), it carries with it not only a catalyst to action but also the authoritative backing of the approving party. It leaves a very distinct trail; that trail is a large part of its strength.

Naturally, for your project plan you want to obtain explicit commitment. That is a sound business practice, and for many projects, it's a legal obligation. You want to obtain the commitment from those approvers who have the authority to kick the project into action. When we looked at Specific Practices 2.6 and 3.1 earlier, we identified some groups that might need to approve your plan, groups such as senior management and the customer. These identities will naturally depend on the makeup and shape of your organization and the nature of the project you are engaged in. But whoever the approvers are, it's important to obtain their commitment. If some of these folks happen to be a little gun-shy in terms of making an explicit commitment, you can remind them of three qualities of commitment that actually work to their benefit:

1. Commitment cements agreement and alignment.
2. Commitment promotes cooperation.
3. Commitment allows for change.

Commitment Cements Agreement

Explicit commitment marks a milestone in project progress. The effort can now move from planning and conceptualization to action and realization. With commitment comes a consensus of agreement. Even with the acknowledgment of risks and contingencies, the parties agree that this is the approach they will take to develop what needs to be developed. And because commitment also signals the end of primary analysis, input, and refinement, it frees the key stakeholders and other resources to change gears, to move from a level of active involvement into more of a monitoring mode.

Commitment Promotes Cooperation

Commitment to the plan promotes cooperation among the stakeholders involved in the project. On adoption, the plan becomes the official management tool of the project. All parties can expect that the project will be staged in the manner described in the plan. This common expectation has the added benefit of aligning the separate parties that may be contributing to the project to cooperate with each other in the spirit of the plan, to drive the project toward its stated objectives. It is not that all thinking and planning stops at this point. It does not (see the following point). But what is in place is an established path that everyone has agreed to travel. Later, should that path prove in any way problematic, adjustments can be made. But they'll be made within the domains of the plan, within that common ground of analysis and choice that everyone can read.

Commitment Allows for Change

This is an important point to communicate to your approver groups. Commitment (and this is probably especially true for explicit commitment) allows for later input, consideration, and change as needed. Many people feel that a signature closes the input loop, that once they put ink to paper they will no longer have any say as to what happens next. Of course, this is the opposite of what explicit commitment should allow. The commitment here actually signals the beginning of a close relationship. Without it, the relationship remains in the what-if stage. Sometimes it is helpful to directly address this issue with your approver groups. The commitment here is simply a signal to move forward, to begin the work of the plan in earnest. The plan itself should describe numerous future opportunities for stakeholder statusing, progress reporting, and feedback.

The Benefits of Controlled Project Planning

A set of processes and practices like those described under this CMMI Process Area can go a long way toward giving your shop the ability to produce project plans in a consistent, repeatable, and controlled manner. This ability carries with it a number of benefits that can be realized in tangible ways. Here are four distinct benefits of a well-designed project planning program.

A Regimen for Realistic Planning

Pie-in-the-sky planning might look good on paper; it might have a quieting effect on people adverse to facing a picture of reality that might be discomfiting in some ways. But it's not usually very helpful, and when adopted, this kind of planning often ends up causing as many problems as it tries to avoid. The benefit of a well-designed planning program, one that coordinates how estimates and plans are put together, is that the organization can now promote its view of sound planning. It can set standards for planning that reflect those elements most important to organizational success and the attainment of business objectives. This way, planning across the organization begins to consistently mirror management's top issues, and thus the plans, in the eyes of the organization, can be seen as more practical and realistic with respect to these issues.

A Definition of Success

The title of this book is *Project Management Success with CMMI®*. Of course, the word *success* can mean many things, depending on what's important to the organization and its customers. So another distinct benefit of a project planning program is that it provides for the organization to embed in the plan a definition of what project success means to the organization. As recommended under CMMI, a project plan will describe budget targets, schedule targets, resource targets, milestone targets, quality targets, and so on. When weighted and prioritized against the views of management and the customer, these plan parameters become the project's success factors. If you operate within an acceptable threshold of this set, you can consider the project successful. Better yet, management and the customer, in sharing that basis for success, should consider the project a success, too.

A Contract of Agreement and Action

This may be the most practical benefit of a planning program. The approved plan—containing the range of contents and controls deemed necessary by the organization—can now serve as a contract of agreement and action by both the organization and the customer. Once a project starts, there should be no need to continually ask about what's next. Parties on both sides should have a common vision and map of how things will progress across every major project phase. Major commitments such as cost, effort, and schedule will have been set into place in such a concrete way that their foundational parameters should be a point of common acceptance. And with the kinds of detail provided in such plan elements as the work breakdown structure, responsibilities, activities, and milestones should all be out in the open, readily available for reference, and familiar to all.

A Common Basis for Decision Making

Another advantageous benefit of a planning program is that it can serve as a common basis for decision making. The purpose of a plan is not to lock down action; it is to control action, and even the best of planned project activities will need to be adjusted over time. When the project course needs to be corrected, the plan can serve as a common basis for change. Without such a reference, recommendations for change can become somewhat subjective, a matter of opinion, and often swayed by individual clout. The plan will help to set boundaries on course corrections. The plan itself will contain the project's mission, objectives, and operational parameters—an objective description of where the stakeholders wish to go. And so, this being the agreed-upon course, the plan can be used to guide decision making, to analyze individual recommendations, to compare them with the known objectives, and then to make a decision that will better align efforts toward achieving those objectives.

Some Example Program Components

If you're thinking about taking the goals and practices recommended for the Project Planning Process Area and creating a process program to support their use on your development efforts, here are some examples of the kinds of components people typically create to support a Maturity Level 2 program.

A Project Planning Policy

This executive policy endorses and promotes the use of your planning forms and procedures for your development projects.

A Project Plan Template

This outline of the contents of a project plan presents the major sections and points of detail that you want your planners to include when they begin to develop a compliant project plan.

A Set of Estimation Guidelines

These are guidelines that you develop for use by people in the organization who need to come up with estimates for such things as the scope, size, cost, and effort of a project. These guidelines need not be complex or overly formulaic. They should provide general parameters people can use to estimate in a consistent way based on the business needs of the shop.

A Procedure to Create the Project Plan

This is a step-by-step guide that your project planners can use to establish and collect estimates, create the narrative content of the plan, set the budget in place, map out the schedule, and then publish this information in an integrated draft project plan.

A Procedure to Review and Approve the Plan

This is a guide for use by the approver groups in your organization. It describes the steps they will take when a draft plan needs to be distributed, reviewed, commented on, refined, and then officially approved.

A Policy on Acceptable Forms of Commitment

This executive policy describes what forms of both implicit and explicit commitment are acceptable to the organization as applied to specific work products.

Look to the Web Site for . . .

- Project planning policy
- Project plan template
- Project plan review and approval process
- Sample estimation guideline

Chapter 4

Project Monitoring & Control

Most of our methodologies center on project management. They are shaped to help steer project activity along coordinated lines and to promote the smooth communications of progress and status over time. This central focus on tracking reveals its importance to project success. The best planning in the world or the most sophisticated infrastructure can't substitute for persistent and detailed mechanisms to monitor what is going on inside a project domain.

Darrel Evans, PMP, Westchester Consulting Services
Software and systems development

We now come to what many shops consider the core activity of project management: project monitoring and control. And if asked to identify the chief duty of a project manager, I suspect that this is what most people would probably list. Project monitoring and control is the most visible aspect of the discipline. It's what project managers spend most of their time doing. It's what the organization and the customers probably want to see them doing. We looked at project planning in the last chapter, and in the next chapters we'll look at CMMI Process Areas that deal with requirements management, configuration management, and so on. As we move forward in our discussions of these areas, I think two things will become clear. First, the considerations and practices we encounter at each of these areas provide us with tools and techniques we can use to further the mission of project management. Second, and perhaps more importantly, they provide us with the planning and infrastructure we need to monitor and control a project effectively.

It might not be too much of an exaggeration to say that CMMI Maturity Level 2 centers on the Project Monitoring & Control Process Area, that it provides the recommendations that can lead to project management success, and that here we also find the hooks and references that link the other six Process Areas into a cohesive and integrated process management and improvement program.

Let's take a deeper look at Project Monitoring & Control.

The Purpose of Project Monitoring & Control

There are twenty-two Process Areas in CMMI-DEV. They can be grouped into four categories: Project Management, Process Management, Engineering, and Support. At Maturity Level 2, we embrace seven of the Process Areas. One falls into the Engineering category: Requirements Management. Three fall into the Support category: Configuration Management, Measurement & Analysis, and Process & Product Quality Assurance. Three fall under Project Management: Project Planning, Project Monitoring & Control, and Supplier Agreement Management. The purpose of Project Monitoring & Control is to set into place activities that will govern how each of these Process Areas relates to and interacts with the others. The organizational triumvirate of people, process, and technology comes to the forefront here. The design, planning, and preparation potentials they have been holding now give way to action. The job of project management must now be to weld people, process, and technology together in furtherance of the objectives and mission of the project. This can be better understood as a management approach that works across four lines: guiding the work of the project teams, protecting the commitments (time, cost, resources, and so on) that bind the project, ensuring full and timely communications across relevant parties, and facilitating adjustments and corrections when necessary. Let's take a quick look at each in a little more depth.

Guide the Work

Most projects are made up of teams of people, or at least areas of specialty. Each is typically chartered with making certain contributions to the project. Analysts provide requirements, architects provide designs, programmers provide code. At any given point in time, a lot of people might be working on the project, each with his or her own view of the shape, purpose, and criticality of the assignment. So it's important for the structure of a project to have someone in charge, someone who is ultimately responsible for making sure that all this work gets done in a coordinated fashion. That someone is most often the project manager. The project manager may not directly supervise many of the team members' day-to-day duties, especially if the organization is matrixed. And the project manager may not have direct reporting lines to many of the resource groups that contribute to the makeup of the project team. But still the project manager is the party responsible for how the project work plays out, tasked with ensuring as much as possible that the work plays out according to plan. In most technology shops (busy, multitasking, with tight resources), this guiding of a team's energy along preestablished lines is essential to project success.

Protect the Commitments

Project Monitoring & Control is by necessity heavily focused on protecting the commitments associated with a project. With any project, commitments come in many sizes and shapes, often with different stakeholders. Schedules represent a commitment, as do budgets, resource levels, and the quality of deliverables. These commitments are almost always contained in the project's plans (or in documents referenced by the plans). The plans are the organization's best guess as to how to realize these commitments, with one balanced against the other. But after all, a plan is just a plan. With project monitoring and control, the team hits the terrain using the plan as a map, and the commitments now take on a three-dimensional shape. The primary, ongoing concern of project management at this stage is to continually check to make sure that these commitments are taking shape in expected ways and that they are balanced against each other according to acceptable thresholds. The next two points—communications and adjustments—deal with the central issue of managing these commitments in line with stakeholder expectations.

Promote Communications

Another important purpose of project monitoring and control is to promote communications across a project's different stakeholder groups. Here is where the art of project management often comes into play. We'll see that CMMI puts forth a series of practices that can be used to foster communications, but very often, the project manager's ability and affinity for communications make the difference here. There are many reasons why projects can get into trouble, but one that will always show up on a top-five list is poor communications. The risk of poor communications is that it can lead to disjointed perceptions as to project progress. When a project is actually doing fine, people might feel that things are in trouble. When the general assumption is that things are fine, things may actually be in jeopardy. Both conditions are best handled by avoiding falling into them. Regular and open communications can help promote a consistent and reliable vision of project progress. The project manager is not solely responsible for filling this communication stream; everybody involved in a project should be a part of this stream. But it's the project manager who often sets the tone for this stream and initiates the kinds of forums that open communications up to all members of the team. Communication is one of the best ways to ensure that everyone has a common understanding of the state of the project at any point in time.

Facilitate Correction, Adjustment, and Focus

A fourth major purpose of project monitoring and control is to establish a foundation for facilitating corrective actions, adjustments, and points of refocus. If all projects went according to plan, there would be little need to assign a project manager. An administrator would probably be more than adequate. But projects—unfolding in the real world as they do—do not always go according to plan. Because of this, the person with his or her hands on the steering wheel needs to be ready to change direction from time to time. The facilitation of change is important here for two reasons. First, change can be (to one degree or another) unnerving, so it needs to be handled in a professional and accountable way. Second, change has the potential to lead to misalignment, so it needs to be assessed, coordinated, and diligently managed. Uncontrolled change has driven more than a few projects to the rocks. Because project managers sit at the center of project activities, because they are the party charged with keeping the tiller pulled in the right direction, they must maintain a vigilant focus on the need for change and on the smooth planning and rollout of change in support of a project's objectives.

The Heart of the Project

The purpose of Project Monitoring & Control can be summarized as providing a way to manage the work required to keep a project on track. And it's probably safe to say that most of the work of project management comes in support of this activity. Most of what project management does is monitoring and control. In the realm of the PMI's PMBOK, a project lifecycle is often segmented into process groups: those that deal with initiating a project; those that deal with planning a project; those that deal with executing and controlling a project; and those that deal with closing a project. If the groups were buckets, what size would each one be?

The largest would probably be the one that would hold the activities required for executing and controlling (Figure 4–1). This is what CMMI refers to as monitoring and controlling. And this really is the heart of project management; it can be seen as the heart of the project. The estimates we derive, the plans we develop—these directly serve project monitoring and control. The controls we establish around requirements and change requests directly serve monitoring and control. So do the measures we produce. So do the quality audits we perform. The supplier agreements we establish directly serve project monitoring and control.

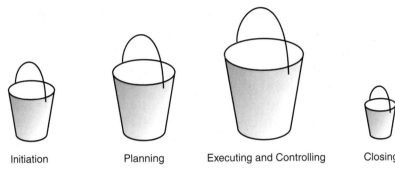

| Initiation | Planning | Executing and Controlling | Closing |

Figure 4–1: *The relative sizes of the four project lifecycle phases*

At its core, project management is a boots-on-the-ground job. Strategy is important, but tactics are essential. The CMMI Process Area called Project Monitoring & Control is all about setting into place those management tactics that will help you guide your project to its predefined goals in an effective and efficient manner.

Project Monitoring & Control Goals and Practices

CMMI defines two Specific Goals and a total of ten Specific Practices for Project Monitoring & Control. Here is the official specification text for each of these elements.

SG 1   MONITOR PROJECT AGAINST PLAN
Actual performance and progress of the project are monitored against the project plan.

SP 1.1   MONITOR PROJECT PLANNING PARAMETERS
Monitor the actual values of the project planning parameters against the project plan.

SP 1.2   MONITOR COMMITMENTS
Monitor commitments against those identified in the project plan.

SP 1.3   MONITOR PROJECT RISKS
Monitor risks against those identified in the project plan.

SP 1.4   Monitor Data Management
Monitor the management of project data against the project plan.

SP 1.5   Monitor Stakeholder Involvement
Monitor stakeholder involvement against the project plan.

SP 1.6   Conduct Progress Reviews
Periodically review the project's progress, performance, and issues.

SP 1.7   Conduct Milestone Reviews
Review the accomplishments and results of the project at selected project milestones.

SG 2   Manage Corrective Action to Closure
Corrective actions are managed to closure when the project's performance or results deviate significantly from the plan.

SP 2.1   Analyze Issues
Collect and analyze the issues and determine the corrective actions necessary to address the issues.

SP 2.2   Take Corrective Action
Take corrective action on identified issues.

SP 2.3   Manage Corrective Action
Manage corrective actions to closure.

Generic Goals and Practices

See Chapter 10 for information about the important Generic Goals and Practices that support project management success for all the Process Areas at Maturity Level 2.

SG 1: Monitor Project Against Plan

In the previous chapter, we looked at the Project Planning Process Area and at the importance planning plays in the overall picture of project management. All sound management, no matter what the business or discipline, relies on planning. It's the way to prepare for forward motion along coordinated lines, the way to harness and synchronize energies. This first goal of Project Monitoring & Control recognizes this value in planning. As we noted in the last chapter, we don't plan just to go through a thought exercise. We plan to establish the mechanisms of management. The plans we develop for a project become the chief tools by which we manage the project. Monitoring actual project activity against what is described in the plans takes on particular importance as we move from planning into project execution.

You may begin execution with a series of plans in place. The PMI view introduces the use of a series of plans, including plans for communications, procurement, scope management, schedule management, cost management, and so on. CMMI takes a less specific view, recommending that your plans—whatever they are—cover costs, scope, schedules, resources, stakeholder involvement, risks, and data management. If you plan to follow the Process Area recommendations we discuss in this book, you may also end up with a requirements management plan, a configuration management plan, a measurement and analysis plan, a supplier management plan, and some form of quality assurance plan. These plans may be substantial works, or they may be simple and concise. They may be separate documents or combined.

Whatever forms these plans take, they will all need to be monitored and controlled. They will need to be tracked. The contents of the charter and the schedule (the work breakdown structure) may be the most visible plan on the table, but that does not discount the relevance of other plans you might have prepared. Together they constitute the performance targets and objectives of the project. The job of project management at this point is to see all the plans through, to guide project activity within the boundaries of the plans, and to use the framework of the plans to make informed corrections should adjustments need to be made.

CMMI describes seven Specific Practices for this first goal under Project Monitoring & Control (Figure 4–2). These move in close parallel to the practices recommended for Project Planning. That makes sense because you are now ready to track against the items you planned, such as the schedule, budget, risks, resources, and so on. Let's look at each of these seven practices.

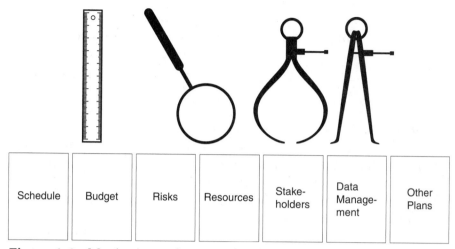

Schedule	Budget	Risks	Resources	Stake-holders	Data Manage-ment	Other Plans

Figure 4–2: *Monitoring and measuring plan parameters as a key to effective project tracking*

SP 1.1: Monitor Project Planning Parameters

This first practice defines what might be considered the primary administrative duty of project management. When monitoring project planning parameters, you track those critical items on which the plan is based. Usually this includes monitoring the following four items:

1. The project scope
2. The schedule
3. The budget
4. Resource levels

All of these have been estimated in the plan. If properly derived, all of the activities, deliverables, and milestones in the plan should have sprung from this foundation data. That's why it's important to keep an eye on these items. You'll often find on very large projects that administrators have been appointed to do just that. On other projects, it's up to the project manager.

Because these four items carry the potential to dramatically impact the evolving shape and condition of a project, they can be thought of as high-impact items. These parameters need to be continually controlled; they need to be managed in such a way that their actual performance values do not fall outside of an acceptable range of variance.

Scope

The scope of the project is most often realized as a set of defined requirements. The work of the project (and thus the budget and schedule) is to realize the requirements as defined. This is an important parameter because it's the predominant influencer on the size of the project. If the scope is allowed to grow over time in an unchecked fashion, you risk having inadequate resources to address the work at hand. And as most of us know, project scope will change over time. Sometimes it shrinks, but more often than not, it grows. Project management needs to be vigilant in its management of scope. Managing scope well will directly affect your ability to manage the other planning parameters equally well.

In Chapter 5 we'll look at the Requirements Management Process Area under CMMI and discuss a group of practices that can help you control scope. Then, in Chapter 6 we'll look at Configuration Management and discuss how its focus on baseline management and change control can also help you keep a handle on scope.

Schedule

The project schedule is another high-impact planning parameter. The schedule will typically house the work breakdown structure, that sequence of activities and applied resources that constitutes each major phase in the development lifecycle. Because it's readily accessible and easily digestible, the schedule may be the highest-profile item in this set of parameters. Referencing it, the team members, management, and customers can all get an idea of how things are going; they'll at least come away with an impression of the project's status, whether that impression is accurate or not. That's why it's essential to track the schedule closely, to regularly assess its contents with what's actually progressing on the project, and to update and rebaseline the schedule when important adjustments need to be made. A current, clear schedule can serve as an invaluable communications tool for any project.

When it accurately reflects project activity and is shown to be a reliable predictor of project progress, you'll enjoy a commonality of understanding among stakeholders.

Budget

If we're talking dollars, sometimes project management has control over the budget, and sometimes it does not. It depends on the organization. But the budget doesn't have to be just dollars. It might be counted as resource weeks, hours expended, or some other representative denomination. Whatever its makeup, the focus remains the same: to track consumption so that project expenditures remain in line with project activities. Next to the schedule, this may be the most sensitive of project parameters. The budget is what the customer counts on to be reflected on the final price tag. Management relies on the budget as an indicator of profit. Because of this, budgets especially need to be continually monitored. Drifts in costs cannot always be corrected through increased allocations; such drifts might call for prompt action from other quarters. Budget management can become a specialty job in and of itself. Project management's job is to keep consumption ever visible to key project stakeholders and to issue reports and updates as needed to ensure the intelligent and considered use of material investments.

Resources

The final planning parameter we'll consider here is resources. When we think of resources, people usually come to mind. And that's probably the most practical way to think of it. But resources can be other items, too: work facilities, computing equipment, software, tools. There is always a cost associated with allocating resources to a project, costs in money as well as costs in commitments and availabilities. The resources assigned to your project need to be monitored against your plans for two reasons. First, if the resources you require are not being made available to you, you may put the schedule and the scope of the project at risk. This may require management intervention. Second, if your resource levels appear top heavy, you may end up with idle workers, people who may be better used elsewhere, on other projects. The balance between work and resources needs to be continually maintained.

SP 1.2: **Monitor Commitments**

Parameters (SP 1.1) and commitments share a lot in common. The distinction is so slim that you can think of the separation as one of convenience. The scope of the project, the schedule, the budget, and resource levels all constitute real project commitments. But out of these some additional commitments are usually born, project attributes that directly impact the expectations of management and customers. These additional commitments need to be monitored just as closely as the project parameters. They may not always carry the same weight when it comes to impacting the shape and momentum of a project, but they do contain the potential to affect the solidity and the value of progress at any point in the lifecycle.

These kinds of commitments typically arise from three domains:

1. Deliverables
2. Quality
3. Communications

Let's take a quick look at each.

Deliverables

The purpose of any project is to create something—a product, a service, something big, something small. It's fair to say that much of project management can be considered product management. Across the life of any project, the teams at work are going to produce a series of products. Some will be components of the actual end product. Others may be support materials. Still others may be reference materials. In all this, there will be a set of key deliverables, those specific work products that signify progress in a significant way and that point to the project's objectives being met. These deliverables are typically identified in the project plan; they may constitute milestones or project benchmarks. These deliverables are also often recognized by management and customers as indicators of progress. When stakeholders can inspect works in progress in a way that confirms the big picture is taking shape according to plan, a certain harmony of understanding will exist. For these reasons, the project manager should keep a close eye on the deliverables scheduled to appear at specific points in the project.

Quality

Quality should always be seen as a project commitment, regardless of the size or scope of the project. A technology shop that is managed by process (such as a CMMI Maturity Level 2 program) should in fact automatically embed quality targets into a project's performance objectives. Customers may not always think to include the idea of quality in their concepts of project tracking; it's all too often an unspoken expectation. But by making it overt, you help make it manageable. In Chapter 9, we'll look at the Process Area called Process & Product Quality Assurance. Through this Process Area, you establish quality targets for your project. The proper content of plans, compliance with process activities, the collection of critical data, the communication of important information, and so on: Each of these can be quantified as a measure of performance that shows adherence to quality expectations. By making such a commitment, you can assure your stakeholders that the work is being conducted in line with standards that will promote reliability, suitability, and—by extrapolation—success.

Communications

The final commitment category here is communications. There is certainly an implied commitment on all projects to regularly communicate with key stakeholders. These stakeholders include your team members, your management, and your customers. Without communications, you run the risk of carrying the project forward in unapproved ways or in unauthorized directions. You risk segmenting the teams into disjointed parties, likely with differing views of project objectives. Communication has a lot to do with the art of project management. Communication avenues should be set into place, communication forums should be established. But the tone and tenor of project communications often comes from the project manager. Thoroughness and openness are the themes here. Protective or partial communications may seem to shield people now and again from unpleasantness, but such insulation is rarely conducive to forward motion. Too much communication is a tough shortcoming to achieve on a project, and even if you do err in this direction, it is better than erring the other way. Note your communication commitments early in the project. Ensure that your stakeholders understand the communication stream. Then see that the stream runs smoothly.

SP 1.3: **Monitor Project Risks**

Risk management is another of the very visible responsibilities of project management. One of the practices in Project Planning (Chapter 3) is to document any risks, assumptions, and constraints that surround a new project. As the project moves into action, these issues will need to be continually tracked, measured, and monitored so that they may be addressed should they begin to materialize as problems. Of course, identifying risks does not end with planning. Risk management is an ongoing part of project management and thus needs to extend into PMC activities.

The job of project management in this realm is to provide for the identification and intake of risks, assess the impact of risk conditions, categorize and prioritize risks, establish risk mitigation strategies, and assign owners to each risk event as necessary.

Risk management can be addressed with varying degrees of sophistication, depending on the makeup of your organization and the needs of your project. From a structural approach, risk management is addressed in more detail through the second goal of Project Monitoring & Control, Manage Corrective Action to Closure.

A Note on Risk Management

A subtheme I'd like to thread through the information in this book is the harmony that exists between CMMI Maturity Level 2 and the PMI's PMBOK. The seven Process Areas of Level 2 open doors to address the same concepts and concerns that the PMBOK's nine Knowledge Areas address. A process program based on the seven Process Areas can readily contain the management domains described in the Knowledge Areas. That brings us to this third practice, Monitor Project Risks. Risk Management is one of the nine PMBOK Knowledge Areas and deals with identifying, prioritizing, and mitigating risks across the project lifecycle. Risk Management is also an independent CMMI Process Area, residing outside of Project Monitoring & Control. The Risk

Management Process Area, however, is not introduced at Maturity Level 2. CMMI considers Risk Management to be an advanced area within the Project Management category and so omits it from Level 2. In the Staged Representation, Risk Management appears at Level 3. The difference is one of degree.

The PMBOK's Risk Management Knowledge Area describes the PMI's full view of managing project risks. The Risk Management Process Area does the same thing for CMMI. But at Maturity Level 2, CMMI introduces risk management in a fundamental way through Project Planning and Project Monitoring & Control. The intention is to set into place risk-handling strategies and procedures and then, as the organization matures over time, introduce a dedicated focus for this management domain.

SP 1.4: Monitor Data Management

Data management deals with managing the data and work products that accumulate over the life of the project. Data management was initially addressed in Project Planning; the project plan includes a plan for data management. That's the point when you identify what essential work products you'll be producing, which repositories will house these products, how access to them will be managed, what security will surround them, and so on. Monitoring this plan is important because product work is the real raison d'être of any project. You will need to confirm that your people do indeed have access to the things they need to perform their work, that the integrity of the work products is being maintained, and that any needed adjustments regarding data management are recognized and acted on.

In the discipline of project management, the chief tool for data management is usually configuration management, that formal system of file, document, and data control that protects work products. We discuss the CMMI Configuration Management Process Area in Chapter 6, where we'll take a deeper look at how data management—and the monitoring of data management activities—can be addressed through the practices recommended for that Process Area.

SP 1.5: Monitor Stakeholder Involvement

In covering SP 1.2, we discussed the importance of monitoring project commitments, including communications. This practice revisits that topic with a view toward active involvement. Stakeholders are those people who have a direct stake in the outcome of the project. Stakeholder involvement is one of the items accounted for during project planning. In the plan (or plans), you identified who the relevant stakeholders are, what portions of the project concern them, and at what points they should be involved in those portions.

The aim now is to monitor this planned involvement, to ensure that you are communicating with your stakeholders and that you are getting them involved at the proper points. Communication becomes especially important here because not all stakeholders are imminently present across all project lifecycles. Some may be quite removed from day-to-day project activities. Yet their insight, views, and opinions are still necessary for project success. Project management, here taking on the duties of leadership and team integration, needs to monitor the involvement of the project stakeholders to promote both integration and smooth collaboration.

Stakeholders usually fall into four categories:

1. Members of internal teams
2. Integration partners
3. Senior management
4. Customers

Let's a quick look at some considerations for each.

Internal Teams

I like to think of members of the project's internal and technical teams as stakeholders. Some organizations don't. The benefit of including team members in this category is that their positions rise in parallel to those of management and the customer, and thus they tend to become more of a partner in project success. Another stakeholder-like quality of the internal teams is that they almost always represent areas of specialized talent, so they make specific contributions to the project at distinct points in the lifecycle. A key to project effectiveness, efficiency, and progress comes with coordinating the work and dependencies of these internal stakeholders.

Integration Partners

Integration partners can be important members of the stakeholder community, but sometimes there is a tendency to overlook them. Integration partners are those people or groups within your organization with whom you will be required to work in order to realize the full scope of the project. They may provide you with computing resources or access to sets of data. They may connect you to other systems or allow you access into their systems. In all of these cases, certain required project activities fall outside of your direct control. By working with these stakeholders, you can ensure that partner cooperation and interactions are coordinated, timely, and maximized.

Executive Management

Your senior management is another stakeholder whose involvement you'll want to ensure. In many cases, management will let you know when they want to drop in and check things out; they'll be proactive in their curiosity. Other times, you will need to push interaction with them. However it's accomplished, management involvement is important to project success. You will benefit from management confirmation that progress is on track. You may need management approval to make adjustments or course corrections. And you may need management from time to time as a liaison between you and the customer.

Customers

The last category of stakeholder is the customer. Customer involvement in the project, while nothing to shrink from or minimize, does need to be carefully controlled, so it should be conscientiously monitored. The operations of your project will benefit from good communications with your customers and through their involvement at preset benchmarks or project milestones. Given the right degree of insight and the right level of information, your customers will be able to ascertain project progress, the realization of its mission, and the performance and quality of production products. This in turn should build within them an appropriate view of progress and a feeling for the stability and state of the project.

SP 1.6: Conduct Progress Reviews

Here is another highly visible job of project management: conducting progress reviews. The ubiquitous form of a progress review is the status meeting. Project teams tend to hold regular status meetings, sessions where team members assemble to report on work activities, accomplishments, and upcoming work.

Progress reviews can play two important roles in the management of a project. First, they serve as a communications avenue. On paper, a project can look like a concentrated entity, but in reality, project teams are often distributed, sometimes widely distributed. Status meetings, especially when they are planned well in advance, provide an opportunity for members of the team to come together and exchange information, to understand how the work is moving along, and to prepare to undertake new activities. In Chapter 3 on Project Planning, we discussed the value in members of the project team—technical members, management, and customers—sharing a common understanding of the mission and scope of the effort. That same advantage holds true here. Regular status meetings help ensure that these members continue to share an understanding of the current state of the work of the project, that there is a synchronicity with everyone's view of progress. This first role of progress reviews can be seen as one in which the members partake of common information.

The second role is one in which project management takes in what might be called priority information. Progress reviews are not the only opportunity for this, but they are a solid opportunity to make it happen. Project management should always be culling the depths of a project, looking for priority information. This is information vital to maintaining the parameters of a project: scope, schedule, budget, resource levels. These data sets represent the actuals of project activity. Project management compares the actuals with what was estimated in the plans and, based on the goodness of fit, makes one of two decisions: stay on course or adjust course. This kind of priority information can come from many sources and at any time during a project. But the use of planned status meetings as a venue to review progress gives project management the opportunity to interact with a consolidated mix of project team members and thus elicit priority information in a proactive manner.

The first role could be said to give the project manager a qualitative indicator of progress. The second role could be said to deliver a quantitative indicator of progress. Together, the two form a pretty complete picture of project status. From this, the project manager can create informative and accurate status reports that document for a specific point in time where the project stands with regard to its overall mission and objectives.

SP 1.7: Conduct Milestone Reviews

Some organizations consider progress reviews and milestone reviews to be the same thing. Others make a big point of keeping them distinct. The degree of linkage is not as important as the activity. These reviews can happen together, or they can happen apart; whatever works for your project teams. Apart from a progress review, a milestone review can be shaped to a particular end. The word *milestone* itself (like a lot of concepts in project management) comes from Roman antiquity: A milestone was a stone that marked distance along a road. Even today we use mile markers on highways. For a technology project, then, milestones are dates or activities of particular relevance to the status of a project. They are points of reference that should evidence some culmination of effort or product in a significant way. Milestones serve as mini-goals that, once achieved, better ensure the project's major goals. Projects typically tend to use two kinds of milestones:

1. Critical path dates
2. Critical path work products (key deliverables)

Critical Path Dates

One of project management's key management tools is the project schedule. Common in technology shops, the schedule usually contains a work breakdown structure—a detailed, ordered listing of tasks with durations, priorities, dependencies, and resources all noted. Most

WBSs reflect the various phases in a project's lifecycle. In a PMBOK-based project, you'll almost always see four high-level phases: Initiation, Planning, Execution and Control, and Closure. Lifecycles based on specific methodologies such as waterfall, RAD, agile, or the spiral method will usually show their own phase structures. In all of these, there will be critical path dates, points at which one major phase gives way to the next. If phase activity is finished before that date, all the better. If not, corrective action may be needed. Most project managers tend to keep critical path dates clearly before them. Customers tend to move according to these dates; senior management often relies on them. By keeping a handle on critical path dates, you exercise the ability to manage according to timelines and thus can potentially adjust resources, activities, and budgets to fit the timelines.

Key Deliverables

A milestone complementary to a critical path date is a key deliverable. From a management perspective, the difference between the two is simply one of focus; the impacts are invariably the same. Key deliverables are major work products produced (usually) at critical path dates. A requirements document is usually a key deliverable; analysis depends on it. A high-level design could be a key deliverable; coding depends on it. The same can be said of a test plan, an integration procedure, the production of user documentation. Like critical path dates, key deliverables signify project stability through the interrelatedness of project dependencies. By anticipating, reviewing, and pushing forward key deliverables—the foundation of project scope—project management can control the work streams that influence budget, schedule, and resource levels.

SG 2: Manage Corrective Action to Closure

The first goal of Project Monitoring & Control represents the monitoring part of this Process Area: Monitor the actual performance of the project against what you described in the plan, and work to keep the two in sync. From time to time, you may have to alter the plan to reflect new or revised activities. At other times, you may have to revise project activities to bring them back in line with the plan. Regular monitoring gives you the insight you need to shape appropriate decisions along those lines.

Now we come to the control part of Project Monitoring & Control. The second goal of this Process Area is to manage any corrective actions to closure. This goal encompasses two concepts: manage risks and redirect fully. We've already discussed risk management, from the view of the PMBOK as well as from the extended view of CMMI, past Maturity Level 2. This goal encompasses risk management but also includes normal project adjustments: actions to realign scope, budgets, schedules, resources, and so on. Both of those concepts are covered in the recommendation to manage corrective actions.

Managing corrective actions to closure is an important extension. Most projects, when viewed from a micro level, are probably off course most of the time. But that's okay—strict adherence to initial plans is not a realistic expectation. The job of project management is to continually realign project activities with performance expectations and discrete project goals (Figure 4–3). The idea is not to take action willy-nilly or in half measures but to make a concerted effort to address issues or conditions that can affect the project and to work to demonstrably minimize their impacts. When the sum total approaches anticipated end values, the project can be said to be a success.

Three practices are defined for this goal: analyze issues that may impact project progress, take action to address the issues, and then manage your corrective actions until the issues have been resolved or placed under control. Let's take a look at each practice in turn.

Figure 4–3: *Corrective action brings project drifts back on track*

SP 2.1: Analyze Issues

This practice can be seen as related to SP 1.3, which recommends monitoring project risks. Analyzing issues deals with looking at risks, performance levels, and any other conditions or situations that have the potential to impact progress and then assessing the likelihood or relevance of these impacts. You can rely on the practices of SG 1 to assist with this. Those practices (SP 1.1 through SP 1.7) recommend monitoring a whole set of conditions and factors: schedule, budget, resources, milestones, and so on. As you keep an eye on these things, you and your team members will more than likely stumble upon evidence of drift, of things here and there moving off course. These are the issues you want to identify and consider analyzing. Not all of them will require your immediate attention (see the next practice), but the only way to know this is to perform at least a basic analysis of each in order to assess the potential for impact and the degree of imminence and to understand what mitigation actions might be available.

SP 2.2: Take Corrective Action

A schoolyard definition of project management might be to keep the project on track. This assumes two things. The first assumption is that projects have the ability to go off track. We all know this to be true. In fact, we might make a stronger pronouncement: At one time or another, all projects will likely go off track. The second assumption is that, left on its own, a project has little power to get back on track. That's the job of the project manager. When the wheels slip the rails, a project manager should react by taking corrective action to put the project back on track. That's the essence of corrective action. The measure of sound corrective action comes through its proportion and its impact: Was the amount of action suitable to the issue at hand, and did the action have the desired impact?

Corrective action usually takes the form of one of three activities.

1. Remove (nullify) the issue.
2. Change project activities in response to the issue.
3. Change the plans to reflect a new reality.

Remove the Issue

The most desirable action project management can take to address a prevalent issue is to remove the issue. That's the best kind of problem you can have: one you can erase, one you can nullify. That might sound like wishful thinking, but many issues in a project can be handled this way and so will have practically no impact on a project's operating parameters. These issues usually turn out to be nonissues; they present as problems, but on analysis they clear up on their own: simple misunderstandings, out-of-scope focus, irrelevance pushed to be made relevant. Many times these problems come our way so quickly and with such little force that we fail to realize that we are dealing with issues this way.

Of course, not all issues can be simply removed. Often you will have to initiate corrective action to mitigate an issue's impact. This mitigation usually takes one of two forms: modifying current activities (moving around the issue) to remain in line with the project plan, or modifying project plans (living with the issue) to reflect the new circumstances.

Change Project Activities

Sometimes the best course of action is to change the activities of the project team. For example, to address a schedule issue, you might add a new set of testing resources. To address a scope issue, you might temporarily suspend change control meetings. The obvious intention here is to bring reality (what's really happening on the project) back in line with what's been accounted for in one of the key parameters of the plan. This often happens when a preset parameter (e.g., the schedule) cannot be missed or modified. In situations like these, you need to modify what the teams are doing; you need to change the level of activity, up or down, to realize expectations present in the plan.

Change the Plans

A third option here is often overlooked. Corrective action can be to change the plans: modify them, rebaseline them, and rerelease them. That's often the most appropriate action to take. We can't always bend reality to match the present or future we would like to see. Certain factors simply cannot be removed or mitigated; they have to be accepted for what they are, problematic though that may be. In these cases, the stakeholders' expectations may have to be realigned and new objectives documented. This is where replanning comes in. A good planning program and process can come to your aid. Most project managers will acknowledge that periodic replanning can probably help any project. The bumps occur when people are trained to expect that plans will not change at all or will change very little. That's probably an unrealistic expectation. A planning program that allows for changes, adjustments, and new baselines can be used to communicate the inevitability of change up front and even encourage participation in change. Of course, the degree of plan changes—adjustments to project commitments—needs to be thoroughly approved by relevant stakeholders, and the frequency of plan changes needs to be controlled. Too little change might indicate that plans are not being properly maintained. Too much change might represent a blurred project management or scope that is not well understood or managed.

SP 2.3: Manage Corrective Action

Issues will arise across the lifecycle of a project. Your analysis will lead to some issues being ignored; others may be placed in an observation state. Some you will act on, and based on your analysis you will decide an appropriate course of action. This corrective action should be managed to closure. That can mean one of two things: Manage the action until the issue goes away, until it no longer has any potential to impact the project, or manage the action until the issue is under control in such a way that its impact on the project, while inevitable, has been minimized. Closure is the key target here. Addressing issues through action is a necessary part of project management, but if an issue isn't firmly wrestled to the ground, chances are that the core problem still remains. Though desirable, our actions won't make all issues go away. But through continued diligence, we can minimize impacts.

This third practice represents an overriding project management philosophy within CMMI: Follow-through is essential. Protecting project parameters, analyzing issues, taking appropriate corrective action, and then following through to make sure the desired impact is achieved—that may well be the essence of ongoing, active project management.

The Benefits of Project Monitoring & Control

As we have seen in this chapter, Project Monitoring & Control sits at the center of project management activities. The recommendations in this Process Area deal with the day-to-day concerns that influence progress and alignment with performance objectives. Project Monitoring & Control can be seen as the center of your CMMI Maturity Level 2 program also. PMC both feeds from the other Maturity Level 2 Process Areas and shapes their activities. Because of the central nature of this Process Area, you can gain many benefits by deriving a set of processes to help manage and direct it.

This section discusses four of these benefits that deserve special attention. They support the major theme of this book, that CMMI Maturity Level 2 can take an organization a long way toward solidifying an effective and efficient project management program that contributes tangibly to bottom line success.

A Platform for Value Management

Value management arises out of an organization's cultural makeup. Whether planned or not, it's an inescapable trait of operations. Each organization focuses on those things it finds most important. Of course, the best way to realize value management is to plan for it, and one effective way to plan for it is through process. A process program can be forged to carry an organization's values; in fact, it should be forged with that function in mind. And this applies to Project Monitoring & Control also. There are dozens of ways to monitor a technology project, hundreds of separate elements that can be controlled. But which ones are important to the organization? What are those critical elements that add up to the organization's definition of success? When you can base your monitoring and control program around processes that capture these values, you move a long way toward ensuring that all members of the PMO, together with members of the project teams at large, work toward these targets in a coordinated way. Further, you establish the tools and techniques that aid in driving toward these values. In short, the organization sets into place a machine (the process program) to bring these values about in tangible, measurable ways.

A Common Language of Progress and Oversight

In Chapter 1, I mentioned the case of the project manager who kept three different versions of his schedule, one for management, one for the team, and one for himself. When he had to communicate with a particular group, he went for that particular schedule, bent to tell a particular story. Consistency of communications was obviously not in the forefront of his priorities. But in a well-run shop, you'll find that communications consistency is given its due place. This is rightfully so. So much of project monitoring and control stems from communications. We communicate to collect information; we communicate to impact information; we communicate to interpret information. The value of a PMC program based in process is that here you can capture the terms, definitions, and meanings used to communicate such factors as progress, status, and success. A common language here especially contributes to smooth management when you remember the diverse groups that make up a project team. Your technical members have a particular view of the world. Your senior management reacts to a different set of priorities. And your customer may have an altogether unique perspective. Your process program can serve as a unifying force among these parties. Through it, the form and manner in which you express concepts of status, oversight, progress, and the attainment of objectives become commonly understood and open to consistent interpretation.

A Project Management Performance Bar

A program that defines organizational PMC activities can be used to set a standard of performance for its project managers. Like any form of management, project management has a distinct qualitative side to it. Personal traits affect whether project management is more or less effective. The abilities to organize, plan, forecast, communicate, and strategize are all influenced by the personalities exercising them. Some project managers are strong in certain areas, less so in others. Some have an affinity for one aspect of the job and less of an attraction to others. As long as humans are appointed as project managers, that will remain the case. A well-designed process program may not be able to settle all project managers along a level performance bar, but it can be very effective in establishing minimum performance standards.

A PMC program like the one described in this chapter will actively ensure the tracking of critical path dates and key milestones, the measurement of important project parameters, the use of specific modes of progress reporting, and the facilitation of communication standards. This framework will help set a standard for performance that all your project managers can share, that they can work to meet. More so, it will give the people surrounding and interacting with the project a regimen they can count on as representing not the individual view but the organizational view of what project management really means.

Consistency in PMO Operations

The last benefit that we'll mention here represents in a very real way the culmination of joining process improvement to project management, of the potential to blend CMMI practices with PMBOK methods. When this is accomplished, a technology organization can achieve consistency of operations across its project management office. Such consistency is a plus for any shop. Project management naturally sits at the center of any development effort, and the domains that project managers manage carry the full business weight of the initiative. Technology projects may push for technical verisimilitude, but they depend on sound business controls. To be fully realized, these controls need to be standardized within a PMO. If their implementation is left instead to the personal interpretation of individual project managers or, worse, is unaccounted for altogether, the PMO is functioning more like central casting than a cohesive organizational unit.

When an IT shop begins to shape the way it monitors and controls its projects through the use of process, and when it embeds within those processes practices proven to deliver positive results, project management will begin to take on the cultural characteristics typical of an integrated team. The members will share a common view of what sound business management really means. They will employ common tools to shape projects and provide insight into their progress. They will judge and report success using an established set of values. And they will communicate with the rest of the organization—those myriad teams and players they are chartered to interface and interact with—using a language and approach that demonstrates harmony, stability, and professionalism.

Reaching that state should be the goal of any project management office.

Some Example Program Components

The way you implement Project Monitoring & Control will be highly dependent on the size, culture, and focus of your organization. Large projects may require one approach; small projects another. Certain industries may need heavy monitoring and control processes. Others may be able to operate with lighter versions. All in all, the components you build to support the program can be, and indeed should be, a reflection of your style of project management and the particular organization goals established for your project and its teams.

But however you work or however your organization is shaped, some elements of a PMC program can be common across technology shops. This section describes three typical components that almost every PMC program can use in some form or another.

Tracking Policy

A project tracking policy, authored and issued by senior management, can establish the boundaries of a PMC program. Through this policy, the organization can define which critical parameters need to be tracked, which groups constitute relevant stakeholders, which communications and reporting mechanisms should be used, which performance measures will be collected, and so on. Policies like this are typically not large documents; they are brief and concise. Yet they encapsulate the mission of project monitoring and control, and they make visible management's commitment to the use of the process assets in order to realize this mission.

Status Report Forms

A standardized status report form is a handy way to make sure that different project managers conduct project reviews in similar ways, tracking and noting a common set of progress data points. You may also choose to develop a status meeting procedure or a set of status meeting guidelines, tips that remind a project manager what to check for when the teams periodically get together. But a form, something your project managers can carry with them into meetings, becomes a visual, tactile clue to prompt the proper meeting agenda and to ensure that a full set of topics or points of interest are consistently addressed.

Project Tracking Metrics

Later in this book, we will look at a Process Area called Measurement & Analysis. This Process Area can be employed to design a metrics program in support of project management goals. The tie-in can be seen here. Since the use of data is the best way to objectively quantify project progress and efficiencies, a PMO will be well served by providing its project managers with at least a foundation set of measures that it would like everyone to collect across all projects. The idea is to standardize on a set of common measures, instruct people on how to collect and analyze them, and then provide some form of reporting mechanisms so that measurement results can be distributed to relevant parties in the organization.

Look to the Web Site for . . .

- Status report checklist
- Risk management log
- Milestone review report
- Progress measurement report

Chapter 5

Requirements Management

Our systems are a reflection of the requirements we develop in tandem with our clients. Requirements encapsulate the business need, the functional expectations, and most importantly the value of the solution. Although the systems we design and build are by nature highly complex, we strive to maintain requirements sets that are straightforward, declarative, and simply organized. And well controlled. This promotes a direct and ongoing line of communications with the customer.

Johann Strenberg, CEO, Tenzer Spring Dynamics
Digital data management for clinical assessments

There are no doubt plenty of technology professionals who believe that requirements management is the single most important job for any project manager on any project. Most of these folks have reached this conclusion because at one time or another they have had to deal with the impact of poor requirements management.

Scope creep, misaligned expectations, backtracking, perplexed customers—these are all conditions that tend to pop up when a project's requirements are left to fend for themselves. These kinds of conditions can cloud a project's mission and objectives. Without active requirements management, a manager's best efforts to control the traditional domains of cost, schedule, scope, and resources can become quickly compromised.

That's why CMMI introduces this Process Area at Maturity Level 2. Requirements management under CMMI is seen as a basic and fundamental project management responsibility.

In this chapter, we'll look at how CMMI defines requirements management and explore how you might implement established requirements management practices on your projects.

The Purpose of Requirements Management

There are many potential ways to define a project's requirements. We'll take a specific look at some of those ways in the upcoming subsection Requirements—What Qualifies? But from a high-level, general perspective, it's reasonable to define requirements, broadly speaking, as those general expectations you share with your customer concerning what you're going to work on together, what you're going to build, what it should do after it's built, and what it's going to take to build it.

Because requirements are usually the main source of these expectations, it's helpful to think of them as a contract of mutual understanding. If you and your customer share this same understanding across the life of a project, chances are good that you'll both emerge in the end still pretty much in agreement.

But if your understandings begin to drift apart over time, your expectations may likewise begin to move farther and farther away from your customer's. What you think about what you and your teams ought to be building may not be what your customer thinks you ought to be building. And at some point, sooner or later, both of you are going to be standing together asking questions such as, "How did we end up here, and what went wrong?"

With a sound approach to requirements management, you and your customers can employ a mechanism to stay in sync, to move together, not drift apart.

No one building a new house would want the architect or the contractor to decide in private that an angled staircase is just as pleasing as a curved staircase and then act on that choice. And a waitperson who brings you beef when you ordered fish is not keeping up his or her end of the bargain. It's the same with a project's requirements. Requirements are a key ingredient to project success. Very often they establish the initial customer relationship. And because they rest at the very core of project activity, requirements should be carefully and continuously managed.

A Core Project Management Responsibility

There are lots of good reasons to proactively manage requirements on your projects. Those managers I know who have learned this lesson the hard way can offer up plenty of reasons, with plenty of gory detail. But if you look at requirements from a fundamental business perspective, it becomes clear that it's important to manage them for five basic reasons.

1. They form the basis for agreement.
2. They define the scope and character of project work.
3. They may establish a legal responsibility.
4. They can serve as objective success criteria.
5. They are naturally subject to change.

Let's discuss these reasons further.

Basis for Agreement

By their very nature, requirements are the basis of the agreement and the understanding you share with your customer: "This is what we are required to do." However, requirements establish this understanding not just with your customers—they also forge a link between you and your management, and between you and your project teams. Requirements are the elements that keep you, your teams, and your customers in a harmony of understanding. The requirements are not the sole contributor here, of course, as there are other factors at work, but the part the requirements play is both crucial and significant.

Because they are typically introduced early in the lifecycle of the project (at least in baseline form), requirements are one of the few touchstone artifacts that can reflect the evolution of the project in visible, tangible form, from beginning to end. And because requirements serve so well as a basis of agreement, it's important to ensure right from the start that they are recognized in that role and that mechanisms are set in place to ensure that the integrity of this basis remains intact.

Scope Definition

This is the classic reason why it's important to manage requirements. They define and bound the scope of all subsequent project work. If you look at the PMI's PMBOK, or at the ISO 9001:2000 standard, or at Six Sigma's emphasis on the Voice of the Customer, you'll see this point emphasized again and again. The requirements—in whatever form they come to you or in whatever form you generate them—determine or impact just about every aspect of project work: the amount of work to be done, the kind of work to be done, the types of resources you will need, the length of time, the amount of money, and so on.

Good project managers know as a matter of practice that it's smart to create plans based in large part on the requirements. (For more detail on this subject, see Chapter 3.) That being the case, if you can control the requirements, you ought to be able to keep a firm hand on your plans. And if your plans remain under control, all those issues of cost, time, and resources should be, by and large, pretty much under control, too.

Performance Obligation

Another reason to manage requirements can take on a special significance depending on the kinds of clients you deal with. With some clients—perhaps those issuing you large contracts or engaging you on projects of high sensitivity—the requirements can actually constitute a legally binding responsibility on your part. They may define a performance standard that you and your teams will be required to live up to. This is becoming more and more common today in organizations of all sizes, as IT projects expand in reach and business criticality.

Because fulfillment of the requirements can be a binding obligation, it becomes especially important to control them in an effective and conscientious manner. Failure to do so, or even a weak ability to do so, could have enormous ramifications not just for your client but for you, your management, and your organization as well.

Success Criteria

This fourth reason sheds light on the real and positive benefits you can reap from successful requirements management. You and your customers can use the requirements as a benchmark for project success. The full realization of the requirements can be equated, at the end of the lifecycle, with project success.

This is one tactic I like to see project teams and customers get together on. If both can agree to look at the requirements as a major part of the success criteria early in the project, chances are you'll pay attention to the requirements across the life of the project. You'll want to keep them current. You'll have a reason to work with your customers to make sure all expectations concerning them are staying in line.

Using the requirements as your success criteria is a great way to forge a common partnership with your customers, one in which obtaining the goal brings equal value and rewards to both parties.

Subject to Change

Now we come to a volatile reason why it's important to manage requirements.

By their very nature, requirements are subject to change.

It might be more accurate to say that they are destined to change. In the fields of systems engineering, software engineering, and technology development, we tend to employ a lot of fairly stabilized tools: programming languages, code compilers, modeling systems, diagrams, charts. But of all these tools, the one we most depend on—the English language—is the least stable, the one most open to interpretation. And because those of us in the U.S. IT industry tend to express requirements in English, there is always going to be a degree of interpretation involved when working with them.

That trait carries with it the basic reality that, over time (a lot of time or a little time), the meaning of requirements may change, information may evolve, new elements might come to light. It's only natural. It's only human. It's difficult for any group of people to capture all at once what a complex system might have to do. It's even more difficult if those groups are new to technology projects or don't work in technology domains.

So under most circumstances, requirements are going to change. They will probably change on a somewhat regular basis. And with change comes another chief responsibility of project management: the introduction of change management. (See the upcoming subsection A Continuous Activity.)

Requirements—What Qualifies?

In a prototypical development organization, it should be easy to identify what the requirements are. They are the specs in the software requirements specification, or the contents in the requirements document, or maybe scenarios in a business needs report. Whatever form they take, the requirements stand out as the descriptions of what the technology teams have to build.

Things can get a little less clear-cut in shops that are not "typical," which is probably most shops. Teams dealing with integrated systems, combinations of hardware and software, and cross-performance interfaces have to analyze closely what their exact requirements are. Attention to domains and detail becomes crucial.

And then there are teams who say they probably have no requirements.

I worked with a major Medicare claims processing company that wanted to adopt CMMI across its IT groups. Most of these groups, it turned out, didn't really build anything, not from scratch. They maintained existing systems.

Early in the initiative, the manager of one of these groups came to me and confessed that, as best he could figure, his requirements were nothing more than the service-level agreements contained in his department's annual contract. We looked at the contract, and he was right. On top of that, his people had only three service requirements: (1) In the event of an outage, restore system functionality within ten minutes; (2) formulate database queries for all registered customers on a first-in, first-out basis; and (3) prepare and issue a set of standard monthly and quarterly reports to Medicare services management.

The point here is that requirements can be very detailed or very high level. They can be extremely volatile or relatively stable. Look at your organization and at the way it establishes its customer agreements. You may base the relationship on a formal contract, an agreement, or a statement of work, or maybe on a traditional requirements document.

If you'd like a way to determine just what your requirements might be, make a list describing what you'll do for the client, and then compare those items with the five points we just discussed. Here they are again.

1. Requirements form the basis for agreement.
2. They define the scope and character of project work.
3. They may establish a legal responsibility.
4. They can serve as objective success criteria.
5. They are naturally subject to change.

If the descriptions tend to fall into or cover most of these points, chances are you're pretty safe considering those to be your requirements.

A Continuous Activity

The CMMI framework makes the point more than a few times that requirements management should be considered a continuous project activity. It is not just an early-lifecycle job. Nor is it a job that's put to sleep and then resurrected when test time rolls around. It's an activity that project management should account for across all phases of the project.

After all, new requirements might be introduced at any time. Existing requirements might have to be modified or extended. Other requirements might turn out to be obsolete or unnecessary. A development project, no mater what its discipline or business domain, is a dynamic entity, internally and externally. Its smooth evolution is one of the chief responsibilities of project management, and this includes the ongoing evolution of the requirements. As we'll see later in this chapter, the Specific Practices defined for the CMMI Requirements Management Process Area give us a set of recommendations we can use to establish this ongoing management in a smooth and integrated way.

No Requirements Development *at CMMI Level 2?*

This is a question people wonder about all the time. Why does CMMI include the Requirements *Management* Process Area at Level 2 but does not introduce the Requirements *Development* Process Area until Level 3? Requirements Development, of course, describes the set of practices used to elicit, define, and organize the requirements.

This order seems backwards to some people. But the Software Engineering Institute has a reason for it. The SEI's take is that a project team will not be able to do a good job of working with its requirements until it first has a way to manage them. So the approach is to first become practiced at managing the requirements and then move forward to develop them in an organized way with your customer.

Requirements Management Goals and Practices

CMMI defines one Specific Goal and five Specific Practices for Requirements Management. Here is the official specification text for each of these elements.

SG 1   MANAGE REQUIREMENTS
Requirements are managed and inconsistencies with project plans and work products are identified.

SP 1.1   OBTAIN AN UNDERSTANDING OF THE REQUIREMENTS
Develop an understanding with the requirements providers on the meaning of the requirements.

SP 1.2   OBTAIN COMMITMENT TO THE REQUIREMENTS
Obtain commitment to the requirements from the project participants.

SP 1.3   MANAGE REQUIREMENTS CHANGES
Manage changes to the requirements as they evolve during the project.

SP 1.4   Maintain Bi-directional Traceability of Requirements

Maintain bi-directional traceability among the requirements and the project plans and work products.

SP 1.5   Identify Inconsistencies between Project Work and Requirements

Identify inconsistencies between the project plans and work products and the requirements.

Generic Goals and Practices

See Chapter 10 for information about the important Generic Goals and Practices that support project management success for all the Process Areas at Maturity Level 2.

SG 1: Manage Requirements

There is only one Specific Goal for Requirements Management: to manage the requirements. Simple enough. Obvious enough.

How you manage requirements in your organization is naturally going to depend on the makeup of your organization, the kind of work you do, the kinds of clients you have, and the policies of your management.

Let's look at the full description of the goal. "Requirements are managed and inconsistencies with project plans and work products are identified." In other words, you manage the requirements to ensure that your team is producing products that truly reflect what the requirements call for at any phase in the project lifecycle.

It is a simple goal, and it is an obvious one, but to get there you'll want to establish some project management procedures and approaches you can share across your teams so you can achieve this goal in a consistent and repeatable fashion. For example, the goal of managing requirements is accomplished in large part by giving project stakeholders the opportunity to review and understand the requirements, then provide input for clarification and completeness (Figure 5–1). Once all parties are in agreement, the baseline version of the requirements can be officially approved.

CMMI defines five Specific Practices that can be used together to help you effectively manage requirements. In the following subsections, we'll take a look at each practice and discuss ways that organizations might typically put these practices into place.

At this point, it's important to remember that we're presenting ideas and approaches we have seen work well in other shops. These practices are not rules. They are not items you must implement in order to officially achieve Level 2 through a formal appraisal. Under CMMI, these are called Specific Practices, but they are meant to be flexible, as flexible as you need them to be.

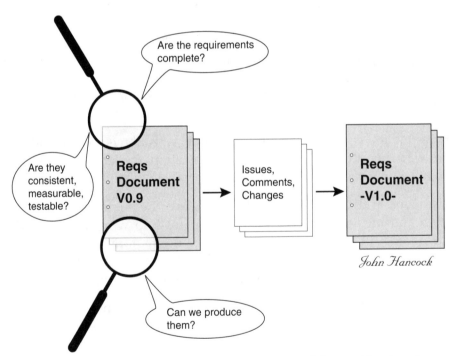

Figure 5–1: *Thorough opportunity for review of the specifications is essential to commitment*

A better way to look at the following material is to see it as a basis for planning how you might implement your own requirements management practices. To do this, you'll want to keep your culture in mind, think about what would work best for your folks, and try to capitalize on things you're already doing well that might fit in this domain.

Let's begin with the first practice.

SP 1.1: Obtain an Understanding of the Requirements

On most technology projects, there is always a temptation to hurry up and go. People might think that if they aren't hearing the tap-tap-tap of keyboards, progress is not being made. This first Specific Practice can be thought of as a reminder to resist jumping into the work until everyone has a comfortable understanding of what the requirements call for.

Enthusiasm is a good thing, but it is better when accompanied by focus. Understanding the requirements will help ensure that all stakeholders—team members, management, and customers—have the chance to establish a common understanding at the outset and to occupy common ground from that point on.

We have found that you can promote understanding of the requirements in a shop by using a set of five simple but effective activities (in any order or with a special focus on any steps you find especially helpful).

1. Document the requirements.
2. Identify the stakeholders.
3. Distribute the requirements for review.
4. Allow time for adequate review.
5. Encourage feedback.

Document the Requirements

If the requirements aren't documented, it's going to be hard to get a good understanding of them, or at least an understanding that can be shared. As strange and as risky as it seems, some technology shops resist putting requirements into writing. Such shops may start off with a documented core set, but then they seem to prefer to talk through the evolution, thinking that a casual approach will be more conducive to a free flow of ideas.

That may be true in some places, but it's not a sound project management practice. The strength of documented requirements is that everyone has access at any one time to the same sets of information. And that's the most effective way to manage how information is collated, disseminated, and refined.

The approach you take to documenting the requirements can take shape from the preferences of your shop. Some teams simply use a word processor and print out versions and updates as needed. Others use some of the more sophisticated automated tools available on the market today. Either approach is fine. The key is to ensure that the requirements exist in an externalized form, that they are not kept in someone's head—or lots of different heads—where they might soon take on a life of their own.

Identify the Stakeholders

The ultimate purpose of understanding the requirements is to get everyone comfortable enough so that they can commit to the requirements and establish a recognized baseline to work from. To do this effectively, you'll probably want to define who "everyone" really is. Chances are, it's not actually everyone. It's often not practical to include an all-encompassing group in the requirements review and approval process. That's why it's usually up to project management to identify the relevant stakeholders for this activity, those people who will be most impacted by the review and approval process.

Stakeholders are typically those people who will have some direct responsibility concerning the requirements: confirming them, inspecting them, working from them. You can look two places when you want to identify the proper stakeholders for your project. First, identify external stakeholders, people outside your project team. These are usually customer contacts or liaisons who own the business side of the project. You work with these folks to confirm that you have the right sets of requirements and that they stay in line with customer needs across the life of the project. External stakeholders may also be the people who help confirm, during some stage of testing perhaps, that you have accounted for all of the requirements.

Next are internal stakeholders. These are the key members of your project team who will be charged with controlling how the requirements are worked through the various phases of development. Internal stakeholders also usually include select members of the management team.

Distribute the Requirements for Review

In the realm of CMMI and in the domain of sound project management, you are not required to force people to understand the requirements. Your job instead is to make sure that all the right people have an ample *opportunity* to understand them. To foster this opportunity, you should probably take on the job—or appoint someone to the job—of handling distribution of the requirements to the stakeholders when the need arises. You can handle this any number of ways: by sending an e-mail with attachments, by providing access into a set repository, by dropping off printed copies on desks. If you've accounted for the task of getting the requirements into the hands of the people who need to review and understand them, you can probably count on the stakeholders to take it from there.

Remember, you might have to redistribute updated versions of the requirements from time to time. It might be a good idea to establish a distribution procedure you can use throughout the project. (For more information on this, see the discussion of the Configuration Management Process Area in Chapter 6.)

Allow Time for Adequate Review

Your stakeholders will need ample time to review the requirements if they are going to acquire a good understanding of them. Some requirements sets are quite large. Others might be relatively small. The amount of time your stakeholders will need to get their arms around the requirements will naturally depend on how many requirements there are. It may also depend on how complex they are, how integrated they are, and any number of other factors.

Keep this in mind when you're sending the document out for review. Try to give your stakeholders a comfortable amount of time to roll this task into their current schedules. If your reviewers feel rushed or if their review time is squeezed, they may not be able to do a thorough job. That might lead to missed issues, gaps, and a level of uncertainty that could slow down getting the right level of commitment.

Encourage Feedback

Your stakeholders will probably do a good job of reviewing the requirements if they feel that their comments are going to be seriously considered. Sometimes in this kind of activity, people have a tendency to hand off the requirements the way they might a live bomb—a little nervously, hoping it doesn't explode. But the great benefit of a review procedure is that you almost always end up with better requirements.

If you encourage people to give as much feedback as they'd like, you may end up getting a lot of it. But you can get work through and assess a pile of feedback; it's the lack of feedback that can introduce risks.

Encourage feedback, then, and give your stakeholders a way to submit it. You can use review and comment forms, e-mails, issue logs, or anything that will make it easy to document issues, concerns, and points for clarification.

SP 1.2: Obtain Commitment to the Requirements

The second practice under Requirements Management is to obtain commitment to the requirements. This is a natural extension of the first practice, understanding the requirements. In the same way that you don't want to begin project work until the requirements are understood, you also don't want to begin work until the requirements have been approved, or at least until a baseline set has been approved.

Commitment is important for a few reasons. First, it creates an atmosphere of acceptance—people have agreed that work is ready to proceed. Second, it implies input—if people are asked to approve, they probably have had the opportunity to not approve. And third, commitment is a visible way to establish consensus. Commitment demonstrates to your management and to customers that the project teams are indeed working together.

The concept of commitment can mean different things in different organizational cultures. In some shops, a verbal "yes" might be sufficient. In others, people might have to sign formal documents. However it's done, the purpose of commitment remains the same: to demonstrate common agreement. In light of that, then, here are five activities that have worked well at other shops for getting people to commit to the requirements.

1. Identify appropriate approver groups.
2. Incorporate feedback.
3. Set a time limit.
4. Ensure that commitment allows for future change.
5. Seek signatures.

Let's take a quick look at each one.

Identify Appropriate Approver Groups

As early as you can in the project lifecycle, try to identify who should probably approve the requirements. Most of the time, these folks will be readily apparent. But when they're not, project management should walk the hallways to identify these people and then integrate them into the process.

You may have identified them already by identifying who the reviewers should be. Sometimes the reviewers and the approvers are the same group. Sometimes, though, you'll want to tap a broad set of reviewers for input and then use a select or different group to be responsible for approval.

It comes down to a question of authority and practicality. The people you want to commit to the requirements should be those stakeholders—internal and external—who have the ability to ensure that, once approved, the requirements will begin to be realized. Their blessing should be enough to assure that. At the same time, you want to be practical. Seeking out too many approvers, to get total consensus, might be a tall order in many organizations. Keeping the approver groups compact and appropriately authoritative will help you obtain commitment as smoothly and efficiently as possible.

Incorporate Feedback

In the section about SP 1.1, we looked at the importance of seeking feedback from your reviewers. Now the idea is to visibly incorporate that feedback into the requirements sets. There's a real value at play here, but it's one that has to be balanced with your judgment. The value is that the approvers will be much more comfortable committing to the requirements when they see that their questions, issues, and concerns have all been explicitly addressed. The balance comes from deciding which changes to incorporate.

If you've given your customers and teams ample time to review the requirements and if you've encouraged feedback, you may have to work through quite a few issues. You don't need to feel obligated to make everyone's recommended changes. A better course—and probably what the reviewers and approvers really want to see—is a serious consideration of all the questions, issues, and concerns. If people feel that the project stakeholders have had a chance to address these points and work through them, they will probably be amenable to the changes you do incorporate and be ready to commit to those as being acceptable.

Set a Time Limit

Project managers have to be effective time managers. Tasks, deliverables, and goals almost always depend on some kind of time table. Keeping the project running according to schedule is a primary responsibility for project managers. That's why it's important to establish a time frame for obtaining commitment to the requirements.

If the window for review and discussion looks like it's always open, the stakeholders may want to analyze and reanalyze, never feeling quite ready to let the requirements go. Setting a deadline—a reasonable deadline—for this process will help your teams focus their efforts toward a degree of consensus. This sounds like a simple point, and it certainly is simple, but its importance should not be minimized. Many, many projects have gone off track early because their teams could not come together over the requirements. Management can help avoid this kind of disconnect by establishing the review and approval process up front, communicating this process to the people who will need to employ it, and then setting the time frame the process will need to operate within. Given this kind of pathway and a predetermined end point, your teams in all likelihood will be able to arrive at the state of consensus your project needs. And you can further support this by using the technique that follows: assuring your teams that commitment now still allows plenty of opportunity for future change.

Ensure That Commitment Allows for Future Change

If the people involved in your project are new to technology development or if you are dealing with a complex solution, you may find that people are hesitant to release or approve the requirements because they feel that once they commit, they won't have a chance to say anything else again. You can relieve them of that concern by assuring them that the requirements management process will be an ongoing and iterative activity across the project and that there will be plenty of opportunity to tweak and adjust the requirements as needed.

The management objective at this juncture is to establish a baseline of requirements. The baseline will serve as the common go-point for the team and as the benchmark for all subsequent iterations. If your customers, technical team members, and other stakeholders feel comfortable that you'll accommodate ongoing input, they'll be much more willing to commit to the release of a baseline. And this will help you work through the next activity: getting approval signatures.

Seek Signatures

There are many ways to obtain commitment to the requirements. The idea to seek signatures is the most traditional way. In the world of business, ink on paper is a good thing. Signing is about as clear a way as any to show commitment. So, if you can get your stakeholders—those you've identified as approvers—to formally sign acceptance of the requirements, you've paved a clean path toward establishing a baseline.

But not all business cultures support such a traditional approach. Distance and location may preclude it. Organizational practice might promote other alternatives. Electronic signatures might be preferred. Your customers and management might be fine with e-mail approvals or even verbal acceptance.

The goal that project management wants to reach here is a recognizable milestone of agreement, some form of empirical evidence showing that commitment to the requirements has been achieved and that subsequent project work can now commence. The kind of "signature" that will work for your project will depend on the culture you operate in. Therefore it's a good idea to define this method of commitment early in the project lifecycle. In the domain of project management, the requirements are not the only data set that will need to be approved. You'll need similar approval methods of your plans, change requests, and project deliverables. Somehow, in some form, you'll need to seek signatures for all of these.

SP 1.3: Manage Requirements Changes

The third Specific Practice for this Process Area is to manage changes to the requirements. The first two practices—to obtain an understanding and to obtain commitment—are in place to help you establish working baselines for the requirements. You might well move through these practices at multiple times during a project. This third practice is defined to help manage the in-between evolution of the requirements.

Managing changes to the requirements implies a project management approach to change control and smooth change integration. We'll look at this topic in more depth when we look at the Configuration Management Process Area in Chapter 6, but for now let's look at five basic considerations you can employ to help manage requirements as they evolve.

1. Know that requirements will change.
2. Control with baselines.
3. Honor your customers' needs.
4. Assess proposed changes.
5. Incorporate changes in an orderly manner.

Let's take a quick look at each one.

Know That Requirements Will Change

This is really a reminder more than it is an activity. Because you may go through a good amount of work to get your teams to baseline a set of requirements, the thought that the set might change could make any project manager cringe. But change is a natural part of the business and development domains, so it's important to recognize that the requirements will change. Part of the focus of the Requirements Management Process Area is to track and monitor changes to requirements over time and to ensure that the work products that support the requirements remain in sync with the latest version of the requirements (Figure 5–2).

An important part of a project manager's job is to know that requirements will change, to communicate that they may change, and then to support the inherent dynamic nature of requirements with a sound methodology to control and manage the changes. If you recognize change as an acceptable part of the project lifecycle, chances are your teams, management, and customers will work with you to make sure change is handled in as smooth a way as practical.

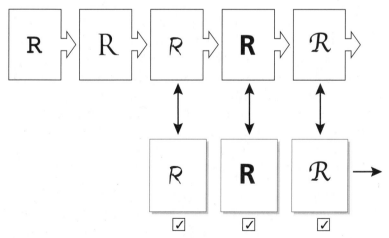

Figure 5–2: *Managing requirements changes as a key to synchronicity*

Control with Baselines

Data management is another important aspect of project management: knowing who needs access to which data, when, and to what extent. The requirements document (for the sake of convenience, we'll call it a document) is one work product that many people will need to access. It's also one of the few products that will move (or should move) through every cycle of a project. Because of its wide-reaching impact, a requirements document should be conscientiously controlled. One of the best ways to do this is through the use of version-controlled baselines.

Using such baselines implies a degree of ownership and centralized management. Project management assigns ownership of the requirements document to a responsible party, who then provides for the distribution of the document, ensures its integrity, and provides for the smooth integration of approved changes into subsequent versions. (For more on the subject of creating and releasing baselines, see Chapter 6.)

Managing baselines this way will help make sure that your project teams are always working with the latest version of the specifications and that proposed changes can be assessed against the latest version as well.

Honor Your Customers' Needs

"All change is good" is an ancient Mandarin proverb. That might not always be true for technology projects, but some degree of change is inevitable. Most of the time you'll find that requests for change come from your customers. Something was forgotten or not accounted for in its full scope, or something changed. Of course, managing requirements in a professional manner means keeping a tight rein on them, making sure they don't run away from the project. But at the same time, this professionalism calls for you to keep your customer's mission in mind, to help the client realize what needs to be built for the business.

Project management should work to strike a balance between two important responsibilities. First is the responsibility to create the kind of product (or service) that will effectively serve the customer's business needs. Second is the responsibility to manage the amount of time, money, and resources the customer can provide to the project. Sometimes these two responsibilities butt up against each other. It's not always an easy job, and it may have more to do with the art of project management than with the technique of project management, but the project manager should always work to balance the customer's needs. This may mean, from time to time, introducing new or extended specs into the requirements mix. It might also mean working with the customer to establish a set of second-phase requirements, one that can be assessed once the current project goals have been met.

The objective here is to maintain an open ear to your client's needs. Understanding that the requirements will be subject to change across the lifecycle of the project will help you and your team members keep that channel open and that balance point set.

Assess Proposed Changes

Open communication is one hallmark of a well-run project. The freedom to communicate fully and openly, combined with proper communication channels, permits project teams, customers, and management to exchange information, updates, and current status in a way that supports consensus and promotes openness. It's also a way to open the gate for a lot of change. Another prime responsibility of project management, then, is not only to control the amount of change introduced during a project but also to evaluate the value and appropriateness of each change request.

Customers might often feel pulled between including all the functionality they would like to have and accepting the amount of functionality they can currently afford. You can help balance this pull by establishing a formal way to assess requirements changes once they are submitted. If you can establish a protocol people can follow to review requirements changes and then determine the impacts on the project and the potential value the changes might bring, you'll have a way to objectify what might begin as a subjective preference. This kind of cost/benefit analysis can be useful for approving some items, tabling others for later consideration, and seeking further information for others.

It's also a good idea to assess these requests through the use of a change review committee, representatives from the various team and stakeholder groups who take on the job of reviewing and approving requirements changes as they arise. (In Chapter 6, we'll look at the potential use of a change control board and a change request procedure as a way to manage the intake of change requests and to assess their potential value to the project.)

Incorporate Changes in an Orderly Manner

The classic phrase used to describe the situation where requirements are poorly managed is *scope creep*. Scope creep can begin to take hold when project managers don't control requirements baselines, when they don't work to assess change requests, or when they fail to integrate change in an orderly manner. Indeed, if the mission of this CMMI Process Area had to be distilled to its essence, it might well be to prevent scope creep. And remember, scope creep can move backward as well as forward. Forgetting to put in approved changes can be just as damaging as putting in any change willy-nilly.

So it's important to implement a way to incorporate change in an orderly manner. This may involve appointing someone on the team to own the requirements baseline and to be responsible for keeping it current. When a certain cycle of changes has been incorporated or when a new date-based version is ready, this owner will ensure that the contents are up to date. And just as importantly, this owner should ensure that the existence of the new version is communicated to the appropriate teams. Smooth change means not only incorporating change into the requirements documents but also making these changes available to the people who must incorporate them into their work.

That being the case, project management should consider ways to control the input of requirements changes into relevant documents (or repositories), establish a method to release new versions of the baselines, and then communicate the impact of the new materials to relevant team members, customers, and management.

SP 1.4: Maintain Bi-directional Traceability of Requirements

The fourth Specific Practice for Requirements Management is to manage the requirements, in part, by establishing bi-directional traceability. Traceability simply means establishing a mechanism to follow the life of each requirement as it moves from phase to phase in a project.

Because (as we have seen) the requirements will change, because you may be dealing with a significant set of them, and because their integration into technical work products can be less than visible, traceability serves a valuable purpose. Basically, traceability is a tool to make sure you don't lose any requirements along the way. And it's a great way to demonstrate at the end of the project that everything the customer asked for at the start has been successfully accounted for.

A lot of discussion always occurs when the concept of traceability comes up. The basic idea is pretty simple. CMMI sees traceability as a thread that weaves through the various phases of the project, connecting a requirement or specification to each distinct activity involved in product realization. The purpose is straightforward, too. It's a technique you can use to ensure that the requirements are being appropriately accounted for every step of the way. The detailed discussions around this practice usually deal with the extent of traceability and how sophisticated it needs to be.

Traceability can be very well managed by any of the requirements management tools available on today's market. But you don't need a special tool to take care of the job. Simple spreadsheets can often work just as well. The idea is to use traceability as a way to regularly monitor the requirements, to follow their integration into your solution. Whatever tool works for your team will meet the intention of CMMI.

Traceability can serve three project management points of focus.

1. Trace to plan.
2. Trace to anticipate.
3. Trace to know.

Trace to Plan

Setting up a structure to help you trace requirements can also help you plan downstream project activities. The structure of tracing will help you plan this work. If, for example, you are using a lifecycle that calls for functional analysis, high-level design, low-level design, coding, integration testing, and acceptance testing, you can use a traceability matrix to plan when logical groups of requirements might flow through each phase.

If you follow this method, you'll find the matrix can also help you organize and group requirements. It can help you prioritize requirements and then negotiate and allocate them across teams.

As your management picture of the requirements begins to take shape in the matrix, you will then realize an additional benefit: a framework for tracking and communicating requirements management and development progress.

Trace to Anticipate

Another strong benefit of using a traceability matrix is that it gives you a way to forecast upcoming activities and to anticipate any potential issues, risks, or bottlenecks. From a purely visual standpoint, the matrix can provide visible clues as to what appears to be on the horizon. Tracing will help you forecast events that may need mitigation and then understand what steps you might need to take to keep your other plans and activities on track. This way, traceability can become an additional management tool to help you allocate and balance resources and capacities in an effective manner.

Trace to Know

Perhaps the most important benefit traceability can deliver is the ability to know with a high degree of confidence where your requirements stand at any one time in the production process. Traceability will give you a foundation to always be able to communicate where you are in the realization process. It will help you know what you have accomplished. It will help you know what you need to get done. And it will help you share this information with others.

By employing traceability, you gain an increased degree of control over the flow of requirements as the product moves closer and closer to deployment.

SP 1.5: Identify Inconsistencies between Project Work and Requirements

The fifth Specific Practice for Requirements Management is to identify and resolve inconsistencies between plans, work products, and the requirements. This final practice can be seen as the culmination of the four previous practices. If you have worked to understand the requirements, obtained commitment to them, managed their changes, and traced them across project phases, you have the ability and the insight to keep the requirements continuously aligned with your plans and work products.

This practice is set into place to help you achieve two project benefits:

1. Harmony with plans
2. Harmony with work products

Harmony with Plans

Requirements are not the only things that will probably change during the course of a technology project. Plans are likely to change, too. In the realm of project management, planning is pretty much an ongoing activity. Schedule intervals may be refactored, resource levels rebalanced, costs reestimated. Because both plans and requirements may coexist in a state of flux, it becomes especially important to keep the two aligned.

The ability to realize the requirements will be heavily influenced by the validity of your planning. And the integrity of the plans will be heavily influenced by how accurately they reflect the requirements. The relationship is one of mutual dependence.

Project management carries the responsibility for project planning, one of its most visible and noteworthy duties. But because of the tight link forged between the requirements and the plans, project management is also necessarily charged with making sure the plans accurately reflect what the requirements call for the teams to build at any point in time.

Harmony with Work Products

Harmony with work products is just as crucial a trait as harmony with project plans. In fact, this may be a more difficult activity to ensure, due to the level of detail that may be involved. That's one reason why proper change control and traceability are so helpful to requirements management. Project management should continually and regularly monitor the evolution of work products to make sure that what is being built—what's beginning to emerge off the assembly line—truly reflects the current state of requirements.

Many project managers address this job by holding regular status and review meetings. Milestone deliverables can then be meticulously compared to the requirements at predetermined points to ensure consistency. The types and number of work products you submit to this level of scrutiny will naturally depend on the type of project you are engaged in. The determining factor will be to identify those work products, in progress and completed, that have the largest potential to impact the validity of the final work. (For more on keeping the requirements aligned with project plans and work products, see Chapter 4.)

Some Other Ways to Achieve the Practices

The five Specific Practices just described can help you and your teams achieve the goal of managing project requirements in a complete and effective manner. We discussed a series of activities or considerations you might wish to use to help each practice work within your organization. It's important to remember that these are simply recommendations. There are many other ways you can set these practices into place. The ones you can call best practices are those that work for your organization and its culture. Here are some other ways we have seen teams set these practices into place.

SP 1.1: Obtain an Understanding of the Requirements

- Host group review and discussion sessions.
- Establish mini review teams.
- Conduct requirements training sessions.
- Sponsor customer-led orientation sessions.

SP 1.2: Obtain Commitment to the Requirements

- Take a vote.
- Employ the "Silence implies consent" rule.
- Designate a single authoritative approver.

SP 1.3: Manage Requirements Changes

- Set up a suggestion box.
- Establish an e-mail address for change requests.
- Recognize only certain stakeholders as change requestors.
- Set time limits on submitting domain changes.

SP 1.4: Maintain Bi-directional Traceability of Requirements

- Use a wall chart to map requirements and project phases.
- Invest in an automated requirements management tool.
- Use a word processor to create a table or spreadsheet.
- Use a relational database keyed to project phases.

SP 1.5: Identify Inconsistencies between Project Work and Requirements

- Hold regular technical status meetings.
- Conduct peer review inspections.
- Sponsor customer-led, in-progress inspections.

The Benefits of Sound Requirements Management

The five practices defined for this CMMI Process Area have been set into place to help project teams stay aligned with what their customers expect from them. Understanding the requirements, obtaining commitment to them, managing change as it occurs, tracing progress and integration, and maintaining harmony among the requirements, plans, and work products are recommendations that not only work well as standalone activities but also fit well together, complementing and augmenting one another.

From the perspective of effective and responsive project management, there are many benefits to managing requirements using these techniques. Control is enhanced. Accountability is made more visible. Risk is lowered. Predictability is raised. Each of these is the result of proactive and planned project management concerning the requirements.

But let's take a look at four benefits that are specifically related to the practice of sound requirements management.

Synchronicity

Synchronicity is the condition that exists when all parts of a system are properly aligned. Things turn smoothly. They work well together. For technology projects, sound requirements management is a way to introduce synchronicity across the various project teams. Because the requirements describe the system to be built and are documented, they can serve as the basis for establishing the scope and deliverables for a project and for establishing the basis for ongoing agreement concerning scope and deliverables.

With a common understanding of the requirements kept in place across the project and its phases, you and your stakeholders can expect to share the same general mission and goals for the project. This synchronicity extends from you to your customer, from you to your technical teams, and from you to your management.

Enhanced Control

A conscientious approach to requirements management adds an extra degree of control to technology projects. Schedules, budgets, and resources are all heavily influenced by the requirements. In the purest sense, these items should be direct reflections of the requirements. If management allows the requirements to drift from the plans set to contain them, a project can quickly lose its bearings. Scope creep, schedule delays, and cost overruns—all the classic project management issues—can easily materialize when a disconnect appears between what one party thinks you are working on and what another thinks, or when the normal amount of change one might expect is handled in a way that appears disorganized.

By working diligently to place the requirements in the forefront of project activities and by providing procedures to address change as it occurs, you can help assure that such a disconnect does not occur. The control you'll exercise over the project will allow you to present a consistent and predictable management position to your customers and senior management.

Management Visibility

One of the strengths of well-tendered project management is that it brings visibility into the management process. Black-box management—hiding the process from sight—is almost always a sign of trouble. By extension, then, one of the chief strengths of sound requirements management is that it's a technique to add visibility, to shed light on the project so that everyone knows what is being worked on and what the priorities are. There are no hidden corners of functionality, no side-door negotiations.

Requirements management as described under CMMI helps you establish a single functional view of the project's mission and scope that can be readily shared with all your stakeholders. And because the view has been supported by protocols and procedures that address and manage change, it becomes open to everyone who may have a stake in the evolution of the requirements.

A Standard for Fulfillment

The fourth benefit of requirements management using CMMI recommendations is the realization of a standard for fulfillment. Most technology projects culminate in some form of verification and validation activities. Verification tests make sure the requirements can be fully traced to the resulting product. Validation tests make sure the product operates in its intended environment.

When you manage the requirements well over the life of a project, the verification and validation activities should emerge with clear and reliable results. The requirements here serve as a standard for fulfillment, as the benchmark you can use to compare the performance of what you have built. This standard gives you a reference point that is objective and can be relied on and referenced by all stakeholders.

Some Example Program Components

In this chapter, we've looked at one Specific Goal and five Specific Practices recommended for the Requirements Management Process Area.

As noted, the single intention that all this detail steers us toward is the consistent and informed management of the requirements as they move from phase to phase in a project. This results in a predictable path people can follow on a project and a path that the organization can use from project to project.

To support this degree of consistency and repeatability, you may want to create a set of assets and artifacts that your organization can use as part of its requirements management program. Here are some typical tools other organizations have used to help them achieve compliance with CMMI and manage their requirements in a common way.

Requirements Management Policy

A policy is an executive mandate that promotes the purpose and intention of your requirements management activities. A policy of this kind is usually a short document (a page or two) that summarizes the general approach the organization will take toward managing requirements. Setting a requirements management policy in place is a good way to establish an organizational standard and introduce your teams to the accepted methods of requirements management.

Requirements Document Review Procedure

In one form or another, you'll want to establish a process your teams can follow to review the requirements. This process will help teams review the requirements for two purposes: to understand them and to commit to them. This does not have to be a complex procedure; it can be a few simple steps. The reason to document the review procedure is to give your people a ready method to follow each time they have to undertake a review activity. If you have a process ready for them to follow, your teams can focus on the review activities, not on figuring out how to manage the review activities.

Requirements Review Checklist

This checklist provides your teams with a way to evaluate the requirements in a consistent way, using common criteria. The checklist might ask the teams to mark whether the requirements appear to be complete, whether they are clear, whether any appear to conflict with others, and so on. The checklist can be used as a review support tool to remind teams of attributes to look for to make sure the requirements are in a useful condition for the project teams.

Requirements Document Stakeholder ID Form

Identifying relevant stakeholders is an important part of requirements management. These stakeholders are those people—internal and external to the project teams—who are both qualified to judge the quality of the requirements and chosen as the logical parties to approve and commit to the requirements. An ID form is a helpful document to use to initially identify and then track the recognized stakeholders for requirements activities. This form can serve as a ready reference for people who may need to contact the stakeholders or work with them.

Requirements Review and Comments Form

A great way to understand the requirements and then obtain commitment to them is to provide your people with an opportunity to review the requirements and submit questions and comments on them. A requirements review and comments form can be a handy tool for supporting these activities. This need not be fancy. A basic form can capture information such as the name of the document being reviewed, the name of the reviewer, and a listing of questions or issues the reviewer noted about the document.

The form is useful in two ways. First, it gives the reviewers a tangible way to document their questions and concerns. Second, it provides a good mechanism for submitting questions and concerns for discussion and consideration.

Requirements Change Request Procedure

We'll take a deeper look at this procedure in Chapter 6. For now, the idea is to provide a procedure that your teams can follow to create a requirements change request, submit it to a recognized review body, and then track the progress and status of the request. Having such a change request procedure is an immensely helpful asset for any project and any organization. Since the management of change in general is such a major responsibility and the management of requirements changes in particular is such a crucial one, having a formalized change request procedure provides a mechanism for the smooth management of all aspects of change.

Requirements Baseline Sign-Off Form

The goal of requirements management is to ultimately arrive at an approved requirements document: a baseline version for distribution. Once the stakeholders have indicated commitment to the requirements, you may want to provide a sign-off form to use for a couple of purposes. First, it provides the paper trail to show commitment. Your stakeholders can use this form to sign on the dotted line (or indicate approval in whatever way works best for your organization). Second, this form can also serve as the official check-in form your configuration manager or document owner can use to begin the work of managing a new version of the requirements.

Look to the Web Site for . . .

- Requirements management policy
- Requirements document review procedure
- Requirements review checklist
- Requirements document stakeholder ID form
- Requirements review form
- Requirements review invitation notice
- Requirements change request procedure

Chapter 6

Configuration Management

ALF operates in a heavily regulated industry, providing clients with analyses of customer data and profiles of consumer trends. In this domain we have a fiduciary responsibility to protect a broad range of information sources and data sets. To do this we employ a robust configuration management program, one designed to ensure data integrity, guard data access, and promote the security of data transfers.

Richard Caulfield, Vice President, Applied Logistic Futures
National data mining and analysis services

Configuration management deals with controlling the configuration and integrity of work products. As a discipline, it's important to project management because projects are really nothing more than the ordered production of work products. Plans are produced, designs are created, program code is developed, test cases are built, and so on. The importance of configuration management comes from the fact that all these products are produced and maintained in a dynamic environment. Rarely is it static. So all these work products are subject to change. Because this change can come from any number of directions (internally, externally; up, down), project management is well served with a mechanism and an avenue that ensure the ongoing integrity of work products.

We looked at this issue in a more limited way in Chapter 5, when we discussed Requirements Management under CMMI. That Process Area deals with changing and controlling technology requirements and other specifications. As a matter of course, most project teams control their requirements using some type of configuration management process. But configuration management is about more than just managing requirements. Configuration management deals with the smooth control of everything from the schedule and budget (management work products) to key deliverables such as system code, documentation, and designs (technical work products).

All of these need to be protected to some degree from ad hoc access and uncoordinated modification. Some projects—some organizations—will probably require what could be called heavy configuration management. Others can operate with light configuration management. In this chapter, we'll look at the recommendations CMMI offers all organizations for configuration management following industry best practices.

The Purpose of Configuration Management

At its heart, the purpose of the Configuration Management Process Area is to establish official product baselines and then coordinate, evaluate, approve, and manage changes to those baselines. These products might come from any number of activity areas.

They could be works in progress. Functional requirements, development plans, and system code are all elements you might elect to place under configuration management.

They could be components of production. Promoting new system modules and data from development into operation environments is an activity often managed through a configuration management system, an approach that statutory and regulatory decrees (such as the Sarbanes-Oxley Act) strongly encourage.

The products could be network and hardware configurations. Network and systems administration is often a key source of configuration management activities. The way networks are laid out, desktops are imaged, users are set up, systems are inventoried—these are all facets of effective configuration management.

Configuration management promotes the protection of work product integrity through the establishment of a configuration management system that can be used to house essential work products, assess and control changes to them, and then serve as a mechanism for releasing current baselines to project stakeholders (Figure 6–1).

Configuration management is usually a well-established practice in most successful technology shops. It is also broadly recognized in today's popular quality standards and frameworks. ISO 9001:2000 cites its importance in section 7 (Preservation of Product). ITIL calls for its implementation in Service Delivery and Service Support. Six Sigma alludes to it in the Control activities of DMAIC. And CMMI includes it as a primary Process Area at Maturity Level 2.

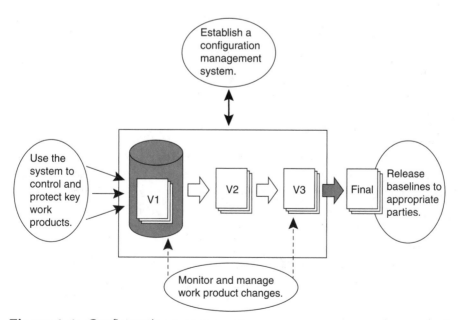

Figure 6–1: *Configuration management as process ensures ongoing product integrity and validity*

A Mechanism of Management

Project management will not fulfill its productivity potential on a project if everything is left to the talents of the project manager. As mentioned earlier in the book, talent is no doubt a good thing (as are initiative, imagination, judgment, and intuition). But project management works best when this is augmented by a process-managed atmosphere, one in which project management goals and objectives are supported by a framework of consistency and predictability. Given this, you can look at configuration management as part of this infrastructure for successful technology projects. It sets up tools and techniques for managing the evolution of work products. It's a tool directly in support of project management. It's a mechanism for management.

In some organizations, the duties of configuration management might be carried out by a specialized team of dedicated managers, administrators, and analysts. In other organizations, the duties might be handled on a part-time basis. Whatever approach your organization elects to take, here are four aspects of configuration management that are typically implemented to one degree or another on all projects:

1. A repository for artifacts and baselines
2. A structured approach for work coordination
3. A platform for change management
4. A control point for data integrity

A Repository for Artifacts and Baselines

Everyone has heard a story about team members who wasted days of effort because they were working from an old copy of the specifications. That's an archetypical configuration management story. Projects produce a lot of products over time, and they produce a lot of updated versions of old products over time. Confusing one for the other can have negative impacts on project progress and project success. That's the impetus behind this central reason for configuration management: It provides a recognized repository for the storage of official project artifacts and baselines.

Projects require different teams, different stakeholders, and various management layers to have access from time to time to particular work products. For the sake of order, this access needs to be controlled; it needs to be bounded by an appropriate level of rules. Configuration management, then, is a way to establish this environment of controlled access. It promotes management of a location (or locations) in which to store project artifacts needed by different teams. And this environment is a place to establish and release baselines: those documents that represent the official and latest versions of the work products. The assumption here is that if a product came from the official repository, there should be no question about its authenticity and relevance.

A Structured Approach for Coordinated Work

A well-designed configuration management system also provides your project with a structured approach to coordinated work.

Lots of different teams work on projects. People create work, review work, approve work. A configuration management system can bring an effective order and structure to this work stream. Under it, people can follow common guidelines for getting to artifacts, for checking them in and checking them out. Audit trails and version histories can be established. Backups and rollbacks can be efficiently facilitated. In short, you can use configuration management to establish a protective environment that gives your teams what amounts to rules of the road for trafficking across project work products and cycles.

When an organization is not able (for whatever reason) to provide a degree of configuration management for its projects, you'll often see a set of problems known collectively as the Renegade Syndrome. You'll have cowboys charging through new territory, shooting from the hip. You'll see artistes who take it as a badge of honor to follow their own rules. And you'll find that the people seen as the most effective are the ones who put out the most fires. These forms of energy, imagination, and dedication are not bad things in and of themselves. It's when they are not focused that their usefulness is dissipated, even directed against each other. Configuration management is a way to harness these energies along common, managed lines. It's a mechanism to introduce standards and consistency, and therefore it's a tool to reduce risk.

A Platform for Change Management

One of the chief uses of configuration management is as a platform for efficient change management. Change is inevitable during a project. We discussed this a bit in Chapter 5. Change can come from multiple angles: from your customers, your management, your technical teams. A major domain of the Configuration Management Process Area then is to facilitate change control, the approach you take when assessing and approving change.

As noted earlier, the configuration management system serves as the repository for baselines and artifacts important to project success. It follows, then, that this is also the appropriate domain for change control activities. The idea is that the repository remains the base for all official versions of designated work products. People should not change these work products simply on their own initiative. Some form of recognized change request should be presented first. Usually this involves some type of change review committee or change control board. The change can then be assessed for validity and impact. If approved, resources can then be identified to make the changes in the repository. If needed, a new baseline can then be released.

This way, the elements of Configuration Management serve two main purposes. First, they establish a repository to house and protect a project's chief work products. Second, they provide controls to access work products in the repository and to update them as needs arise.

A Control Point for Data Integrity

As noted in the three previous points, the chief mission of any configuration management effort is to protect the integrity of its contents and to prevent unauthorized change to key work products. This level of protection and integrity is becoming more and more important to more and more IT shops.

In recent years, high-profile corporate scandals such as those at Enron and MCI WorldCom have shed light on the tenuous nature of corporate data, especially financial data. The inappropriate handling and mismanagement of data can lead to disastrous results. To address this, Congress passed the Sarbanes-Oxley Act (SOX), which established standards—configuration management standards, by and large—for the ways data can and should be handled in large publicly held companies. SOX says management must now take ownership of the integrity of their company's data. Because it usually falls to the role of IT departments to house and manage this data, this responsibility naturally extends to IT.

Right now, SOX statutes apply only to certain types of companies. But because the spotlight shines so brightly on this issue, many nonpublic companies are moving to adopt this ownership position. A well-designed configuration management system can protect your data, allow for only authorized changes, and ensure management and customers that what you are working on is demonstrably compliant with what the requirements asked of you. Configuration management can serve as the foundation on which to build a SOX-compliant data access and control system. It can become an effective and efficient control point for corporate data integrity.

To Tool or Not to Tool

The complexity and sophistication you apply to your configuration management system will naturally depend on your organizational culture and the types of projects it undertakes. In practicality, a configuration management system can be a file cabinet. It can be a safety deposit box. Or it can be a very expensive software tool. There are lots of choices out there when it comes to acquiring and setting up a configuration management system.

CMMI does not make recommendations on the kind of system best suited to your shop. It lets you and your management make that call. So look at your organizational needs. Look at the goals and practices for this CMMI Process Area. Then you can make an informed choice about the solution that works best for you.

Configuration Management Goals and Practices

CMMI defines three Specific Goals and seven Specific Practices for the Configuration Management Process Area. Here is the official specification text for each of these elements.

SG 1   ESTABLISH BASELINES
Baselines of identified work products are established.

SP 1.1   IDENTIFY CONFIGURATION ITEMS
Identify the configuration items, components, and related work products that will be placed under configuration management.

SP 1.2   ESTABLISH A CONFIGURATION MANAGEMENT SYSTEM
Establish and maintain a configuration management and change management system for controlling work products.

SP 1.3   CREATE OR RELEASE BASELINES
Create or release baselines for internal use and for delivery to the customer.

SG 2   TRACK AND CONTROL CHANGES
Changes to the work products under configuration management are tracked and controlled.

SP 2.1   TRACK CHANGE REQUESTS
Track change requests for configuration items.

SP 2.2   CONTROL CONFIGURATION ITEMS
Control changes to the configuration items.

SG 3   ESTABLISH INTEGRITY
Integrity of baselines is established and maintained.

SP 3.1   PERFORM CONFIGURATION AUDITS
Perform configuration audits to maintain integrity of the configuration baselines.

SP 3.2   ESTABLISH CONFIGURATION MANAGEMENT RECORDS
Establish and maintain records describing configuration items.

Generic Goals and Practices

See Chapter 10 for information about the important Generic Goals and Practices that support project management success for all the Process Areas at Maturity Level 2.

SG 1: Establish Baselines

The first CMMI goal under Configuration Management is to establish baselines. Simply put, a baseline is a starting point. It's an official point of reference. The Sunday newspaper that shows up in stores late Saturday afternoon is a baseline. The final edition that's delivered Sunday morning is an updated baseline. Lots of stories were looked at and sorted through by the news staff between those two editions, but that pile of loose information could never be called the newspaper. The newspaper is the stuff selected and then printed under an official banner: *The Washington Post*, *The St. Albans Advertiser*.

It's the same in the field of technology and project management. Baselines are the official versions of documents and work products that the project teams use to plan their work and reference progress. Projects may work from a lot of baselines, or they may elect to use just a few. It depends on the project. Baselines can be documents such as software specifications, project plans, and high-level designs. Baselines can also be work products such as software code, system compilers, and individual components and parts.

Baselines are essential to sound project management because they promote commonality and order. By *commonality*, we mean that the baseline—because it is the official and authorized version of that thing—serves as a common point of reference for the whole team. Through it, people work from the same set of information and therefore share the same lines of understanding. By *order*, we mean that the baseline serves as the focal point for project progress. Work goes through baselines; it does not go around or over baselines. So the baselines help establish a common work path for project teams, one that can be measured for progress.

CMMI defines three Specific Practices to help you establish and maintain baselines for your projects. Let's take a look at those now.

Configuration Management versus Version Control

Version control and *configuration management* are two terms often used together, sometimes one for the other. But there is a difference. Configuration management is a somewhat formal discipline. It employs tools, procedures, and rigors to protect access to and distribution of certain products. Version control can be thought of as a softer form of configuration management. It does not employ as much rigor or as tight a level of control.

Sometimes when you look at a project document, you'll see a version history table somewhere near the front. This table is updated by the author or the owner whenever changes or additions to the document are made. This is a form of version control.

Configuration management would put that plan through a much more scrutinized approach. Changes and additions would be subject to reviews and approvals, access to the plan would be formally controlled, and the release of new versions would be likewise managed and monitored.

In this chapter, we are discussing the practice of formal configuration management. Because it is a formal procedure, you may not want to place every project document or work product under configuration management. Version control might turn out to be the appropriate level of control for many, or even most, of these items.

SP 1.1: Identify Configuration Items

The first practice is to identify your configuration items. In other words, early in the project lifecycle (hopefully as early as the planning stages), you identify which work products your teams will place under formal configuration management. You might elect to configuration manage a lot of products and artifacts. You might elect to configuration manage only those items you deem to be critical or essential. The decision will be contingent on your project: its size, scope, and relative importance.

You can use some common criteria to help you decide which types of items you might want to configuration manage. Here are three you might find useful:

1.   Customer-centric products
2.   Management-centric products
3.   High-impact materials

Let's take a quick look at each one.

Customer-Centric Products

Project work products that are customer-centric are good candidates for configuration management. By *customer-centric*, we mean those products used to establish and maintain work directions and expectations between you and your customers. Take the project budget, for example. This contains your project's expense levels, burn rates, degrees of capitalization, projected costs, and actual costs. All of this information is probably highly important to your customers. After all, it's their money in the budget. You wouldn't want people—whoever they are—playing around with the budget at will. You'd want some tight reigns on it. You would probably want to place the budget under formal configuration control.

Another good example—and perhaps the only obviously essential and required item to configuration manage—is the Product (capital P) you are building for the client. This might be source code for a software system. It might be the parts that will go into a data center. Whatever the Product might be, it defines the essence of the customer relationship, so it is a prime candidate for configuration management.

Depending on your type of project and your use of these products, some other customer-centric items might include the following:

- Requirements documents
- Commitments made with the customer (for resources, budgets, schedules, deliverables)
- Acceptance test plans
- Milestone review schedules

Management-Centric Products

As a project manager, you'll be controlling your own domain of activities, and chances are you'll be using a set of what we might call management-centric documents to help you do this. Management-centric documents include those materials that help you monitor progress on the project, direct activities along productive lines, and control the commitments you've made to your management and the customers.

A good example of a management-centric document is the project plan. Your customers might have very little interest in the fine details of this plan (or its component plans). But to you and your teams, it's the chief management tool for the whole project. The plan is what your people will follow to get where you want them to be. You would probably want to see the plan controlled in a way that ensures orderly change, consistent revision and distribution, and appropriate interpretation.

Another example is the technical designs. Since these will largely dictate how the programmers (or the cable technicians, the assemblers, and so on) will construct products, it might be important to configuration manage these as well. Technical designs are certainly crucial to overall project management.

Look to your project for other items that you deem to be management-centric, items that will be important to you for controlling project progress and measuring success. Here are some other common management-centric products that you might want to configuration manage:

- Project plans
- Resource assignments
- Progress reports
- Milestone reviews
- Approval and signature sheets
- Official client communications

High-Impact Materials

As a final consideration, think of any high-impact materials you may work with during the project. High-impact materials are those kinds of documents or products that have the potential to represent the project as a whole, even in the abstract.

A clear example of high-impact material is the project contract. This is a legally binding document that probably contains a description of the project and a description of what you will be building for the client. Change requests might also be thought of as high-impact material. Change requests carry the potential to alter the scope, direction, or focus of the project—in big ways or in small ones. Project managers can naturally expect some volume of intake with change requests over the course of a project. They can also expect to make periodic adjustments to project parameters such as schedule, budget, work products, and resources. If these adjustments occur through change requests, it might be a good idea to maintain an audit trail of this material.

Here are some other potentially high-impact materials you might want to consider for configuration management:

- Project contracts
- Statements of work
- Risk resolution logs

SP 1.2: **Establish a Configuration Management System**

The second Specific Practice under Configuration Management is to establish a configuration management system. Early in this chapter appears a note: To Tool or Not to Tool. That issue returns here. Does the practice of establishing a configuration management system imply the need to instantiate a sophisticated, maybe expensive, configuration management tool in your shop? No, but it does present the idea to set in place the policies, techniques, and procedures that will help you control your configuration items and ensure their integrity across the life of the project. That's the essence of any configuration management system.

Here are four tips you can use to help you think through your project's need for a configuration management system.

1. Evaluate your project's configuration management needs.
2. Assess the available tools (and acquire your solution if needed).
3. Configure your selected system.
4. Establish a configuration management plan.

Evaluate Your Project's Configuration Management Needs

The amount of rigor you'll likely want to see in a configuration management system will depend in large part on the needs of your project. All projects are different. A project made up of a three-person team working for eight weeks will probably not need the same kind of configuration management system that a project with a hundred people working for nine months will need. And that brings us to a basic question: What is a configuration management system?

Most people would consider it to be some type of filing system tool, sophisticated or not. That's correct, but that's only part of it. A configuration management system usually consists of the tool, along with a methodology for using the tool. This may include such things as procedures for submitting change requests, the appointment of a committee or board to review change requests, a policy to create and release baselines, and guidelines for storing, backing up, and publishing documents and other work products. (For more on this, see the upcoming subsection Configure Your System, as well as the section on SG 2.)

The extent to which you implement all these items should be based on the needs of your project. So look to what you've been asked to build for your customer. Identify the items you'll probably want to formally manage. Evaluate their management needs, and then make the decision as to the scope of system you'll need.

Assess the Available Tools

A configuration management system does not have to be a fancy automated tool. It can be something as simple as a controlled library, even a system folder. But today's technology projects are typically sophisticated enough that the use of some form of automated tool would be recognized as a good idea. As you begin your project, or better yet, in anticipation of your project, you should—as part of project management due diligence—begin to formulate your configuration management system needs and the solutions available to you.

Of course, your organization may already have a solution in place. Many shops have standardized configuration management solutions. They have purchased packages and created systems that are deployed across all their development environments. If that's the case, and if there's no real reason to deviate from the standard, you can move on to thinking about tailoring the system for your needs.

In the event that you don't have a solution in place. you should work with your management to evaluate available tools and acquire a suitable solution. There are many, many configuration management products on the market today. Some are proprietary, some are open source. Some are straightforward and basic, others are highly sophisticated and adaptable. Select the product that will serve the needs of your current project and that you think will accommodate the needs of the future projects your shop will handle.

Configure Your System

Once you've determined what you will configuration manage for your project and you've acquired your configuration management tool, it's time to configure the system. Sometimes larger IT shops will have a configuration management team, and project management typically works with that team to configure the configuration management system. Smaller shops might not be so specialized; the job of configuring the system might fall to the project team itself. Either way, the same kinds of tasks will need to be accounted for.

You'll want to set up the tool to provide for the proper staging areas, the proper access controls and user rights, file lists, approver groups, repository names, backup schedules, and other such housekeeping needs.

You'll want to review (and tailor as necessary) the controls that insulate the system. This includes such items as change request procedures, baselines schedules, promotion guidelines, and approval and permission forms.

And you'll want to make sure that your change control board (or whatever form this group takes in your organization) is in place and that its members have been identified and prepped.

You may need to account for other factors for your project. Take a proactive position on these activities. If project activities begin in earnest without your configuration management system being available, you may have product control problems early in the lifecycle, and they may be difficult to bring back on track after that. (For more discussion of the makeup of these management materials, see the upcoming section on SP 2.1.)

Establish a Configuration Management Plan

If you've looked at everything recommended so far for your configuration management activities, you may begin to notice a traditional project management pattern emerging. The need for a plan is beginning to take shape.

Planning is one of the key focal points of project management. And the Configuration Management Process Area comprises a key set of project management activities. Therefore, it's a good idea to develop a configuration management plan for your project. We'll discuss this in more depth when we look at CMMI's Generic Goals and Practices in Chapter 10, but right now let's take a quick look at some considerations we've already identified for configuration management:

- What work products you'll configuration manage
- What system you will use
- Who will manage the system
- What policies and procedures will be followed
- What configuration management activities will be performed
- When these activities will be performed

These are elements we typically see in a plan. Here we represent the who/what/when of configuration management. Collecting all this information in a plan (either in your master project plan or in a stand-alone configuration management plan) will go a long way toward helping you anticipate and coordinate your project's configuration management activities.

SP 1.3: **Create or Release Baselines**

This third practice under the first goal of Configuration Management is to create or release baselines. In other words, use the configuration management system to control those products you've identified, and then use it as the device through which the products—their official forms and versions—are distributed to your teams and stakeholders. That promotes three subpractices.

1. Follow the plan.
2. Commit to the system.
3. Recognize the source as primary.

Follow the Plan

Every project should probably operate with some kind of configuration management plan in place. Large projects may need extensive plans. Small projects can probably make do with simple plans. These plans define what will be controlled and should also identify how (and even when) baselines will be stored, modified, and released.

A configuration management system will not perform to its potential or serve the full needs of a project if the plan created around it is not followed. The plan should be seen as the guide for what products are managed; for who has access into what repositories, with what rights; for the steps required to update work products; and for the procedures used to release baselines.

If these activities are left solely to the discretion of the individuals on a project team, you'll probably quickly discover that each one will take a different approach to how products are managed, and soon issues with version control and mastering will be sure to surface. Following the plan will help everyone on the project team use the system in an agreed-upon way, a way that will be consistent and predictable across the project life-cycle and that supports the next point: committing to the system.

Commit to the System

The main value of a baseline is that you can regard it as the authoritative version of a set of data, whether that data is source code, a plan, or a list of stakeholders. It's authoritative *because* it is the baseline. Other versions of that data, when they reside outside the configuration management system, should be treated as drafts, proposals, or benign references. Until they are formally moved through the configuration management system and the change control process, they should carry no official weight.

A project team should commit to the configuration management system as the source for authoritative versions of key products and documents. Organizations that are new to process or new to the rigors of configuration management might be tempted, for the sake of expediency or parsimony, to work with documents or products outside the system, to avoid the need to check them in and out and to avoid the paperwork and reviews. But this approach is sure to cause problems, if not in the short term then certainly in the long term.

One responsibility of project management is to communicate to the team what tools and techniques will be used to manage project data and to actively promote and manage the use of these tools and techniques. This includes the configuration management system. And because the configuration management system is the caretaker of key project data, special emphasis should be given to its considered and conscientious use.

Recognize the Source as Primary

Here we encounter the issue of whether it's better to be right or to be official.

If members of a project team are modifying source files or documents outside of the configuration management system, it's possible to end up with an official version, one protected in the system, that is out of date. This begs the question: Which one does project management recognize? There's no pat answer here, of course. The dogmatic position may not be practical in a real-world business environment. On the other hand, the laissez-faire position might threaten project control to the same extent.

This brings us back into the domain of project management. As a project manager, you should introduce the function and purpose of the configuration management system to your team members, your customers, and your management early in the project lifecycle. You should communicate the importance of primary sources and product integrity and the way in which the system will support these concepts. Then you should, in your own activities, look to the configuration management system for the primary sources of relevant project data. In all likelihood, your teams, customers, and management will follow your lead.

SG 2: Track and Control Changes

If you had to boil it down to its essence, you could view configuration management as covering two broad project areas: the storage of key work products and documents, and the activities that govern change control. We looked at the first area in our discussion of SG 1. The second goal under Configuration Management is to track and control changes made to the project. While this goal is definitely related to the first, it is often handled by a different group than the one that maintains the configuration management system.

In large technology organizations, you'll often see a group exclusively devoted to change management. Perhaps it is known as the change control board, or the enterprise change management group, or the change review committee. This group's primary responsibility is to address change requests that come into a project and to determine which requests should be approved for project work. Effective change management is a big part of project success. When projects get into trouble, it's commonly because some element of change has drifted out of control, so project management needs to be vigilant about change management over the course of a project. The project manager should ensure that the appropriate level of oversight and methodology is available when the project begins.

In this section, we'll discuss the two practices CMMI recommends for tracking and controlling changes, and we'll look at some activities you can consider when thinking about how to put these practices in place for your projects or in your organization.

SP 2.1: Track Change Requests

The first practice is to track change requests. The word *track* here suggests a degree of organized control. In casual organizations, change requests may be allowed to fly in from all corners. They may be accepted as verbal exchanges, as e-mail suggestions, in any form or fashion. That's a friendly approach, but it's probably not very amenable to accountability or business analysis. Because a change—any change—can turn out to have significant business impacts, accountability and analysis are important project management responsibilities. That's why most management standards (including PMBOK, CMMI, ITIL, and ISO 9001) support a formal way to manage and track such requests.

Here are three tips to help you track change requests in a somewhat formalized way.

1. Establish a change review board.
2. Establish a change request procedure.
3. Establish a change review and approval procedure.

Establish a Change Review Board

Call it a change control board, a change committee, or whatever you want. It can be made up of one person or three or sixteen. The intention is to establish an authority whose responsibility is to review change requests, assess their impacts, and then approve, deny, or table them. This committee really serves as an extension of project management and should be seen as an adjunct to project management.

Sometimes organizations already have an established change board in place. One job of project management is to work with that board. Other organizations may not have a set board in place, so it may fall to project management to establish one for the project at hand.

Whatever approach you take, the idea is to make ownership of change review duties clearly visible to everyone. Solicit membership to the board, make explicit appointments, and then augment the board with the procedures it needs to take in and assess change requests (as described in the next two subsections).

Establish a Change Request Procedure

In addition to establishing guidelines for how the change review board should operate, you'll also want to make sure that there is come kind of change request procedure in place. This may include a change request form people can use to submit ideas for change, a series of documented steps they can follow to fill out the forms and submit them to the board, and maybe some guides on how to present or explain the request to the board.

The extent and the activities you define for the change request process will naturally depend on the needs of your project and on the makeup and structure of your organization. The objective is to give your customers, team members, and management a formalized approach they can all use to consistently submit and manage the changes that arise during a project.

Establish a Change Review and Approval Procedure

Your project's change review board will need guidelines on how to operate. These guidelines might be contained in an organizational charter, or you might put them in an executive policy. Wherever they are, they should clearly spell out the procedures the board will follow to review, assess, and decide on pending change requests. The objective here is to remove, as much as possible, subjectivity from the review and approval process. The decision as to the acceptability of a change request should be based on documented, objective criteria. In line with this, you might want to set in place guidelines on how to assess the impact of a change request: what criteria (e.g., complexity, relevance, importance, cost) will be used to judge the impact of adopting the request. You might also want to establish guidelines for how to conduct a review meeting: how individual change requests will be pulled and presented to the board for review. And you may want to create guidelines that define how the board will vote on change requests: what constitutes a quorum, how many members must be present, whether majority vote rules, and so on.

SP 2.2: Control Configuration Items

The second practice is to control your configuration items, which simply means controlling the changes incorporated into your baselines, managing the new versions for release, and then accounting for an audit trail that tracks prior versions. This practice is an extension of SP 2.1, Track Change Requests. Here you are controlling, in essence, which requested changes will go into the baselines, which ones will be tabled for later consideration, and which ones will be denied or returned for further analysis.

Here are three techniques you can use to help manage configuration items in a controlled manner.

1. Establish ownership.
2. Establish version histories.
3. Establish guidelines for updates and releases.

Establish Ownership

The idea of control implies ownership. For your project, you'll undoubtedly be managing a set of different files and documents in your configuration management system. Some may be plans, some source code, some designs, and so on. To manage changes to this material, each item should be assigned an owner. The owner designation can be made to an individual or to a group, and it grants authorship rights over the materials in question. Owners typically are granted full access rights into their areas of the configuration management system. Others are granted more limited access rights, such as read-only, print, or copy.

By assigning owners, you can establish change control at a high level for your project teams. You'll also be providing logical points of contact for particular project data sets, identifying people to whom others can turn to ask questions, make suggestions, or receive updated information.

Establish Version Histories

One advantage to storing project files and documents under formal configuration management is that the configuration management system will typically keep a complete version history of the material under control. If you need to recall a previous version of a document, for example, the system should be able to readily produce it for you. The same ability should apply with earlier versions of source code and data files.

This is both an important aspect of controlling baselines and a valuable component of project management. Configuration management is not just about releasing the latest version of something. The history of that something is just as important. The prior versions, when taken together, can tell the tale of the project. This version history is valuable because it contains an audit trail of major decisions and project changes, and it captures the usual evolutionary paths all projects tend to move down.

For your project, you should confirm that your configuration management system can maintain version histories. If the system cannot do so automatically, you might consider establishing a document retention, storage, or backup policy that supports the retention of previous versions of selected materials for set periods of time.

Establish Guidelines for Updates and Releases

Change is a given for any technology project, and one of the key jobs of project management is to control this change. The CMMI Configuration Management Process Area focuses on this idea. But given this, there is a real need to use your judgment to determine what rate of change is needed for your project. Just as too little change can be a problem, so can too much change. If you are not releasing updates to your baselines often enough, you run the risk of having your team members work with outdated materials. Likewise, if you're constantly releasing new and updated material into the work stream, you could be setting up inadvertent impediments to progress, stifling your teams with too much change.

SG 3: Establish Integrity

Data integrity has become a crucial factor in many technology shops today. The Sarbanes-Oxley Act may be the biggest driver for the renewed interest in this area. SOX sets up a series of controls and reporting expectations regarding the ways a public company manages its financial data and systems. The fines and penalties for falling out of compliance with SOX can be significant. Because of this, many companies, public and nonpublic, have established in-depth data integrity policies for all its systems, not just financial.

This third CMMI goal for Configuration Management relates to the importance of data integrity. The purpose of this goal is to confirm integrity—to periodically verify that the contents of the configuration management system are current, that they are properly indexed, and that the system is functioning properly.

Project management is largely about data management: creating data, refining data, setting up access to data, publishing data, and ultimately delivering data to the customer. Since these functions spin at the center of all projects, it's up to project management to make sure the data sets retain their integrity across all phases of the project. CMMI defines two Specific Practices to help an organization establish data integrity for its projects. Let's take a look at these practices now.

SP 3.1: Perform Configuration Audits

The first practice designed to help establish integrity is to perform audits of the items in the configuration management system. Here are three techniques you can use to help you perform audits in a consistent and repeatable fashion.

1. Establish an audit procedure.
2. Schedule audits in the configuration management plan.
3. Conduct visible audits.

Establish an Audit Procedure

Practically speaking, you can design an audit to look at anything. But for an audit to be valuable, it needs to possess two characteristics. First, it needs to look for items or conditions that are meaningful to you and to your project management objectives. Second, it needs to be performed in a consistent way; all audits should be performed according to common guidelines. To make sure both of these characteristics are accounted for, it's a good idea to define an audit procedure for use by your configuration analysts (or the team members responsible for the configuration management system).

The audit procedure should document such things as what products and conditions to audit for, what steps are required to access and move through the system, and what reports need to be generated based on the audit activities.

With a standardized audit procedure in place, people can conduct audits in a consistent and reliable manner, not only across the various audits for your specific project but also, if desired, across the various projects under way within your organization.

Schedule Audits in the Configuration Management Plan

Earlier in our discussion of this CMMI Process Area, we looked at the usefulness of developing a configuration management plan for your project. One component of this plan could be a schedule defining when configuration audits will occur. Scheduling audits provides three benefits to project management.

First, a schedule for audits will help ensure that proper audits are conducted. If you have a plan to execute the audits, you'll be better able to anticipate and account for upcoming audits. You'll also be assured that you've accounted for the right number and intensity of audits across the full life of your project. Second, you'll be better organized to make sure that your auditing resources are available when audit times draw near. Without an audit schedule, you might find that people are committed to other responsibilities and that their audit responsibilities fall in priority or get lost in the mix of project work. Third, with an audit schedule, you'll find that your teams are better prepared for the audits. Knowing when the audits will occur may help your teams stay in compliance with your configuration management policies and procedures.

Conduct Visible Audits

The third activity for this practice is to conduct visible audits. In other words, make the auditing activities and audit reports visible within the organization. Visibility will communicate the value of the audits and will also promote the concept that audits serve as quality checks that provide valuable status information to the entire team.

SP 3.2: Establish Configuration Management Records

This practice under the third goal concerns the establishment of records. If you and your teams have used the configuration management system as the chief repository for work products and you've performed periodic audits, you should have the data available to establish appropriate configuration management records. The value of these records is that they can help you set in place three sound project management practices.

1. Document audit trails.
2. Document version histories.
3. Document audit records.

Document Audit Trails

Well-practiced project management always operates with audit trails. It's a professional necessity. We've mentioned in this chapter that project management is in many ways product management and document management—managing the evolution of information as it's carried across project phases.

The records you establish through your configuration management system and create through your audits will provide the kinds of audit trails you need to maintain project integrity. The audit trails can be used to document project changes: changes in scope, resources, schedules, budgets, and so on. The audit trails can also help you trace the degree and direction of progress, helping you assess efficiencies, effectiveness, and value. Finally, audit trails can be used to confirm the validity of choices and decisions made across the project lifecycle.

Document Version Histories

Another key strength of establishing a configuration management system and a formal configuration management program is that the history of your product evolution remains clear. When needed, you can access previous versions of source code, source files, and documentation. The value of this is twofold. First, the histories support your use of audit trails. You maintain, in effect, a complete change history of your files and documents. You can easily access these previous versions to understand how change impacted your project and at what points certain decisions and choices were made. Second, the histories provide for data protection. With your histories intact, the chances that you might lose, overwrite, or misinterpret information are greatly diminished. Keeping your histories intact is both a valuable and practical form of data protection.

Document Audit Records

Maintaining a history of audit records and audit reports can provide an organization with a good base for tracking the effectiveness and efficiencies of its configuration management system. It can also provide project management with change control and churn data that can support overall measures of productivity, earned value, and opportunities for improvement. The audit records also provide an audit trail to track product integrity. These reports can be used to demonstrate that proper and adequate measures have been taken to ensure that project management activities include oversight of product integrity.

Taken as a set, the audit records can also serve as your documentation that audit trails were established and version histories maintained.

The Benefits of Sound Configuration Management

People are often surprised at the lack of sound configuration management practices in place in many technology organizations. The control of code, documentation, and other key products is often simply left to individuals who modify, copy, and update on their own prerogatives. That approach may have its place in small shops, in skunk groups, or in teams working on low-risk, low-impact systems. But for the business mainstream, lack of configuration management means risky business. In fact, the benefits of configuration management are so obvious, practical, and compelling that it's hard to imagine why any project team would not enthusiastically endorse their deployment.

Of the many benefits to implementing a well-designed configuration management program, this section presents four that are especially worth considering.

Referential Integrity

As already noted, project management is largely about product management: managing the quality and completeness of the products that your project teams produce. And delivering solid products is often the measure of project success. That's where configuration management comes in. A well-designed configuration management system will help ensure that your products are complete and current and that they truly reflect the work of your teams.

Without a configuration management system, the referential integrity of your work products can quickly come into question. Teams may be prone to work with different versions of related information. Old specs may sneak into new work. Required components might be left out or ignored. Expectations may get clouded. The vendor–customer relationship can disconnect.

Trust may be the single most important product you can build for your customer: trust that you have everything under control, trust that you're managing everything that has been placed in your care. When you operate your efforts through the discipline of configuration management, you set in place the controls to maintain that integrity and reinforce that trust.

Change Control

Uncontrolled change has bedeviled more projects than most project managers would like to remember. Rampant change, misdirected change, unassessed change: They all can have significant impacts on project budgets, schedules, resources, and scope. But under the domain of configuration management, change can be controlled. In fact, a defining trait of a configuration management system is its ability to control access to information and to manage the release of new information. And then there's the fact that the major operational offshoot of a configuration management system is a change control system, which shapes the processes and procedures you follow to elicit change requests, evaluate them, and act on them.

Instituting formal change control provides a protective management umbrella for a project. It sets in place an insulating layer that can shield the inner workings of teams from unnecessary intrusion and distraction. And when change is necessary, as some change invariably is, change control can provide an avenue down which you can navigate new requirements, assess their impacts, plan for their smooth incorporation, and then provide for their proper integration.

Statutory Compliance

The Sarbanes-Oxley Act has probably done more to promote sound configuration management than anything else in the last ten years. The reason is simple. Corporate executives can face jail time if they don't provide for the responsible control of the information that flows through their data systems. Jail time and hefty fines make bad news on Wall Street.

The criticality for a company to meet statutory and regulatory obligations is a powerful reason to ensure that you're operating under sound configuration management practices. A well-designed configuration management program will provide for mechanisms to control, monitor, and track change; support the right kinds of approvals and authorizations needed to move data through systems; help establish the separation of duties; and provide an audit trail not only for your data but also for the history of access to your data.

When you look at the investment required to establish and maintain a configuration management system and then compare that to the cost of falling out of compliance with state and federal laws, the positive return on investment crystallizes into hard numbers.

Workflow Control

Good configuration management can also provide workflow control for your project teams. This is a distinct benefit for any project, but it becomes especially important for large projects. Projects are often made up of disparate teams, each with its own project focus and perhaps with its own worldview. In the absence of a configuration management system, these teams might tend to channel and filter work through a variety of different pathways. It's highly likely these paths may not connect or may easily disconnect.

The value of configuration management is that it can establish workflows that must be followed by the different teams, and thus it can be used to control, coordinate, and harmonize work. By instituting such mechanisms as repositories, check-in/check-out rules, access rights, rollback and backup capabilities, change procedures, and audit trails, the configuration management system defines how people access, modify, integrate, and release data. The order inherent in the system helps promote order outside the system.

Some Example Program Components

Your project will have its own configuration management needs, but some common elements appear in configuration management systems across many different kinds of organizations. The components described in this section are usually set in place in some form or fashion to help structure and support configuration management activities. As you plan the configuration management system for your projects, keep thinking of configuration management as an extension of project management, as a tool for project management. One of the chief responsibilities of project management is the smooth and ordered control of work products across the project lifecycle. Configuration management is a way to ensure that this responsibility is effectively addressed.

Configuration Management Plan Template

In this chapter, we discussed the need to identify configuration items, manage them through the use of a system, track changes, release baselines, and perform periodic integrity audits. The need for all of these activities implies the need for a configuration management plan.

Many organizations establish a configuration management plan for use on their development projects. And to promote the consistent and repeatable use of configuration management planning, organizations may create a template that planners and analysts can use to create a standardized configuration management plan. Using a configuration management plan template is a proven way to define what configuration management activities are endorsed by the organization. It's also a valuable functional aid, guiding both new and experienced configuration managers in how to prepare for an upcoming project.

Change Control Board Charter

Change control is a typical part of general configuration management activities. To support orderly change control, many organizations establish what's commonly known as a change control board. Some call it a change review board, some a change request committee. In all cases, the basic function is the same. This team of people is charged with reviewing, assessing, and approving change requests.

Because this team needs to operate in a predictable way, against a set of accepted criteria, it's helpful to establish the board through some type of team or group charter. The charter will typically define the role of the team, the rules it will operate under, and such basics as meeting schedules, analysis procedures, and voting regulations.

Change Request Form and Procedure

We've noted throughout this book that the one constant of project management is change. Change is inevitable, and requests for change may come from all quarters: from the client, from technical team members, even from your management. So it's handy to manage this flow of change through some type of change request form and change request procedure.

A change request form serves two management purposes. First, it gives everyone a guide for thinking through a request for change in the same way and for providing the same kind of information regarding the change. Second, it gives the change control board a single mechanism its members can use to evaluate and assess the need for the change.

To augment this, you should consider establishing some type of change request procedure that defines the steps that should be taken to access, create, submit, and track the status of change requests. Change can become a headache for project management when requests seem to be leaking in from every door, window, and air vent. By establishing a change request procedure, you define a single intake path for change, one that you should be able to manage and control and one that will also provide a path that your people can follow to submit change in an orderly manner.

Change Assessment Procedure

You and your stakeholders will want the change control board to be able to assess change requests in an objective and fair way, one based not on subjectivity or preference but on criteria designed to evaluate value. One way to promote this is to work with your management and with the board to define a standardized assessment procedure. This procedure is usually included as part of the charter. It defines the steps the board will follow to select, analyze, and vote on proposed changes.

Change Assessment Criteria

The change assessment procedure details the steps taken to review and approve change requests. In support of this procedure, you might also consider establishing change request assessment criteria. The board can then use these factors to weigh and evaluate each change request. For example, one set of criteria might be to determine the following with each request: the cost of implementing the change, the benefit the change will deliver, the risk of implementing the change, the risk of not implementing the change, and the source of the change request. All of these factors can then be weighted and scored to produce a form of value indicator, and that indicator can then be used as a gauge for granting or withholding approval.

Well-run change boards tend to operate with such evaluation criteria at hand. They provide an analytical approach to determining a cost/performance benefit for change requests in a way that can be applied across a broad range of change requests.

Baseline Update and Release Procedure

Another type of component typically included as part of an overall configuration management program is a baseline update and release procedure or policy. As mentioned earlier, baselines are the most current version of your project's key work products and deliverables. These items are protected within the configuration management system. Any proposed change to a baseline must first be reviewed and approved, usually by a change board. The intention of an update and release procedure is to control the flux of change with these key materials. Too little change and people may end up working with out-of-date documents. Too much change and people may become confused as to what is the most current version and what they should really focus on.

The update and release procedure can establish guidelines and schedules for revising, publishing, and distributing baselines. This procedure can be used to control the rate of change introduced into the organization. It will also help set the rhythm for assessing and incorporating change, as well as for helping your technical teams anticipate and prepare for change.

Look to the Web Site for . . .

- Sample change control board charter
- Configuration management plan execution process
- Configuration management plan creation process
- Configuration management policy

Chapter 7

Supplier Agreement Management

Our outsourcing partners provide us with a level of on-demand expertise that enhances our flexibility and responsiveness. This same scalability allows us to maintain a market position that emphasizes cost-effectiveness. For these part-nerships to work on an ongoing basis, they need to be based on a foundation of mutual cooperation and contribution and managed against a set of standards both parties can commit to with confidence and the assurance of success.
Bennett Bruon, CIO, General Data Services Corp.
Provider of interlan switching services

Development projects often require the use of outside resources to help them create what they are required to create. A project team may need a special skill set that is not readily available in-house. The team may need to interface with other parties working with the same customer. The chief mission of the project might be to assemble components pro-duced elsewhere. In cases like these, the role of the supplier takes on special significance, especially when it comes to project success.

Most people readily recognize the role project management plays in directing and controlling internal resources. Here the chain of command is usually pretty clear, and lines of authority are well established. But this same direction and control can weaken, or fall off altogether, when it comes to working with suppliers. Management might feel hesitant to extend management authority to an independent third party. Sometimes both sides might question who should manage whom. And sometimes the physical distance between parties lessens the connection. Whatever the tendency or situation, project management should nevertheless work to focus its energies just as keenly on suppliers as it does on internal resources. When suppliers make significant contributions to project work, they should not be thought of as independent entities. They should be considered part of an integrated team. And being part of the team, they should operate in ways consistent with the processes and standards that apply to the project team as a whole.

The CMMI Process Area called Supplier Agreement Management promotes this integrated view of suppliers. It sets in place goals and practices to help you coordinate and collaborate successfully with your suppliers.

The Purpose of Supplier Agreement Management

The purpose of the SAM Process Area is to ensure that you establish a supplier relationship that promotes the steady, coordinated realization of your project's objectives. This typically involves a three-tiered approach. First, look at the types of critical acquisitions you are required to make for your projects, and then shape a set of performance and management criteria for each. Second, identify those vendors who have the ability to supply the types of products or services you need while performing to your criteria. Third, establish a working relationship with selected vendors that promotes openness and visibility through in-process inspections and coordinated integration.

Through this three-tier approach, the organization can set in place procedures to help it make smart buying decisions. It will also enjoy a set of guidelines that will help identify value-add suppliers and forge long-term working relationships with them.

Project management will enjoy similar benefits. It will have a set of agreed-upon controls that will help effectively manage the supply chain across the life of the project. And with all of these elements taking shape, management will have the mechanisms it needs to ensure the delivery of quality components and final products to the customers.

Let's look at four attributes of effective supplier agreement management.

Shop Smart

Smart shopping is a good idea for any business, and Supplier Agreement Management sets in place practices to make your company a smarter shopper. There can be a tendency sometimes to make purchases based on personal relationships—that's the strength of good salespeople. You want to buy from *them*. But SAM takes a more empirical approach. It helps you define the attributes you want to see in a product or a service; it then promotes comparative shopping to find the best deal. With this homework done, you can make the decision that makes the best sense.

Most people when they, say, shop for a car, take the SAM approach. They work up a list of features they like, they search through advertisements, maybe talk to friends. Then they visit dealerships, go for test drives, and negotiate for the best deal. That's the SAM way. Businesses should shop using a similar approach.

Control the Supply Chain

The phrase *supply management* is big these days. At the enterprise level, companies spend hundreds of millions of dollars on it annually. Supply chain management is all about availability, inventory levels, price points, delivery capability, and a host of other factors. At the project level, supply chain management is just as important. There is the need to ensure that the delivery of supplier products or services is timely, that they arrive when they are needed. Supporting this, there is also the need for efficient collaboration, especially when you are working on complex projects or when multiple suppliers, some perhaps dependent on others, are involved. And this leads to the importance of cooperative coordination.

SAM sets in place the kinds of practices that help you control your project's supply chain. It takes a position that might be treated passively and actively integrates it into project management oversight, raising it to a level visible by management. In fact, when you think about it, all of project management is really about supply chain management: making sure that the components needed for project success are there when you need them, that the various pieces integrate smoothly, and that schedule, cost, and resource efficiencies are maintained.

Forge Reliable Supplier Relationships

The practices found in SAM can help your organization forge reliable relationships with the suppliers who perform to your standards. It can help you separate the wheat from the chaff, too; it can help you avoid the vendors who might promise the world up front, perform poorly, and then try to slip back in again. Identifying productive vendor relationships will go a long way toward making a business successful, especially if its need for outside resources is pronounced.

The practices under SAM set up concrete performance expectations and open a window into supplier activities. Once you have worked with a supplier who meets those expectations and welcomes (properly applied) oversight of their activities, you know you've found a vendor on whom you can depend, one you can work with to meet objectives and tackle problems.

By setting this bar for performance, SAM can help lead you into beneficial supplier relationships. In the same ways that you are obligated to be responsive to your customers, so are your vendors obligated to be responsive to you. And when you find vendors who want to cooperate and collaborate with you in this manner, you've got a good start toward forging a long-term, successful partnership.

Protect Quality

Perhaps the penultimate purpose of Supplier Agreement Management is to protect project quality. When you engage suppliers, you are electing to relinquish a degree of quality control. You are turning over to a third party work that your customer entrusted to you. And whether or not that third party is well qualified, the future of the work now rests largely in their hands. SAM is designed to slide the control factor back your way. The idea here is to establish performance and quality standards up front as a basis for the purchase agreement, so that the supplier will begin the work with your standards in mind. Their efforts and energies can then be directed to meet those standards.

SAM also opens the door on what might be a black-box relationship. Again, early in the purchase process, you and your supplier agree to your participation in the production process. Your supplier gives you access to the shop floor, so to speak. You have the right to periodically monitor ongoing work, to confirm that your standards are being followed, and that work in progress is up to standards. Through this open-door approach, you are better able to protect the quality of what you will ultimately deliver to the customer.

The Brother-in-Law and the Guy Who Knows a Guy

Most large companies tend to have some sort of purchasing department. And often these are very well-run organizations, with vendor qualification criteria, contracts, and agreement shells in place, all supported by the resources needed to monitor vendor activity. However, in smaller development shops, or perhaps in less formal organizations, purchasing might not be so well controlled. Supplier Agreement Management is really an entry point for applying basic vendor management practices. SAM is there to help you avoid less than professional practices, such as giving your brother-in-law the contract because your niece needs braces or trusting your friend to get you a great deal from a guy who knows this guy who knows how to get it. These kinds of practices might work from time to time, but they aren't the smartest path for ensuring that what you end up with will align tightly with your customers' needs.

Supplier Agreement Management Goals and Practices

CMMI defines two Specific Goals and eight Specific Practices for the Supplier Agreement Management Process Area. Here is the official specification text for each of these elements.

SG 1   ESTABLISH SUPPLIER AGREEMENTS
Agreements with the suppliers are established and maintained.

SP 1.1   DETERMINE ACQUISITION TYPE
Determine the type of acquisition for each product or product component to be acquired.

SP 1.2   SELECT SUPPLIERS
Select suppliers based on an evaluation of their ability to meet the specified requirements and established criteria.

SP 1.3   ESTABLISH SUPPLIER AGREEMENTS
Establish and maintain formal agreements with the supplier.

SG 2   SATISFY SUPPLIER AGREEMENTS
Agreements with the suppliers are satisfied by both the project and the supplier.

SP 2.1   EXECUTE THE SUPPLIER AGREEMENT
Perform activities with the supplier as specified in the supplier agreement.

SP 2.2   MONITOR SELECTED SUPPLIER PROCESSES
Select, monitor, and analyze processes used by the supplier.

SP 2.3   EVALUATE SELECTED SUPPLIER WORK PRODUCTS
Select and evaluate work products from the supplier of custom-made products.

SP 2.4   ACCEPT THE ACQUIRED PRODUCT
Ensure that the supplier agreement is satisfied before accepting the acquired product.

SP 2.5   TRANSITION PRODUCTS
Transition the acquired products from the supplier to the project.

Generic Goals and Practices

See Chapter 10 for information about the important Generic Goals and Practices that support project management success for all the Process Areas at Maturity Level 2.

What Makes a Supplier a Supplier?

This is a valid question. If you are a systems engineering shop, do you need to apply supplier management to the folks you buy mechanical pencils from? Or if you supplement your in-house development staff with contractors, do these folks need to be managed with SAM? When is a supplier a supplier under SAM?

If, like a contractor, a supplier works in your shop under your direct management and control, you can consider him or her enough a part of your team that SAM would not be necessary. Likewise, if—like mechanical pencils—you do farm out the control but the purchase is not one you would consider critical to quality or to the mission of the project, SAM might not apply either. It is when you turn over control of a major piece of work to a supplier outside of your direct domain that SAM should come into play. When that supplier becomes a partner in your success, SAM is there to help govern that success.

SG 1: Establish Supplier Agreements

The first goal of Supplier Agreement Management is to establish agreements with your suppliers. This means you get your organization ready with the management tools it needs to work successfully with chosen suppliers. These tools typically include performance criteria, a list of qualified vendors, established policies and procedures for purchasing, and blank contracts (Figure 7–1). You need to determine the types of acquisitions you will need to make and then identify those vendors qualified to provide the products or services. Supporting this is a set of vendor management policies and procedures used to govern the purchase process and vendor relationships. Finally, blank contracts tailored to the specific needs of certain kinds of purchases should be ready to be completed when a purchase decision is at hand.

To support this goal, you can use three Specific Practices: determining the acquisition type (or types), selecting qualified suppliers for each type, and establishing the agreements or contracts that will be used to engage suppliers. The extent to which you carry out these practices will naturally depend on the type of development shop you run. Large industrial companies or heavily regulated organizations that make capital-intensive purchases will probably require a high degree of rigor and oversight for purchasing practices. Smaller shops that might have

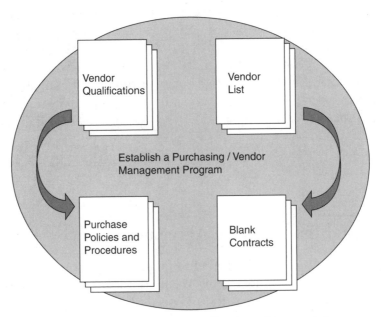

Figure 7–1: *Vendor management as a collection of integrated concerns and capabilities*

looser operating boundaries may be free to take a lighter approach. But no matter what type of shop yours is—large or small—the spirit of SAM remains the same. And the same general considerations should be given for each practice. Let's take a look at each of the three practices and discuss some common ways you might apply them in your shop.

SP 1.1: Determine Acquisition Type

As described in the earlier sidebar, What Makes a Supplier a Supplier, there are some kinds of purchases SAM may surely be applied to and other kinds that you decide do not really need SAM's oversight. This first practice of determining the acquisition type helps you make that distinction. The idea here is to look at the kinds of things you acquire from suppliers, determine which of those you would consider critical to quality or to the mission of the project, and then establish the management tools that will protect them. The phrase *Determine Acquisition Type* would probably be better expressed in the plural: *Types*. Each type of acquisition might require its own tools, forms, contracts, and so on. Here are three tips you might find useful for working with your organization to determine the acquisition types you expect to need.

1.   Identify what you acquire.
2.   Determine the levels of impact.
3.   Wrap your program around key acquisition needs.

Let's take a quick look at each one.

Identify What You Acquire

The first step is to identify those things you regularly or periodically acquire. You want to think through this so you can corral what your SAM process will need to focus on. Organizations of course acquire all kinds of things. Paper, envelopes, toner, consulting hours, design work, development work, and on up the scale. The idea is to look at what you outsource, at what capabilities you need to farm out from time to time. Look at those instances that require you to count on someone else to fulfill one or more of the commitments you've made to your customers. These are the types of acquisitions that usually result in you having to relinquish a degree of quality control.

Once you've done this analysis, it's a good idea to document these categories. This will give you a firm base on which you can build a SAM program, a base that can be managed and adjusted as business needs change and develop.

Determine the Levels of Impact

Once you have categorized the kinds of acquisitions you make, you can analyze them to determine their relevant impacts on customer quality. All acquisitions have the potential to affect customer quality, but it's a good idea to undertake a degree of differentiation here. Not all outsourcing carries equal impact. Think back to the example of computer cabinets versus ballpoint pens.

The focus here is to apply SAM intelligently. It doesn't have to cover everything. Determine which outsourcing needs and acquisition types have the potential to shape project success. To do this, you might assign something like an impact factor to each of the categories you've identified. Or you might rank them in order of priority. When you've done that, you can then establish a threshold or policy that lets you focus on the critical items. This kind of measurable criteria can be useful in objectively managing the program you set in place. Then you can periodically revisit the categories and reassess the impact ratings you've assigned.

Wrap Your Program around Key Acquisition Needs

Now you can establish a policy that says which categories will fall under the SAM umbrella. In other words, you can apply SAM to the categories you deem essential, to those that have the strongest effect on customer quality and project success. And that brings us to an important point.

We mentioned earlier that you don't have to apply SAM to all acquisition types. Perhaps it's best to apply SAM to just those types that do hit customer quality. But even here you don't have to always apply SAM. Organizations—especially those just starting down the supplier management path—are free to focus on the acquisition types they feel need to be specifically managed, perhaps the acquisitions with the *highest* customer impact. As you grow and evolve your program, you can always add more controls or expand the scope of SAM.

Of course, you should revisit and reevaluate this scope over time. But the point is to apply SAM to whatever it is you need SAM to do for you.

SP 1.2: Select Suppliers

The second practice is to select your suppliers. This practice is often slightly misinterpreted. It does not mean you should make a purchasing decision now. The intention is to *prepare* to make a purchasing decision. In other words, for each of your important acquisition types, identify those vendors who are qualified to deliver what you will need. This is often realized as a preferred vendor list. Many larger companies use a preferred vendor database, and not just anybody can get listed in that database. It's a select list of suppliers. Usually suppliers have to meet certain qualifications to be eligible. They must be able to visibly demonstrate that they have the resources, abilities, track records, and stability deemed necessary to be considered reliable.

Your job here is to define that performance criteria, solicit qualifications from the vendor community, and then identify the vendors who meet your criteria. The criteria can be as welcoming or as stringent as you deem appropriate. Either way, here are three tips you might find helpful in identifying and selecting those suppliers you can call on for each acquisition type.

1. Define performance criteria for each purchase category.
2. Assess potential suppliers against the criteria.
3. Establish a preferred vendor list.

Define Performance Criteria for Each Purchase Category

Here you set the standard of performance for your vendors. Define the elements, factors, or traits required to ensure reliable performance for each specific acquisition type. The criteria you define will be heavily related to the acquisition type. Programming services will likely differ greatly from hardware components. They may certainly share some traits, but for SAM to be as effective as it can be, it's best to finely tune the criteria to the specifics of the type.

Some examples of criteria an organization might require vendors to fill include the following:

- Supply resources with an average of ten years of experience with C++
- Have a physical location within fifty miles of the organization's offices
- Have at least five years of experience operating the business
- Charge hourly rates within published industry averages
- Show a track record of customer satisfaction
- Have a specific Dun & Bradstreet rating

You are in charge of the criteria you select. Work to make them appropriate to the needs of your project teams and in line with general performance in the marketplace.

Assess Potential Suppliers against the Criteria

Once you have established the performance criteria, you can begin to qualify vendors against the set. You can do this several ways. You can assess a vendor over the course of a contracted engagement. You can ask vendors to prequalify through some kind of application process. You can embed qualification into a bidding process. However you choose to do it, you are working to identify the vendors who have the abilities and resources to deliver for you.

This practice should not be thought of as a one-time event, like an "Apply now!" announcement. This activity should remain in continuous motion. Naturally you want to identify as many qualified vendors as you can; this increases your options. It may take some time. Keep the practice ongoing, and over time you'll amass a growing database of reliable vendors.

Establish a Preferred Vendor List

You should now be able to establish a preferred vendor list. This might be a card file or a database, but in either form, you'll have it ready when it's needed. It's a good idea to make this an official list. Consider creating an executive policy that states the list is the only source for making acquisitions within the defined categories. Promote use of the list. Exercise its use. You'll gain two advantages by doing this. You'll ensure that purchasing decisions are less subjective, and you'll be able to better manage your community of vendors, shaping the list to maximize both performance and expectations.

Once you have a list of qualified vendors, you are almost ready to initiate the purchasing process. But first you need to have your agreements ready, the blank contracts you can fill out, sign, and seal in order to lock a deal in place.

SP 1.3: Establish Supplier Agreements

The third and final Specific Practice for SAM's first goal reads like the goal itself: Establish Supplier Agreements. Through this practice, you prepare assets that will help you create the types of formal agreements you need to manage a supplier relationship. The two practices discussed earlier moved you in this direction. In SP 1.1, you categorized the types of acquisitions you make and then identified the critical ones you want to wrap under SAM. In SP 1.2, you established the performance criteria you'd like to see honored for each purchase type and then identified the vendors able to perform to those criteria.

Now we come to what might be thought of as the legal aspect of SAM: preparing blank contracts and other types of purchasing agreements and forms. These should be tailored to the categories of acquisitions you've already identified, since each might carry with it its own characteristics and performance criteria. They should also contain the types of agreement statements that will guide such considerations as payment schedules, delivery schedules, changes and modifications, and company contacts. You will end up with a set of materials—usually contracts and forms—that will in most cases be legally binding. That's why you want to make sure that what you're creating will pass legal muster.

Here are two quick recommendations to help you establish such agreements in your shop and position them so they are ready to be used.

1.   Create blank contracts.
2.   Create a purchasing policy.

Create Blank Contracts

Establishing supplier agreements means creating the right kinds of agreements you need to execute purchases. You'll usually do this by creating boilerplate contracts specific to each purchase type. At this point, you might consider getting legal assistance or the help of a purchasing specialist. You want your contracts to serve a few purposes for you. First, you want them to contain the requirements you've decided on regarding delivery, pricing, schedules, and activities such as process and product inspections (see the second goal for this Process Area). To help with this, you'll want to embed the performance criteria, inspection requirements, acceptance requirements, and other requirements into the body of the agreements. You will also probably want to leave room for special or unique project criteria. Next you'll want the agreements to be legally binding, in line with accepted commercial practices and palatable to your suppliers—in other words, fair.

The degree of expert help you might need to create these agreements will naturally depend on the types of purchases you'll be making. Sometimes ready-to-go forms will do the trick for you. Other times you'll need a more complex type of contract, designed to a finer level of detail. Take care to set these agreements in place. Once you are content that they reflect your needs, they'll go a long way toward supporting a mutually beneficial customer–supplier relationship.

Create a Purchasing Policy

The practices recommended here for the first goal of Supplier Agreement Management lead you to set up a supplier management program in your organization. You've categorized purchase types, defined performance criteria for each type, and identified the vendors who are potentially qualified to supply you with those needed goods or services. With all that in place—and with contracts ready to be executed when a purchase decision is to be made—it's a good idea to create an organizational policy governing this program. The idea here is to officially notify the organization that these agreements are the starting point and the management point for purchasing activities. In other words, the purchasing program is the standard way to acquire noted goods and services for a project, and there's no going around the program.

The policy need not be an extensive tome. It can be a simple one-page document, issued from executive management, describing the importance of coordinated supplier management and endorsing the use of the management tools you've created.

SG 2: Satisfy Supplier Agreements

The first goal of Supplier Agreement Management is Establish Supplier Agreements, that is, get your agreements in place so they're ready when you need to execute them to make a purchase. Now we come to the second goal, Satisfy Supplier Agreements. This is a logical extension of the first. With SG 2, you enter into an agreement with your selected vendor, and you work together in partnership to fulfill that agreement.

The idea of partnership is important to the purpose of this Process Area. The best client–vendor relationships are those that are mutually beneficial, that provide the right kinds of opportunities and rewards for both parties. Good agreements are always two-way streets, or rather, two-lane highways leading in the same direction. The idea that you work with your suppliers in partnership promotes this bilateral view of the work at hand. The word *Satisfy* in this second goal alludes to this concept of bilateral cooperation and collaboration. Your job is to satisfy the points of the agreement that push forward your project goals and objectives and also to ensure that your team fulfills its obligations to the suppliers.

The policies and procedures you establish to support your supplier management program will promote smart shopping for your project teams. By assessing qualified vendor offerings and establishing purchase agreements, you create a relationship. To promote this relationship, you and the supplier work together to ensure that recognized supplier processes are being followed, that work in progress meets quality standards, and that product acceptance and integration can be smoothly accomplished (Figure 7–2).

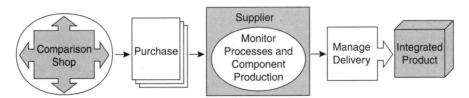

Figure 7–2: *Agreement execution ensures both proper production and proper delivery*

Five Specific Practices are recommended to help you achieve the goal of satisfying supplier agreements. We'll discuss each one in this section.

SP 2.1: Execute the Supplier Agreement

The first practice recommended for the second goal is to take steps to execute the supplier agreement. Taken at face value, the term *execute* simply means to make the deal official, to sign the contract. But that interpretation leaves something of a gap between SG 1 and SG 2. The practices under SG 1 gave you the items and the resources you need to make a purchase. To rush into this first practice under SG 2 would be to hurry up and sign, maybe with your brother-in-law or with that guy who knows this other guy. But the practice actually wants to guide you a little more slowly, in a more considered direction.

The idea here is to make a thoughtful and intelligent buying choice and only then to execute the agreement. A couple of subpractices can be inferred here.

1.   Comparison shop using predefined criteria.
2.   Seal the deal with a prepared contract.

Comparison Shop Using Predefined Criteria

Earlier in this chapter, we discussed how you can prepare for supplier management, and one activity was to define the performance or quality criteria you want to see reflected in what you purchase. That activity will pay off for you now. Here you use those definitions as a basis for comparison shopping. We can go back to our car-shopping analogy. Many people shop for a new car using a systematic approach. They write down the features they would like to have, and then, as they shop, they compare different models against those features. You should do something similar with your supplier and purchasing decisions.

If you have set your criteria in place and identified your pool of quali-fied vendors, you should be able to engage in a prepared round of effective comparison shopping. This is one of the real strengths of this CMMI Process Area. Working with qualified vendors, you apply objec-tive criteria to determine which one offers the closest match to your current needs.

Seal the Deal with a Prepared Contract

After you have evaluated what's available in the marketplace, you should be ready to make an informed purchase decision. This is another place where your preparations will pay off. For the first goal of this Process Area, you established supplier agreements, the blank con-tracts specific to a purchase type that you can pull off the shelf, fill in the blanks, and execute a deal.

It's important to take time to review the contract (the purchase order, requisition, or whatever form the agreement takes) to make sure it truly reflects the terms of the agreement. You might want to confirm that it contains such details as the performance criteria, inspection require-ments, delivery schedules, acceptance requirements, and other factors you wish to employ to manage the relationship successfully.

Once you and your supplier have had a chance to review the details of the agreement and perhaps modify it to the satisfaction of both par-ties, you are ready to sign on the dotted line and begin the relation-ship pro forma.

SP 2.2: Monitor Selected Supplier Processes

This second practice combines with the third (described in the next subsection) to represent an innovation you can enjoy through the use of SAM: the idea that you should shape your relationship around an open-door policy of periodic supplier progress inspections. This is an often overlooked management opportunity. The objective is to ensure that the full terms of the agreement are being met at each stage of product (or service) development. The best way to confirm this is to look at some of the key activities the supplier is engaged in to make sure they are being conducted in a way reflected in the agreement.

To support this practice, you might want to look at Chapter 9, where we discuss the Process & Product Quality Assurance Process Area. That Process Area deals with periodic inspections of your project team's compliance with process and product procedures and standards. You will probably find that a lot of what you build for PPQA will serve you well in your SAM activities.

Here are three techniques you can use to manage this insight into supplier performance.

1.   Establish an audit plan.
2.   Conduct audits.
3.   Report results.

Note that you can also use these tips for SP 2.3.

Establish an Audit Plan

It's important that you work with your chosen supplier to determine up front what critical processes or activities you need the supplier to follow and then develop an audit plan (it could be big; it could be small) to monitor those key activities. You may even wish to make this a part of the agreement or to at least reference it in the agreement. Then, when the project moves forward, you can execute this plan.

The benefit of establishing an audit plan is that it's a way for both parties to prepare up front to meet performance expectations. It's also a way for people at your supplier's firm to accommodate your inspections. If they are aware of when you'll be auditing and what you'll be auditing, they should be prepared to work with you to conduct smooth audits and confirm quality.

The plan need not be complex. It should simply document when the audits will occur, what will be inspected at each one, who will be conducting the audits, what supplier resources will be required, and what performance measures will be acceptable as an outcome.

Conduct Audits

Once you have an audit plan in place, the next step is to follow the plan and conduct the audits. The purpose of these audits is to ensure that your suppliers are following the processes that support your quality and production standards. For example, if you have contracted for the development of software modules, you might expect that your supplier's technical team will perform periodic design reviews. To confirm this, you might want to audit for the existence of design review notes, meeting minutes, design revisions, or other such artifacts. The kinds of audits you conduct will depend on the product you have contracted for and the contents of the audit plan. It is important to conduct the audits as planned, to make resources available to see the plan through, and then to use the results of the audit to measure and interpret supplier performance in an objective fashion.

Report Results

The last tip for evaluating supplier processes is to document the results of the audits and report these results to relevant parties. This is important for three reasons. First, it aids with the management of your project. Positive results, shared with your project team and the supplier team, will confirm that that end of the effort is going as planned. It helps show that progress is on track. Likewise, negative results can be used as an impetus to make necessary adjustments, to bring activities or expectations back in line with project needs.

Second, the audit results can demonstrate that the supplier team is fulfilling its part of the agreement. If you have mapped your performance expectations into the content of your contracts, the audits should serve as a barometer that indicates how well you and your suppliers are operating within the realm of the agreements.

Third, you can amass the audit results over time to compile a pretty good history of a supplier's ability to perform. As noted earlier, one of the objectives of Supplier Agreement Management is to establish a community of suppliers who are reliable and dependable, on whom you can call over time to help address your project needs. The audit reports help you document vendor performance with this in mind.

SP 2.3: **Evaluate Selected Supplier Work Products**

This third practice works in harmony with SP 2.2. Here you evaluate selected work products while they are still moving through the supplier's production process. The rationale for this is pretty clean. You want to periodically confirm that the pieces that will make up the delivered product are being produced in a way that meets performance specifications and quality standards. Looking at the processes and production activities certainly helps meet this goal, but it's a good idea to augment this with actual inspections of the product as it evolves over the life of the project. Conducting both early and periodic inspections will help guarantee that what you get in the end really does match up to what you contracted for. It also helps ensure that if you do discover any unacceptable variances, you'll have found them at a point where correction can be undertaken in a more cost-effective and efficient manner.

Here are three techniques you can use to shape periodic inspections of in-process work products in a controlled manner. (You can also apply the three tips for process inspections noted earlier.)

1. Evaluate in-process production.
2. Establish pass/fail criteria.
3. Establish a corrective action procedure.

Evaluate In-Process Production

As with the auditing process activities discussed earlier, here you look at work in progress with the same aim, so let's quickly review those points. By looking at work in progress, you have the ability to ensure that components delivered to you have been assembled using quality components and constituent parts. If you can uncover defective parts or ill-designed components early in the process, you stand a good chance of setting things quickly back on track, a much better chance than if you discovered the problem after the product had been more fully integrated. Finally, in-process inspections allow you to ascertain the supplier's ability to produce and support quality to a required level of granularity.

Establish Pass/Fail Criteria

When you and your supplier agree to in-process work inspections, the question will naturally arise: How does one pass an inspection? It's a fair question and one that you and your supplier must decide how to answer long before the inspections can be conducted with any integrity. One way to do this is to define pass/fail criteria for each kind of inspection agreed to. For example, if you are subcontracting for electronic capacitors, your pass criteria might be no more than three defective capacitors for every thousand-piece lot—any more and the lot can be rejected. Another example might be shaped for software code. Unit test results might stipulate that a code module must test 99% clean before it can move to integration, and if it must pass through any more than five cycles of unit testing to reach this point, the module can be subjected to supplier-funded outside testing.

The nature of your pass/fail criteria will naturally depend on the kind of work you are subcontracting out, the type of relationship you have with your supplier, and the type of agreement you have made with the supplier. But a well-thought-out collection of pass/fail criteria (or go/no-go, hold/release, or green/red criteria, whatever terms best fit your culture) will help set you and your supplier along common lines of expectations, so that the results of the work inspections will be agreeable to everyone. And that should help keep work progressing along productive and predictable lines.

Establish a Corrective Action Procedure

Once you are inspecting supplier processes, products, and product components, you will benefit from establishing some documented corrective action procedures to deal with those times when the supplier does not meet your pass/fail criteria. The corrective action procedure is used as a way to get things back on track. It's an agreed-upon way to handle the defective parts and to ensure that only operating parts get into the production stream. You might have a procedure to repair the bad parts or to discard them and start over. You might have a retest procedure. You might call in a third-party assessor. Any approach that gives you the comfort level you need to move forward is a valid corrective action procedure, as long as it is also acceptable to your supplier. (It should probably also be in line with industry-accepted practices if those apply.)

The value of the corrective action procedure is the same as defining the pass/fail criteria and establishing an audit plan for each of your suppliers. It helps establish common ground between you and the supplier, the common ground on which you can play out performance, quality, and delivery expectations.

SP 2.4: Accept the Acquired Product

This fourth practice recommended under the second goal is to accept the product you have acquired. Of course, you can also reject the product. The idea here is to establish formal acceptance criteria so that, when your supplier makes the final delivery, you have a protocol in place to ensure that what you are getting is exactly what you ordered. The use of a thorough acceptance protocol is important for an obvious reason: Such a protocol protects you from taking in a faulty product and then being stuck with it. From a contractual standpoint, acceptance probably implies agreement. You agree that the supplier has done the job and upheld that end of the bargain. An acceptance process—one designed to closely examine the product's goodness of fit and suitability for use—will ensure that what you take in really does represent what all parties agreed to.

You can use two techniques to control how your shop accepts products from its suppliers.

1. Establish acceptance criteria.
2. Establish an inspection process.

Establish Acceptance Criteria

Earlier in this chapter, we discussed the value of categorizing the kinds of purchases you make and then defining appropriate vendor performance criteria for each. This can serve as the foundation for establishing product acceptance criteria. These might emerge as a series of checklists or a series of test cases. It depends on the product. But by defining this early in the game, you come away with two advantages. First, you can share with the whole organization what your quality criteria are. You establish a common level of expectation internal to your shop. Second, you can then embed the acceptance criteria into your purchasing agreements. This way your suppliers will begin their relationships with you with the acceptance criteria foremost in their minds. Third, when a vendor knocks on your door with the product under his or her arm, ready to sign it over to you, you're ready to inspect it with a set view toward performance.

Establish an Inspection Process

This may be the most immediately valuable part of your supplier agreement program. Using the acceptance criteria as a foundation, you establish an inspection process to apply to all incoming products. As we noted earlier, this may be a straightforward visible inspection. It might a burn-in of a random sample. It might be a series of tests you execute against predefined test cases. The process you come up with will need to reflect the attributes of the product and the performance criteria you want to verify.

The strength of an inspection process is that you can confirm performance early in the integration cycle, so you can find and correct problems when they are easiest to spot and when they can be cleanly rectified. If you skip this step, you run the risk of embedding problems into your final assembled product. At that point, finding the root cause can become problematic. Worse, determining the party responsible for fixing things can get cloudy. Inspecting incoming parts up front gives you a clean audit trail to control quality, performance, and accountability.

SP 2.5: Transition Products

The fifth and final practice recommended for the second goal of Supplier Agreement Management involves transitioning products. This is not so much a supplier-engaged activity as one that you own. To transition is to take someone else's product and turn it into yours. Many times, even though you may have designed the outsourced product, it comes to you with the supplier's stamp on it—sometimes literally. The idea now is to brand the product with your identity. You want to be able to seamlessly integrate the component into the whole product you deliver to your customer.

Transitioning activities can usually be thought of as integration activities. But that really depends on the nature of the product (or the service) you've acquired. You might transition something by simply plugging it into what you've built (such as a chip on a circuit board). Or you might transition by compiling vendor programming code into your core modules (as with software).

However you do it, here are two tips you can use to transition in a controlled manner.

1. Establish integration guidelines.
2. Establish branding guidelines.

Establish Integration Guidelines

Integration guidelines are documented procedural steps that your folks can use to transition a collection of components into a seamless whole. The integration guidelines you develop should be shaped very specifically to the types of components you assemble. Look at what your organization builds, acquires, and delivers. Analyze the steps needed for product integration. Then establish the guidelines you can use to put the parts together in a reliable way, consistently, over time.

These guidelines will prove useful from another vantage point, too. You can use them as part of the acceptance criteria for the acquired product. If you can share these integration guidelines with your suppliers up front, they will know what integration capabilities must be met well in advance of delivery. They will know what plugs, stubs, or hooks need to be in place to help ensure proper integration.

Establish Branding Guidelines

Finally, you should consider establishing branding guidelines. Think of an automobile, for example, the Ford Mustang. The Mustang is a collection of thousands of parts, all built to fit together—and built by hundreds of suppliers. But the identity of the car remains Mustang. You have to look deep down to discover Ace Electronics or Pearson Upholstery trademarks. The same should hold true for your product. The solution you deliver to your customers should not be seen as a piece of successful teamwork, even though that may well be what it is (and perhaps should be). That's not what your customer contracted for. People don't buy Mustangs because they trust Ace Electronics. They buy Mustangs because they trust Ford Motor Company. You too should establish proper branding guidelines for your assembled product. Within the bounds of your agreements, raise your identity to the surface. This is the best way to show that you stand behind the product and that you take ultimate responsibility for its performance.

The Benefits of Supplier Agreement Management

The practices recommended under Supplier Agreement Management can deliver distinct benefits to your project and to your organization as a whole. When you are required to outsource key components of work—and by default relinquish a degree of control—these practices can give you the insight and mechanisms for oversight to ensure that your outside partners are working in line with your objectives, expectations, and standards. They can also provide your organization with tools it can use to conduct purchasing activities in a manageable, consistent, and accountable way.

Here are four tangible and tactical benefits of a SAM program worth considering.

Consistent Management of the Supply Chain

Supply chain management is a big discipline, and CMMI's SAM Process Area doesn't position itself as an enterprise solution for the needs of this area. But for project teams that don't have a formal supplier program, or for organizations that do not have large or established purchasing departments, the use of SAM brings distinct benefits.

First, the practices in SAM can be designed to promote the timely coordination of suppliers. This becomes especially important in large, complex projects or in instances where a team has to outsource different components of its work to multiple vendors. The insight SAM gives you into work-in-progress and management processes provides you with the hooks you can use to link project activities across a team of vendors.

Second, SAM provides you with practices that support productive collaboration between you and your vendors and even between the vendors themselves.

Both of these capabilities enable you and your project teams to apply consistent and predictable management techniques to productively control the supply chain.

Heightened Purchasing Efficiencies

The central purpose of the SAM Process Area is to establish protocols that lead you to make the best purchase decisions for your project and for the organization as a whole. If you structure your program in a way that truly reflects tactical purchasing needs, you should end up with a program that heightens your ability to make efficient purchases. An efficient purchase can be thought of as one that delivers expected quality in a dependable way at a fair market value. And that, in a nutshell, is the focus of SAM. By looking at your acquisition types, analyzing performance criteria, and evaluating qualified vendors, you bring into your organization the ability to not only effectively seek out the optimum purchasing opportunities but also manage them in an ongoing manner to ensure maximum efficiencies.

Mutually Beneficial Supplier Relationships

Any organization benefits from having a pool of qualified and dependable suppliers to work with. Project success can be enhanced when you are dealing with suppliers who know how to work with you, have the skills to complement your abilities, and are willing to work within your project management approach. A Supplier Agreement Management program can help set in place the controls and oversight mechanisms to establish and grow these kinds of relationships. A SAM program helps you define what performance qualities are important to your shop and establish those attributes you need to succeed. By using these as the foundation for a relationship, you're better able to identify up front those candidates who will best meet your needs.

In the same way, your SAM program will help your suppliers. All suppliers appreciate the value of return business and an ongoing market relationship. Your SAM program will help establish a common basis for expectations between you and your vendors. A vendor whose approach to work and project management dovetails nicely with yours will be able to contribute to your objectives in ways that benefit both parties.

Visible Performance and Quality Control

I have worked with more than a few project managers who prefer the black-box approach to supplier management. They adopt a type of "Don't ask, don't tell" policy. They don't want to know the details of the work they turn over to a vendor. They just want to get something back without the hassle of having to manage it. But that's not a smart way to do business. That's business by nonmanagement, by magical thinking.

Supplier Agreement Management takes you in the direction of integrating supplier activities with your management view, so that your supplier's work becomes visible to the project team and to your management as well. When performance and quality procedures are made visible, not only do you have more control over them but they also become easier to manage. With the black-box approach, you're left to manage against broad strokes, at high orders of magnitude. With a cooperative supplier management program, you increase your level of granularity. This makes adjustments and course corrections much easier to deal with and also increases your ability to confirm that outsourced work is on track.

Some Example Program Components

Supplier Agreement Management, like all the other Process Areas discussed in this book, is meant to be shaped to the needs of your organization. In fact, its shape will highly depend on the kinds of work your shop engages in. Farming out software development requires a different take on suppliers than contracting for documentation work does. A shop that heavily depends on outside resources will probably need a program much different from a shop that only occasionally needs to outsource. But whatever kind of a program you have, you'll want to have some basic components at the ready to help your SAM program work in an orderly and consistent fashion. This section describes some examples of common SAM program components.

Supplier Agreement Management Policy

A supplier agreement management policy is an important program component to have because it sets an executive direction for making outside acquisitions. The policy says, in effect, "Executive management directs the organization to use its SAM procedures whenever key purchases have to be made." In other words, don't enter purchasing negotiations outside of SAM. Once you have built a supplier management program, you'll have in place the kinds of categories, performance criteria, and purchasing agreements that will protect your company from less-than-ideal purchase decisions. The policy, authored and signed by executive management, is the high-level endorsement you can rely on to ensure that your standards in this arena are followed.

Acquisition-Specific Supplier Agreements

Here's what I see as the "lawyer part" of your supplier program, although I am sure there are many cases that don't need to get a lawyer involved. The forms you want to produce are acquisition-specific supplier agreements, or in other words, blank contracts. In your program, you'll determine the different kinds of acquisitions you make. For each of these, you'll determine the performance and delivery criteria that you'll want to bind your selected suppliers to. All of this detail needs to be reflected in your agreements, probably in a way that is legally valid and binding for both parties. The agreements, after all, will be the chief tool used to manage the relationship. Often a purchasing specialist can help you develop these. But the objective is to have the blank contracts ready in advance of a purchase, so when you are ready to make a deal, you have the agreements available.

Corrective Action Procedure

Another good tool to develop for your supplier program is some form of corrective action procedure. As we discussed earlier in this chapter, an important aspect of the relationship you forge with your suppliers is the opportunity to periodically assess work in progress and quality processes. Through this avenue, you and your suppliers can remain in sync across the development lifecycle.

Of course, it's possible that from time to time you might begin to drift out of sync. In that case, it's useful to have a corrective action procedure ready to set in place. This procedure—which you and your supplier should agree to up front—can cover such actions as defining what quality points you'll look for, what steps should be taken when these points are not confirmed, which supplier contacts should be involved, and what to do when there's apparent disagreement on the best corrective course. With this in place, you should be able to avoid most bottlenecks and hard disagreements, as well as their disruptions to project progress.

Product Acceptance Procedure

A very valuable tool for any supplier management program is some type of product acceptance approach. This could be a simple checklist or a more complex inspection procedure. Whatever form it takes, its purpose is the same: to establish an official way to accept an acquired product into the company. The idea behind acceptance is that you acknowledge the suppliers have fulfilled their end of the bargain; what they delivered to you meets agreed-upon expectations. If you're acquiring items such as components, the acceptance procedure might be handled through an inspection checklist. If you're acquiring hardware parts, you might establish a burn-test for a representative sample. If you're acquiring software, you might set up a series of acceptance test cases and execute them prior to sign-off.

Look to the Web Site for . . .

- Purchasing policy
- Supplier process audit procedure
- Supplier work product audit procedure

Chapter 8

Measurement & Analysis

Designing and building navigation control systems for unmanned flight vehicles requires a high degree of precision and accuracy. When you look at it from sea-level, we are a data management organization. Our requirements are data points and thresholds, our designs and specs are measures and tolerances, our performance models are numeric to the nearest one-thousandth. Without measurement and analysis none of our projects would fly.
Debbie Michelen, Director of Quality,
Reliance Control and Simulation Systems Navigation
Controls for the aerospace industry

If you look at the PMBOK from the Project Management Institute, you'll quickly realize that a very large portion of the techniques promoted in that document have to deal with measuring where you are in an ongoing project. The PMBOK itself is divided into nine Knowledge Areas: Integration, Scope, Time, Cost, Quality, Human Resources, Communications, Risk, and Procurement. If you look at the details for each of these, it becomes hard to separate measurement and analysis as an independent project management activity. In fact, measurement and analysis might be the one overarching management responsibility for a given project. The *job* of project management is to measure. By measuring, you can know; once you know, you can anticipate; and through informed anticipation, you can guide effectively.

PMBOK texts and documentation (from organizations such as the PMI and George Washington University) emphasize a host of measurement and analysis considerations. Earned Value factors (such as AC, PV, CV, and CPI) can be used to predict efficiencies. Network diagramming requires an empirical representation of task durations. Resource leveling, quantitative risk analysis, reserve planning, and estimation all presuppose that you are measuring—or at least setting up a base for measuring. So, because measurement and analysis has the ability to support project success in very real and tangible ways, it needs to be given an appropriate emphasis in your projects. Sometimes the measurement needs of your project will require only a moderate strategy. At other times you'll want a robust approach. But both cases will benefit from the same foundation. In this chapter, we'll look at the CMMI Process Area called Measurement & Analysis, and we'll investigate how its recommended practices can help you establish an informative management, analysis, and reporting capability for any project.

The Purpose of Measurement & Analysis

CMMI-DEV treats Measurement & Analysis as a separate Process Area, but that's only a convenience of organization. The practices described for this Process Area promote an integrated approach that supports the PMBOK view. (In fact, the earlier version of the model, CMM, integrated measurement recommendations within Process Areas.) Just as in the PMBOK, Measurement & Analysis provides you with what might be called heightened empirical judgment. When you forgo taking measurements and analyzing the results, you are pretty much left with intuition, instinct, experience, and personal judgment as your management tools. Those aren't bad tools, and CMMI is not out to dissuade you from employing those personal assets. They are essential to project success. But they are, after all, personal, so they vary from person to person. Measurement—the process of collecting data and analyzing it—is a powerful complement here. Empirical data carries a high degree of objective validity. It's hard to argue with the numbers when you get the numbers right.

That brings us to the purpose of this Process Area. It's a two-sided coin. One side of this Process Area is designed to meet the management needs of your project. Early in the lifecycle, usually as a part of project planning, management establishes the data collection needs and then sets in place a plan to collect and analyze this information at set intervals. As with all plans, the measurement plan is supported with the resources needed to make it a viable activity across the project lifecycle. The other side of this coin is designed to establish and strengthen the organizational capability to amass measurement data over time and across projects and thereby develop a predictive tool. Through this, the organization's ability to manage not only from a tactical position but also, more importantly, from a strategic position greatly increases.

If you know anything about the improvement methodology Six Sigma, you're probably familiar with the phrase *data-driven decision making*. The idea as contained in Six Sigma is that you shouldn't work to change a product (or a process) until you understand how it performs. You acquire this understanding by measuring performance. Based on the data you collect, you can then make an informed decision as to how you might improve performance.

The same philosophy holds true for project management. The best way to understand what course you are on is through measurements. The best way to understand how to implement a course correction is through measurements. And the best way to interpret and report on progress is through measurements. The Measurement & Analysis Process Area as described under CMMI is intended to boost your data-driven decision-making capability. The goals and practices described in this chapter will help you identify important business metrics, define collection and analysis procedures, establish a measurement repository, and report analytical results to relevant stakeholders. Through this approach, you'll be able to embed within your project the resources and techniques that will support data-driven decision making.

But before we get into the goals and practices of this Process Area, let's look at the tactical ways that Measurement & Analysis can support data-driven decision making for your projects.

Establish Success Criteria Up Front

This may be the most important tactical advantage to a good Measurement & Analysis program. You (and your management and customers) can define up front what measures are going to indicate project success. Here the traditional numbers usually come into play: schedule, costs, scope, and resources. If you can set performance thresholds at the start of a project and then manage to these thresholds, there should be common agreement over the course of a project as to how well things are going. Of course, you can use any metrics that make sense for your project. But the idea is to set these criteria in place before the project kicks off and to do so with the input of those people who will be the true judges at the end—usually your customers and executive management. With these yardsticks in place, you have not only established what the success criteria will officially be for the project but also armed project management with the viewpoint and tool set it needs to drive toward this success.

Bound the Focus of Project Management

This second trait is a complement to the first. A good measurement program can help set the bounds that project management should be focused within. It defines what control points are important and therefore implies which ones you don't have to worry so much about. Again, schedule, costs, scope, and resources will probably take precedence here to one degree or another. But how those factors are tracked and interpreted can take many forms. In fact, in the absence of a good measurement program, the problem is not that they will not be tracked. The problem is that they will likely be tracked using many different and individual forms. The variety in the differences can easily make it difficult for a consistent picture of progress and status to gel.

Without a basis of key measures defined, you may also find that your project managers are measuring a little bit of everything, taking what's thought of as the safe course by going overboard on measurements.

Add to this the fact that they may not even be collecting the same data across projects and you can see how quickly mountains of data can pile up. But if those measures have no real business need or strategic focus, chances are that those mountains, carrying only the impact of a mole hill, won't help you manage the project toward success.

Provide Empirical and Consistent Progress Markers

So far we've looked at the value of Measurement & Analysis from the viewpoint of project success: the end point where you have the evidence you need to demonstrate you've met the goals you set out to achieve. We also looked at the value here from the perspective of fence lines. A good measurement program provides the boundaries to guide what factors and data points project management should focus on. But there's a third viewpoint to take, one just as helpful as the first two. A measurement program can provide your teams with a set of standardized and empirical benchmarks that help regulate progress across the project lifecycle.

Your project's lifecycle will most likely be chartered as a series of discrete phases. The reassurance you provide that your project is on track at the macro level can be supported by the data you provide to management and customers that you are in control at the phase level, at the micro level. By using a series of phase measures, or even a series of interphase measures, you can begin to collect, analyze, and amass the kinds of data that continually and systematically demonstrate adherence to project plans, constraints, and expectations.

Establish a Basis for Improvement

Finally, we take an organizational view of Measurement & Analysis. It's probably clear to project managers that well-designed data collection and analysis can lead to heightened project control and surer project success. But there's another reason to establish an MA program in your shop, and that has to do with organizational success. From a project perspective, we rely on measurements to help operate within the expectations of our customers, those people who pay us to perform at certain levels of efficiency. When we can show that we're meeting expectations, we can verify that we've done a good job. But there's an equal benefit for the organization. Measurements can (and no doubt should) be used by the executive branch of a company to map out where the organization as a whole wants to move.

In the most obvious example, you can see this in a public company's annual report. The financial data presented along with past-year comparisons, trending charts, and management analyses make up a strategic vision based on data, most of which probably came out of project work within the company.

Whether you're working in a public company or not, large or small, Measurement & Analysis can serve as the foundation for methodically establishing a series of concrete corporate objectives, charting a course to attain those objectives, and then measuring incremental progress toward them.

Measurement & Analysis Goals and Practices

CMMI defines two Specific Goals and eight Specific Practices for Measurement & Analysis. Here is the official specification text for each of these elements.

SG 1   ALIGN MEASUREMENT & ANALYSIS ACTIVITIES
Measurement objectives and activities are aligned with identified information needs and objectives.

SP 1.1   ESTABLISH MEASUREMENT OBJECTIVES
Establish and maintain measurement objectives that are derived from identified information needs and objectives.

SP 1.2   SPECIFY MEASURES
Specify measures to address the measurement objectives.

SP 1.3   SPECIFY DATA COLLECTION AND STORAGE PROCEDURES
Specify how measurement data will be obtained and stored.

SP 1.4   SPECIFY ANALYSIS PROCEDURES
Specify how measurement data will be analyzed and reported.

SG 2 Provide Measurement Results

Measurement results that address identified information needs and objectives are provided.

SP 2.1 Collect Measurement Data
Obtain specified measurement data.

SP 2.2 Analyze Measurement Data
Analyze and interpret measurement data.

SP 2.3 Store Data and Results
Manage and store management data, measurement specifications, and analysis results.

SP 2.4 Communicate Results
Report results of measurement and analysis activities to all relevant stakeholders.

Generic Goals and Practices

See Chapter 10 for information about the important Generic Goals and Practices that support project management success for all the Process Areas at Maturity Level 2.

SG 1: Align Measurement & Analysis Activities

The first goal is to align the activities of Measurement & Analysis. This is an essential goal, a primary target. It will ensure that your measurement program is effective and yields tangible, actionable benefits not only for project success but for organizational success as well. The key here—and the end that all the practices are aimed to achieve—is to align what you want to measure with the information needs of your organization. In other words, define a measurement program that will produce information you find helpful, information you can use to determine where you are and then plot where you'd like to be.

Surprisingly, this approach—which is best understood as a simple, logical tack—is often overlooked. Organizations and teams may be so anxious to begin the process of measuring that they give little strategic thought to what they should measure. And because there is never any shortage of things to measure, the ready temptation can be to measure too much stuff. The other view is to see Measurement & Analysis as an impediment, as an obligation that project management only reluctantly adopts. As a consequence, the emphasis might be on minimum performance. The teams work to round up what might be called the usual suspects, but they don't really use that information as a basis for decision making.

The right approach, of course, is the balanced approach, to design appropriately scaled MA activities that reveal the story of what's important to your projects and your organizational objectives. Measurement programs work best when they are designed to promote the business missions of the project and the organization. Designing such a program involves a series of discrete judgments: What measures are important to the business? What can we measure to support that? Where can we find the data? How can we analyze the data? Who should we send the analysis results to? Those considerations form the basis of a valid MA program (Figure 8–1).

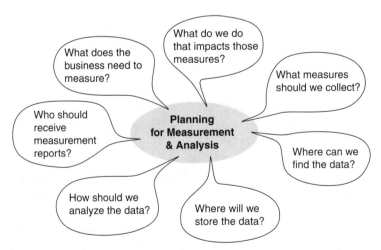

Figure 8–1: *A well-designed measurement program accommodates a range of considerations*

So this first goal can be rephrased in simple terms: Shape your MA activities to gather the kinds of data you can use to make wise business decisions. CMMI defines four Specific Practices to help you achieve this goal. Let's take a quick look at each.

SP 1.1: Establish Measurement Objectives

The first Specific Practice for this Process Area is to establish measurement objectives. As we have noted in other chapters, the term *establish* in CMMI implies a couple of things. First, it implies that you are going to document the objectives, that you'll write them down so they'll be readily accessible by others. Second, it implies that you will make these objectives available to others not only through access but through distribution, too.

This first part is strategic in nature, so you'll want to put some executive thought to work here. What kind of information does the organization find valuable for measuring progress, success, compliance? What are the long-term goals of the company? What are the short-term goals? What might be important to the marketplace? What might be important to the board of directors?

Work with your management to determine what objectives make the most sense for your shop. Meanwhile, here are three activities that can help you determine what your measurement objectives might be and which ones might serve you best.

1. Tie the objectives to business success.
2. Choose demonstrable objectives.
3. Make sure the measures are containable.

Tie the Objectives to Business Success

This may be the best thing you can do for managing your process program as a whole and for managing individual projects, too. Tie your measurement objectives to business success. There are all kinds of things you can measure, and you can easily come up with a host of objectives. But if you want to establish a way to show that what you are doing really is moving the company in the right direction, link your measurement objectives to the goals of the business. Talk to people in senior management. Ask them what their goals are. Is the mission to expand the amount of project work the shop can undertake? Is it to meet the schedule needs of the customer base? Does the company want to reduce expenses, leverage existing systems, become recognized for its quality products? Once senior management has articulated these objectives, you can pull them down to the level of project management. You can establish measurement objectives at this level that mirror the strategic direction of the company. The data you then begin to collect will be readily available to paint a picture of progress toward those goals.

Choose Demonstrable Objectives

Once you know the business objectives of the organization, you can establish measurement objectives at the project level that support them. Here it's important to define demonstrable objectives that can be readily quantified. Often you'll encounter a different kind of measurement objective: "Collect the data that shows we're the best system shop in the industry." That's certainly an honorable goal, but it's not very demonstrable. It's too qualitative in nature. In order to make it concrete, you need to define just what it means to be the best. Is this the ability to meet deadlines within 5% of the target? Is it the ability to stick to within 6% of estimated budgets? It might be the ability to deliver defect-free products. Or it could be some combination of any of these. The point is to position your objectives along quantitative lines, to anchor your program on demonstrable objectives. This will take some thought on your part, and you may have to move from qualitative beginnings to more concrete results, but it will make your measurement program much more manageable and workable as you exercise it across projects.

Make Sure the Measures Are Containable

It's important to ensure that your measurement objectives are containable. The idea here is to not get carried away with all the numerous and sundry things you can pitch into a measurement program. Thinking up viable and demonstrable measurement objectives takes some strategic thinking on your part, but it's not terribly difficult work. You might face the temptation to establish a lot of objectives, a broad range of goals that holds the potential to paint performance pictures from all kind of angles. But that's probably not the best move—especially for beginning measurement programs.

A better approach is to keep your measurement objectives focused. Select a few key indicators that will serve your strategic purposes, build those up, and then—as you grow and develop—you can always add to them. By constraining the objectives up front, you'll also be working to bind the amount of data you'll collect once the program begins, the kinds of measures you'll be required to work through, and the analyses you'll want to undertake. In short, constraining the objectives at this stage will help you create a very manageable measurement program.

SP 1.2: **Specify Measures**

The second practice for the first goal is to specify the measures. This step should arise naturally out of the practice just discussed. Once you have established the objectives for your program, you're ready to think about what kinds of measures can be used to meet those objectives. For example, if your shop has an objective to make on-time delivery for 90% of all project work, one measure you might want to specify is schedule slippage. You might then want to add a derived measure to this, average schedule slippage. This will tell you the organization's schedule performance across all projects.

You'll notice that there is often a one-to-many relationship between objectives and measures. One objective may call for a set of measures. At the same time, remember that one measure can often be used to support multiple objectives. The trick is to think through your objectives and then think through your normal project activities and management points. From these, your measurements should emerge as logical and valuable data points.

Here are two tips you can follow when you're deciding what exactly you're going to measure.

1. Tie the measures to what you already do.
2. Choose measures that are readily available.

Tie the Measures to What You Already Do

It's probably a good idea to avoid introducing a measurement program that will require your project teams to work in many new ways. Sometimes that may be a necessary component of change. But most measurement programs can usually be designed around current organizational practices. When you base the measures on things you already do, you come away with two advantages. First, your new measurement requirements will tend to blend seamlessly into current work streams; they'll avoid the need for new work paths. Second, the measures will more than likely be familiar to team members and, as a result, logical and rational. That will promote collection and use of measures across projects.

Choose Measures That Are Readily Available

As you begin to define the kinds of measures you want to collect, remember the value to be found in low-hanging fruit. Often the measures that are readily available, that don't require a high degree of derivation or digging, are the ones that give you the kind of full-scope picture you're seeking. Data points such as current expenditures, schedule compliance, team size, and number of requirements may not look especially exciting or revealing; they may seem too focused on the big picture. But these kinds of numbers—usually readily available without a lot of extra effort or exploration—really can provide you with the project management insight to guide a project, and they can combine and amass over time to give you and senior management a very solid picture of organizational performance and trends along what can be considered mission-critical lines.

Naturally, there are many wells within a project from which other numbers can be drawn. If these are of significant value to you, by all means, define them. But you need not feel an obligation to establish a deep or complex measurement program. A program sized well for your needs, one that you can develop and evolve over time, will serve you and your teams much more effectively than an over-engineered program that's difficult to implement.

SP 1.3: Specify Data Collection and Storage Procedures

SP 1.1 recommends defining objectives for the Measurement & Analysis program. SP 1.2 recommends using those objectives to define what measures to collect. Now we come to SP 1.3, which focuses on specifying the procedures for data collection and storage. At this point, you document where and when the measures are to be found and where they will be stored once collected. The importance of this practice increases as your measurement program grows in sophistication. If you think of the objectives as the *why* of your measurement program and the measures as the *what*, you can think of this practice as the *where*: "Where do I go to find this data, and where do I put the data once I've found it?"

You can describe these activities as a series of steps if you'd like, or you can define them in a policy narrative. The form is not as important as the function. The key is to take the guesswork (and the legwork) out of finding the data and then to establish a definitive and official location for housing the data.

Here are two steps to consider as you decide how to specify data collection and storage procedures.

1. Locate the data.
2. Establish a data repository.

Locate the Data

By following the advice offered earlier—to select measures that are more or less readily available—you can make this an easy and basic step. If the data is plainly located on the surface of project activities, defining where to get it should be pretty obvious. If, however, you need to build a more complex MA program, this step will itself take on its own level of complexity. You want to provide your team with a map of where to find the data, whether it's on the surface or more deeply buried. With this map in place, people won't have to discover from project to project where the information they need to analyze resides.

Establish a Data Repository

Next you want to define where the data should be stored once it has been collected. You can take a couple of approaches to this task. If your organization is perhaps new to process or if you are almost exclusively focused on project management (as opposed to organizational process management), you might elect to create a measurement repository for each project. If your shop is taking the broader view, you might want to create a central repository that all projects can use. The choice is yours; CMMI at Maturity Level 2 supports either approach.

Likewise, the type of repository you create depends entirely on your needs. Some teams employ a simple spreadsheet. Others elect to use a relational database. Others like to use some of the more sophisticated statistical analysis packages available on the market. But whatever solution you choose, the point here is to establish it as a standard, inform people what it is and where it is, and then give the appropriate team members access to it.

SP 1.4: **Specify Analysis Procedures**

The fourth and final practice for the first goal of Measurement & Analysis is to specify your analysis procedures. This step is the culmination of creating the measurement program. Here you describe how the measurements you collect and store will be analyzed; in other words, what formulas and derivations you'll apply to the raw data in order to produce meaningful results.

The purpose of defining the sets of analyses is to ensure that your various teams can apply the same ones to common sets of data. This will give you results you can use not only to compare one project to another but also to roll up into an integrated picture of organizational performance.

For this last practice, you will do well to keep the first one in mind, the objectives you established for your measurement program. The intention is to use your analyses to reveal information that sheds light on the objectives, turning raw numbers into the information you need to interpret progress toward your objectives.

You'll find that some analyses can be very simple. Cumulative totals, averages, and ranges are all simple methods that can produce very useful results. You also have access to a host of much more sophisticated techniques. As an example, formulas for Earned Value are popular in the PMP realm. And there are the very sophisticated avenues of statistical and quantitative analysis: standard deviations, regression analysis, chi-square analysis, T-tests, and so on. Select the analysis procedures that are right for your projects and your shop, shape these procedures, and then share them with your project teams.

With all four of the practices for the first goal in place, you have established the foundation on which you can exercise your Measurement & Analysis program. And that's what the second goal is all about.

SG 2: Provide Measurement Results

This second Specific Goal for Measurement & Analysis rides on the first Specific Goal. SG 1, Align Measurement & Analysis Activities, recommends four practices you can use to establish an MA program that addresses the business objectives of your shop and defines a series of metrics that can be collected, stored, and analyzed to that purpose. The second goal acts on the first goal. SG 2, Provide Measurement Results, involves using the measurement program you have defined. Carry it out on project work, and then provide the results to project team members, project management, and organizational management.

Like SG 1, this second goal has four Specific Practices associated with it. As we look at these practices, you'll see that they spring from the practices recommended under the first goal. In the following subsections, we'll discuss briefly what the practices for SG 2 can mean for your shop and its MA program.

SP 2.1: Collect Measurement Data

The first Specific Practice for the second goal is to collect your measurement data. The recommendation here is simple: Exercise your program as you defined it. You have already established measurement objectives, and based on those, you have defined a series of measures to collect. You've also indicated where and when to find this data. Now it's time to act on your plans. Assign people from your project teams to carry out the Measurement & Analysis activities. As project work moves forward, these people will begin to collect the data according to the specified procedures. As the data is collected, the numbers can be stored in the repository you have provided and then analyzed either iteratively over time or at preset analysis points. The next practices support either approach.

SP 2.2: Analyze Measurement Data

Once you have collected the data you defined for your program, you can apply the analysis techniques you've also defined. As mentioned earlier, the purpose here is to provide a consistent set of analyses across common sets of data, so that projects are analyzing data in ways that allow cross-team comparisons and also organizational roll-up. The analyses will quickly begin to produce the set of results that demonstrates project progress against the series of objectives your program is based on. As we'll see in the next practice, you'll want your team members to retain these results along with the raw data. This will provide you with the information you need to follow the fourth practice, which we'll discuss soon.

SP 2.3: Store Data and Results

The third practice for this second goal is to store the data and the results. You can do this before you perform the analyses or afterward. The purpose here is to store both types of data: the raw data that you collect and the results from the analyses you perform. The logic behind the second type is obvious. Storing the results is necessary because the results are the pieces of information you'll want to use to satisfy the fourth practice of communicating the results. The results will form the basis of any measurement reports you create for the organization. Because there is an obvious strategic link here to the measurement objectives and because results over time can begin to shape themselves into reliable trend lines, you should store the results in a repository.

The same is true for the raw data. Sometimes after this data has been analyzed, organizations delete the source information. But keeping the raw data is often just as valuable as keeping the results. Sometimes it's more valuable. Amassing raw data over time is another way to establish ongoing and developing trends. It is also valuable because you can always apply new analyses to this data, no matter how removed it is from current project work. Storing both the raw data and the results of the data analyses—either in the active repository or in an offline or archived form—is a practice that will support and strengthen your MA program.

SP 2.4: Communicate Results

The last practice recommended for the Measurement & Analysis Process Area is to communicate the results obtained during the earlier practices. This step represents the apex of your measurement program. This is where the payoff comes to fruition. Surprisingly, it's not uncommon for this step to get lost under a pile of data. If the organization has created a measurement program with vague objectives, has defined an overly ambitious series of measures, or has aimed to apply sophisticated analysis techniques out of the reach of its team members, you'll see a measurement program that stalls at the results step. Lots of plans may have been made. Lots of data could have been collected. But generating and communicating useful results, since it takes much work to do so, may fail to gel as a regular part of measurement activities.

But when you design a well-fitting measurement program (perhaps by using the practices we discuss here), you will be able to generate useful, reliable, and, over time, predictable results. It is then important to communicate these results to relevant stakeholders. These stakeholders may include team members, who want to know how they are performing with respect to targets, management teams, which need to know whether broader objectives are being met; and even your customers, who might appreciate quantitative indicators that show their objectives and parameters intact.

The Benefits of Measurement & Analysis

The PMI's PMBOK places a particular emphasis on tracking project data and reporting progress results in a quantitative fashion. In the

Execution phase of project implementation, measures of project scope, time, cost, quality targets, and other baselines are continually revisited. And in the closeout phase, the push behind customer acceptance calls for a summation of these kinds of key performance indicators. In this vein, Measurement & Analysis can play a significant role in tracking and managing project success.

Measurement & Analysis can also play a broader role and deliver what might be termed higher-level benefits to an organization. A strategically designed MA program, one built against a set of well-considered business objectives, can help focus the macro activities in an IT shop and steer it toward the business goals set by executive management.

Let's take a quick look at three benefits your shop can realize from its measurement program. The first two deal with managing projects and monitoring progress. The third deals with the higher, organizational perspective.

A Tool for Ongoing Project Control

The first advantage of a Measurement & Analysis program is that it provides you and your teams with a tool for managing ongoing project progress. Without this kind of program, your project managers are basically left to rely on individual initiative. Intuition, judgment, and experience are great traits to have, but they are rarely equally represented across your project managers. An MA program delivers a consistent and repeatable mechanism for tracking progress, applied in the same way across projects and recognized by the organization as a whole. This standardized approach allows your project managers to communicate using a common set of terms and benchmarks and to report issues and status using consistent formats.

This advantage will likely come to light very early in the adoption of your measurement program. All projects—both big and small—are made up of a series of discrete phases, an ordered collection of actionable steps. Your measurement program, targeting specific benchmarks along this lifecycle, will allow you to control performance, regulate thresholds (for time, cost, scope, and so on), and make timely adjustments in a focused manner as needed when actual performance deviates from expected performance.

A Standard for Reporting Project Performance

The benefit just described might be thought of as an internal project management advantage of your measurement program. It gives you the techniques that let you adjust the activities and momentum of your project team in order to remain on track. In that way it provides internal value for project management. Now we come to this second benefit: a standard for reporting project performance.

This benefit is one of commonality across stakeholders. Any run-and-gun project manager will tell you there are all kinds of ways to report progress or to circumvent issues of stalled progress. One of the strengths you get from a well-thought-out measurement program is that you establish up front the benchmarks of performance, that is, the definitions of what sustainable progress means and the thresholds that highlight weakened or compromised performance. Across the life of any project, you will want to report progress on a regular basis to a known set of stakeholders. It's helpful to give each of these groups the same kind of progress perspectives. At the same time, it's valuable to be able to use a common set of indicators to compare progress and performance across projects, especially when the organization is working on multiple important projects at the same time. A Measurement & Analysis program can deliver these capabilities effectively and efficiently.

A Foundation for Understanding Organizational Performance

Now we come to the third distinct benefit of a well-designed MA program: It provides a foundation for understanding organizational performance. In the two previous subsections, we discussed the specific benefits Measurement & Analysis can bring to project management: control and commonality in reporting. Here we turn to the bigger picture. After you have been exercising your program for a while, across multiple projects, you'll begin to amass sets of data that can be used to demonstrate affinity to the organization's strategic objectives. This data can highlight broad strengths and weaknesses and paint a picture of macro progress. For many organizations, this kind of picture comes only from regulatory and financial data reporting, and those pictures often emerge after it's too late to really do any substantial adjustments.

Your MA program can shore up the picture here, giving you a predetermined set of data at needed points of analysis. You can use the program as a steering tool, a wheel to help keep the rudder of organizational energy positioned on course.

Some Example Program Components

The activities you probably want to support in your MA program are pretty straightforward. Define what you want to measure, collect those measurements, store them someplace safe, analyze the data, and then report measurement results to the people who need to know them.

To help bring about those activities in an orderly and predictable manner, it helps to support the program with the right kinds of tools and resources. Assets such as policies, processes, templates, forms, and training materials can be used together to constitute a viable and valuable MA program. In this section, we'll look at some typical MA program components, tools that almost any program will find of use in the pursuit of its objectives.

MA Plan Template

Many organizations using PMI-based practices or CMMI promote the use of a Measurement & Analysis plan for project use. The plan can be included as part of the overall project plan, or it can be developed as an extension to a governing project plan. Either way, the end result is the same. The MA plan is typically developed in the planning phase and describes what measures will be taken during the project, who will collect them, where the data will be stored, what analyses will be performed, what results will be produced, what reports will be distributed, and who will receive the reports. It's the traditional what/who/when contents of any well-designed plan.

An aid to this planning is to provide your project teams with an MA plan template. The template contains the placeholders for the content you want all the plans to contain. In many cases, much of this content can be boilerplate: fixed text that applies to all projects and therefore requires little change from plan to plan. The people working on measurements can quickly adapt such a template to the needs of the current project, setting in place a complete and compliant MA plan with minimal effort.

MA Business Objectives

This component—the documented business objectives that your MA program is designed to address—cannot easily be described as typical. However, I view this component as essential to the success of any measurement program. On top of that, I see it as an essential contributor to the success of any process program. Here's why.

The business objectives, by definition, should come from executive management, the strategic arm of your organization. Because of this, your executives are obligated to think through the mission of the business, to determine empirically what they ought to aim for and how they ought to hit that mark (or those marks). That kernel of information then becomes the link between strategic direction and, at the project level, tactical motion. You can then take these objectives and shape your MA program around them. Once the program is in use, the data and results that spring from it should readily paint a picture of progress, toward both your project's tactical aims and the organization's strategic ones.

MA Collection and Analysis Procedure

The third practice under SG 1 of Measurement & Analysis recommends establishing data collection and storage procedures. The fourth practice recommends establishing analysis procedures for the data you collect. Together, these two practices make up the core activity for your measurement program: get the data and analyze it.

Many IT shops that operate using CMMI take these two and build a single process around them, a set of steps that project teams can follow from project to project to collect specific pieces of information, store them in a recognized repository, and then analyze them using specific formulas. A documented procedure can set all this in place for you. It can describe who should do the collecting, where the different data points can be found, and when in the lifecycle they should appear. It can describe the proper location for storing the data, the name of the official repository, and its physical location. And it can document the formulas and the instructions for applying the right formulas to specific data sets.

The use of a common procedure will help your teams carry out their measurement duties in an efficient manner that also complies with organizational standards and expectations. It will also serve as the foundation on which you can grow and develop your measurement program.

MA Reporting Procedure

The fourth practice under SG 2 of Measurement & Analysis recommends that you communicate the results of your analyses of the measurement data. A good tool to develop for your teams is some form of reporting procedure, a communications approach that describes the steps your folks should take to deliver results to appropriate parties. The procedure will help establish a consistent and repeatable reporting pattern. It can describe how the data should be formatted, what templates or forms are available for this formatting, who should be included in the target audience, and what distribution avenues should be used to communicate the results to this audience. By documenting a procedure to cover these activities, you can establish a common reporting mechanism across projects in your organization and use it as the basis for growth and expansion as your measurement program develops over time.

MA Repository

An MA repository is simply a holding tank for the data you collect and the analysis results you produce. It's hard to imagine any kind of measurement program without some type of repository. In its most basic form, this could be a filing cabinet. More typically, shops use databases, spreadsheets, or one of the many statistical analysis solutions available in the marketplace. The repository usually serves one of two purposes. One purpose often chosen is to use repositories solely for project data, measures that reflect the activities for a particular project. You can easily have multiple repositories, one for each ongoing project and many archived repositories from past projects. The other purpose serves an organizational need: to have a single repository that all projects use to deposit measurement data and record analysis results. Each approach is valid. Choose the format that best meets the needs of your IT shop.

Look to the Web Site for . . .

- Measurement & Analysis policy
- Measurement & Analysis process
- Measurement & Analysis metrics set
- Measurement & Analysis job roles

Chapter 9

Process & Product Quality Assurance

A big part of what Altair Solutions does for its client base deals with compliance consulting. Fine-tuned process effectiveness can only come about through process refinement. The mentoring and auditing programs we put in place are designed to help an organization realize how its processes and policies are working, and how they are helping an organization reach its goals. This insight forms the basis for improvement decisions and actions.
Kit Winner, Senior Partner, Altair Solutions, Inc.
Process improvement consulting

CMMI's Process & Product Quality Assurance Process Area sets in place practices that help a project team, or an organization, ensure that its activities stay in line with company policies and standards. The classic view is that this Process Area represents the audit arm of an organization, but it's actually a lot more than that. It's an avenue used to deliver coaching and mentoring services. It's a mechanism for documenting the value in a process program. It's a way to discover improvement opportunities. And it's a great tool for promoting consistency and predictability within the culture.

I suspect that most project managers—probably most technology professionals—would not typically associate PPQA with project management. And to be sure, its focus doesn't fall readily into the central domains of Initiation, Planning, Execution and Control, and Closure. But if you look at Control (or maybe look into Control), you can begin to see how PPQA can serve as a very real and legitimate extension of project management responsibilities.

The basic premise behind the dominant project management disciplines (the views from PMI, George Washington University, ESI, AMA, IEEE, and others) is that successful projects are born out of established work paths, and these paths are founded on processes based on series of proven practices. The effective control of those processes and practices can take you a long way toward project success. In light of this, you can think of the job of a project quality assurance (PQA)[1] analyst (a generic term for one who carries out your PPQA policies; this could be one person or a group, part time or full time) as a lieutenant to the project manager, a support arm that helps the teams stay on process and within the fold of the desired practices.

In this chapter, we'll look at Process & Product Quality Assurance and discuss how project managers can use PPQA to strengthen their project teams and harmonize project activities with organizational standards, practices, and policies.

The Purpose of Process & Product Quality Assurance

The purpose of PPQA is pretty straightforward: to help project teams stay on the course of established processes. The tie-in with project management becomes clear when you appreciate that staying on process is just as important as staying on schedule, staying on budget, staying on track with resources, staying in touch with customers and with management. In fact, it's probably process that helps project managers do all of those things.

Of course, we need to make two assumptions here.

---

1. That term, PQA, is mine. You can call the role anything you want. The central idea is that someone is provided to work with project management to mediate process compliance.

In Chapter 2, we discussed two philosophies that a project team must adopt in order for a framework like CMMI to deliver its maximum benefit. First is a commitment to process, the attitude that it is better to manage a project through process than without it. Second is a commitment to time, the belief that the best way to shape a process program that will more and more ensure project management success is by exercising that program over time. You can look at Process & Product Quality Assurance as the part of your process program that shores up these two beliefs. So for PPQA to serve a role for a project team, two assumptions are required.

The first assumption is that there are processes in place to follow. If you look to references such as the PMBOK or CMMI (or ISO 9001, ITIL, or other well-known models), you can get an idea of the kinds of processes that are helpful to planning and running a project. Without processes, PPQA has nothing to look at. The second assumption is that your team sees value in following the processes, as does your organization—and that you want to manage based within the bounds of established policies and processes.

If those beliefs and assumptions are valid, PPQA is positioned to add value to your project management efforts. How does PPQA do that? How does it work to achieve its purpose? In its most basic form, PPQA sets PQA analysts into the project stream to perform three jobs:

1. Perform periodic project audits to assess compliance.
2. Help teams get back into compliance should they fall out of compliance.
3. Use engagement opportunities to coach, mentor, and improve.

Let's take a quick look at how these jobs support project and organizational management.

Project teams tend to work for the project manager, so they should want to adhere to the work paths the project manager establishes for the team. Project managers tend to work for executive management, so the project managers should want to adhere to the work paths the organization has adopted.

That brings us to the topic of process ownership. If you are currently managing projects using some form of process program, or if you are considering building one similar to the descriptions in this book, you should appreciate the fact that management ultimately owns the process program. Your teams will use it. As project manager, you will control and monitor it, but senior management is its true owner. The logic behind this is pretty straightforward. The process program reflects the values of the organization; it supports the execution of key activities and the production of key work products important to the organization.

It's natural and logical that management should want to check up from time to time on how well people in the organization—namely, members of its project teams—are taking to the process program, to verify that the program is useful and well managed.

The Process & Product Quality Assurance function can be seen as the eyes and ears of management, a reporting avenue management can count on to receive objective insight into the program's use. Viewed from this perspective, we can see that PPQA can support management's objectives about process adoption by supporting established workflows, promoting organizational consistency, providing online coaching and mentoring, and providing a window on improvement.

Support Established Workflows

The PQA analyst working with a project team has one chief responsibility: to ensure that the teams follow established workflows. As project managers plan and run projects, they should be well aware of these workflows. In fact, the workflows will likely be embedded in the plans and schedules, and they may also serve as reference points for project tracking activities. Following the workflows helps make project activity more predictable, and that aids project management.

The job of the PQA analyst is to periodically confirm that the teams are staying on process and following the workflows. The project manager will keep an eye on this obligation also, but by necessity he or she also needs to focus on many other obligations (resources, schedules, and so on). The PQA analyst can be seen as a lieutenant to the project manager, providing insight and encouragement for workflow compliance. And by supporting workflow compliance at the project level, the PQA analyst promotes its continued use at the cross-organizational level.

Promote Organizational Consistency

A PPQA program helps promote the consistent use of standards and management techniques across the organization, a practice that will only strengthen project management's position. This idea of consistency (and repeatability) is often underappreciated. But the capability it delivers to an organization—and to its project teams—can be substantial.

A good process program will help guide the conduct of project teams. It reflects the culture of the organization; it defines a specific way of doing business. Think of KFC, the chicken outfit. This is an organization with a great process for making fried chicken. Every KFC restaurant, from Kansas City to Paris, France, follows that process, so you can count on the meal you get in one location to taste just like one you'd get anywhere else.

Consistency gives your organization its culture. Consistency also gives your projects a predictable environment to operate from. The PQA analysts you assign are charged with promoting this consistency. They provide executive management, project management, and project teams (not to mention customers and other stakeholders) with a reporting avenue that enables this consistency within and across project activity.

Provide Online Coaching and Mentoring

Here's another obligation for the project manager: Keep your team members effective, efficient, and well focused. But a project manager may or may not have full control over who is assigned to the project team. You may get some veterans, you may get some novices; some top performers, some mediocre talents. This is another area where you can get support from the PQA analyst.

By definition, PQA analysts are people with a lot of knowledge about your organization's process program and performance standards. And this makes them a great resource for coaching and mentoring your team members in the ways of process.

The PQA analyst's main job is probably auditing, but this does not preclude a proactive involvement. The preparatory nature of coaching and mentoring delivers two distinct benefits to project management: It serves as ongoing job training for project members, and it prepares your members to demonstrate solid compliance when it comes to audits.

Provide a Window on Improvement

Project management is all about realizing project commitments, profitability, and increased efficiencies—in other words, lessons learned. Most managers support this by conducting team reviews at the Closure phase of project activity. This is typically handled through lessons learned or postmortem sessions. These can prove very valuable for identifying ways to do things better on future projects.

PQA analysts will also prove to be a valuable source of lessons learned and improvement potentials. This is because PQA analysts have regular insight into how project teams are using and managing organizational processes. Their work positions them to be early identifiers of compliance problems, of poorly designed processes, of cumbersome work products, or of issues surrounding training and capability. The audit process can be seen as an opportunity to elicit improvement ideas, open improvement windows, and identify improvement targets.

Coaches or Cops?

Here's a choice that can make a real difference in the success of your projects and in the success of your process program. Does the organization see the job of the PQA analyst as being that of cop? Of collaring process violators and ticketing them back into compliance? Unfortunately, plenty of technology shops adopt this angle. The problem is, it's not a very effective approach. The cop angle tends to emphasize compliance failure over the benefits of process use. It also tends to set up a wall between project teams and process teams, pitting "us" against "them."

The much better angle is to view your PQA analysts as coaches. Their job is to promote the value of process, to make themselves available to help people stay on process, and to periodically take measures of compliance benchmarks. (See the upcoming related sidebar, Auditing Process, Not People.)

Process & Product Quality Assurance Goals and Practices

CMMI defines two Specific Goals and four Specific Practices for the Process & Product Quality Assurance Process Area. Here is the official specification text for each of these elements.

SG 1   Objectively Evaluate Processes and Work Products

Adherence to the performed process and associated work products and services to applicable process descriptions, standards, and procedures is objectively evaluated.

SP 1.1   Objectively Evaluate Processes

Objectively evaluate the designated performed processes against the applicable process descriptions, standards, and procedures.

SP 1.2   Objectively Evaluate Work Products and Services

Objectively evaluate the designated work products and services against the applicable process descriptions, standards, and procedures.

SG 2   Provide Objective Insight

Noncompliance issues are objectively tracked and communicated, and resolution is ensured.

SP 2.1   Communicate and Ensure Resolution of Noncompliance Issues

Communicate quality issues and ensure resolution of noncompliance issues with the staff and managers.

SP 2.2   Establish Records

Establish and maintain records of quality assurance activities.

Generic Goals and Practices

See Chapter 10 for information about the important Generic Goals and Practices that support project management success for all the Process Areas at Maturity Level 2.

Let's look at how you might implement these practices in your organization.

SG 1: Objectively Evaluate Processes and Work Products

The first goal established for Process & Product Quality Assurance is to objectively evaluate your processes and work products. Under this goal are two very similar practices: to evaluate processes and to evaluate work products (and services as they apply). The job of PPQA is to provide objective insight into the use, value, and effectiveness of your process program. The focus is straightforward enough. Across the life of a project, your teams engage in an ongoing stream of activities as they work to produce a series of deliverables and end products. In a project that adheres to established project management tenets, these activities and products will be planned well in advance. They will be mapped out in documents and schedules. Costs and timelines will be attached to them. Management and customers will be looking for them at set intervals.

Naturally, the chief job of project management is to ensure that these activities and products come about as planned, according to schedule. So in a very real way, the project manager is a process and product quality analyst. CMMI sees indisputable value there. But CMMI recommends that you augment this capability with an objective viewpoint, one you can periodically bring into the picture to confirm, without conflict of interest, that process is indeed being followed and that work products are being produced according to organizational standards. The idea is to use PPQA to help project teams stay on process, to identify where improvements might be made, and to report to management as to the adoption depth of the program components (Figure 9–1).

Since both of these practices require basically the same kinds of considerations, we'll treat them together in this section. We'll also discuss some tips for making the most of your PPQA program.

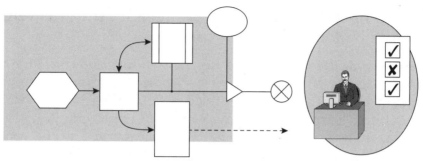

Figure 9–1: *Insight from outside provides a path for continuous improvement*

Objective *versus* Independent

The words *objective* and *objectively* pop up eight times in the goals and practices for PPQA. Many people think *objective* means the same thing as *independent*. Their idea is that you can't objectively evaluate something if you're too closely connected to it. For auditors to be effective, it's probably best that they are independent, that they have no conflict of interest between the item being audited and the audit results.

That's a valid interpretation. And if you can implement your PPQA program using resources independent of the project, so much the better. However, it's not required.

CMMI is shaped to realize its audit goals through the use of objective criteria. This can be seen in such things as checklists, predefined audit forms, and published guidelines. The reasoning here is that integrated resources can perform valid audits using this criteria; the objectiveness of the evaluation tools removes subjective interpretation as much as possible. Through this definition, small IT shops as well as larger ones can implement quality assurance practices without having to delegate separate and independent resources.

SP 1.1: Objectively Evaluate Processes and SP 1.2: Objectively Evaluate Work Products and Services

These two practices look at how you create products and what form the products take as they appear. In essence, someone (or some group) will periodically visit the project team and perform some kind of inspection, assessment, or audit. (It's not important what you call it.) How you shape these practices can be highly customized to the needs, shape, and structure of your project teams. The core qualities you want to account for in each evaluation should be fairness, reasonableness, objectivity, and openness. You might also find four activities helpful when shaping how you evaluate processes and work products.

1. Select key processes and products.
2. Establish an audit procedure.
3. Provide an appeals avenue.
4. Establish a common PPQA plan.

Let's take a quick look at each one.

Auditing Process, Not People

Here's an important reminder: PPQA is not about judging the performance of your team members. That function is best left to organizational management and your human resource experts. PPQA is simply about assessing how management tools (processes, templates, tools, policies, and so on) are performing for the organization and how well the project teams—taken as a whole—adhere to and apply these resources.

So work to make sure that your audit forms, reports, and policies reflect this distinction. Make sure that your PQA analysts audit with this in mind. And be sure to communicate this approach to all the project teams within your organization.

Select Key Processes and Products

Some IT shops have robust PPQA programs. They include all the major processes and work products in what they audit. Other organizations have more focused programs. They look at select things. The approach you take should reflect the needs of your organization. You don't have to audit everything all the time. You probably do want to audit those activities and products that will have significant impact on project success or will help the organization at large accomplish its mission. So select (and document for all to reference) just what your PQA analysts need to examine.

If you're basing your program on the Process Areas we discuss in this book, you might want to take a periodic look at what each of these asks you to do or create. If you've established detailed plans and schedules for project management, you might want to look at portions of those from time to time. The focus here is on adopting an organizational approach to PPQA. Identify what you think is important to audit, and then apply that over time to projects across the organization.

Establish an Audit Procedure

One quality you'll want to embed in all your audit and reporting activities is consistency. Consistency is essential for several reasons. It's a way to ensure audits are perceived as being fair—folks see them going the same way for everyone. It's a way to gauge how effectively the process works. And it's a way to support multiple PQA analysts working across different projects. The best way to establish and promote this consistency is to establish and deploy an audit procedure. The audit procedure is best represented as the documented steps and activities your PQA analysts will follow each time they embark on an audit with members of your project teams.

The procedure you establish should probably describe such details as how your analysts will notify teams of an upcoming audit and how they'll communicate what processes or work products will be assessed; what standards of performance will be used; which tools (such as checklists, forms, and so on) must be used; what kinds of reports will emerge from each audit; and which audiences will receive the reports.

In short, this procedure can represent a major component of your audit process.

The documented audit procedure can also serve as a great tool for communicating with the project teams. By openly sharing it with the teams, you can give them the information they need to prepare for and work within the audit process effectively and with little anxiety.

Provide an Appeals Avenue

From time to time, your PPQA activities will no doubt reveal issues concerning noncompliance. Your analysts will need to record, report, and follow up on these. But this does not have to be a one-way street—in fact, it should not be one. Any time a team is audited and a noncompliance event is found, the team should have a way to appeal what appears to be a negative finding, to voice their opinion as to compliance before a final conclusion is reached. It's helpful to think of the team's input as a critical prerequisite to any compliance decisions.

If there is still disagreement after an official opinion is rendered by the PQA analysts, the teams should still have the opportunity to address management with their thoughts on why the decision might be inaccurate. The audit process will not appear so daunting if those being audited know they'll have opportunities to appeal any conclusions they don't agree with.

Establish a Common PPQA Plan

Planning is a core function in any project management discipline or approach. In Chapter 3, we looked at the essential value of project planning and how project success depends on it. In Chapter 6, we saw the importance of planning for configuration management, for how you'll control the evolution of project work products. And now we see the opportunity to develop a Process & Product Quality Assurance plan. (Some shops simply call this the project quality assurance plan.) The rationale behind developing the plan is pretty easy to see. To rely on PQA activities as a way to gain objective insight into compliance issues, you'll probably want to plan and schedule the resources and activities required to see this effort through.

Many IT shops treat the PPQA plan as simply an extension of the overall project plan. Other shops prefer to develop a stand-alone plan that nevertheless ties in with the project plan. Either approach is valid, as long as each project team has some form of PPQA plan it can reference.

The PPQA plan you produce for the project should contain the traditional elements of any good plan, with these elements now built around audit activities:

- Which project items will be audited and when
- Which project team members will be required to participate
- What the compliance goals and objectives are (see the next subsection)
- Who will handle the audit duties
- How audits will be conducted
- What appeals procedure is available
- What reports will be issued and to whom

Some PPQA Tips

The techniques described for SP 1.1 and SP 1.2 should help you shape your PPQA program along effective and practical lines. But you might also wish to weigh some softer considerations as you think through the purpose of auditing and the value it can bring to the organization. You can employ the tips described here to make the most of your Process & Product Quality Assurance program.

Establish Compliance Goals

Here's a tip I have seen work well in many IT shops, big and small: Establish compliance goals. This is a great way to set an attainable success bar while promoting your process program within your organization. When establishing compliance goals, people often jump to thinking of numbers like 95% or 90%, numbers from our schooldays recognized as denoting superior performance. Of course, everyone would love to get As on evaluations. But that might not always be practical, especially if your process program is new or if your people are new to process. In these instances, I find it beneficial to set a lower goal.

Starting out, the organization might establish a compliance goal of, say, 75% for the first six months. Then whenever an audit reveals that the team hit that mark, the project gets an A. If the team members worked hard but managed to reach only 65% of the goal, perhaps they get a B, still respectable. This is a way to reward efforts to improve, to get better, while not overburdening teams with expectations set too high.

Once most of the project teams are operating comfortably in this range, you can increase the compliance goal, say, from 75% to 85%. Over time, you should see the whole organization migrating naturally to higher and higher levels of compliance.

As you establish these compliance goals, make sure you build these targets into your audit activities and audit reports, and make sure you communicate these management goals—they should be phrased as management goals—to your project teams.

Audit Like a Partner, Not a Judge

This is an important angle to consider. We mentioned earlier that you can think of your PQA analysts as lieutenants to project management captains. They provide a very complementary level of oversight and status for your projects. But sometimes it's tempting to turn the role into that of a judge, banging down the gavel on anything that appears out of order. That approach, however, never proves to be very productive. No one wants a judge looking over his or her shoulder, especially if that judge pops in only from time to time, free from the rest of project turmoil.

A better approach is for your PQA analysts to think of themselves as partners with the project teams. Their job is to promote compliance, to provide coaching and mentoring to those who might need it, and to recognize efforts that demonstrate strong compliance. This angle should be communicated in your analysts' demeanor, that is, in the ways they interface with team members and help teams who have drifted get back on course.

If you think of the PQA analyst role as one that supports project success, emphasizes compliance over noncompliance, and shows the willingness to sit in the trenches with the project team to see process through, you'll find that a constructive partnership is built early and strengthens over time.

Reward Compliance

A final consideration for supporting a successful PPQA program is to reward compliance. In the realm of project management, success usually means that costs, schedules, and product integrity all met or exceeded expectations. The same sort of standard should apply to process program compliance. After all, the underlying assumption is that process is the path we take to success. So if the project was successful, it was probably in part because the team followed the process path.

Especially in organizations new to process, it's beneficial to recognize and reward compliance success. Rewards in this vein can come in many forms. You might recognize teams in front of their peers. You can issue plaques or certificates. You might host luncheons. And of course you can provide that age-old, proven incentive: money.

Rewarding compliance has two distinct benefits for the organization. First, it communicates to the project teams the value the organization sees as a whole in process compliance. Second, it gives people a tangible reason to adopt and embrace process in a way that helps cement its practice across the organization.

SG 2: Provide Objective Insight

The first goal of Process & Product Quality Assurance is to periodically evaluate processes and work products. The second goal stems from the first. Based on the results of the evaluations, you provide objective insight to the organization as to how the project teams are succeeding with process compliance and work product standards.

Such insight can potentially come from multiple sources in the organization. One of these is project management itself. If project management is diligently maintaining managerial control over project activities, it stands to reason that a project manager could provide a degree of insight into process and work products performance. The same holds true for the members of the project teams. Who better, some might say, to really know about such things than the people right in the middle of all that activity? Both of these sources can and should provide this kind of insight. But in the realm of CMMI for development efforts (and this is supported by other project management disciplines as well), a supplementary degree of objective insight can prove invaluable.

It's easy to see that given only their own means to rely on, project management and project team members could have a tendency to be biased, even if the bias is blind, when it comes to reporting compliance findings. So it helps if objective measures can be set in place to augment and further support these observations. As mentioned earlier, objective insight can be realized through the use of independent evaluation criteria and, when and if available, the use of independent resources.

There are two Specific Practices related to this second goal. Let's discuss each in turn.

SP 2.1: Communicate and Ensure Resolution of Noncompliance Issues

In the first goal for this Process Area, CMMI recommends that you periodically evaluate compliance with established processes and conformance to work product standards. SP 2.1 is a direct follow-up. Here it is assumed that sometimes, as a result of an evaluation, you'll uncover noncompliance issues. Perhaps process wasn't followed exactly as it should have been. Maybe a document or a plan wasn't produced with the correct content. Discovering and even recording these noncompliance events is important, but the responsibility goes a step farther. It is just as important to communicate the noncompliance and then follow up to ensure that the issues underlying the deviation have been resolved or at least addressed.

The key here is to shape this activity not as a judgment or act of fault-finding, but as an opportunity for improvement and a way for the organization to gain insight into the value and use of its process program.

In this light, then, here are four tips to help you communicate and ensure resolution of noncompliance issues in an appropriate and constructive way.

1. Remember that noncompliance can be a good thing.
2. Keep the goal in mind.
3. Communicate the value of compliance.
4. Follow up with support.

Remember That Noncompliance Can Be a Good Thing

Yes, noncompliance can be a good thing. It is not always an undesirable trait. It can be helpful to remember this because many PPQA programs tend to automatically label all noncompliance issues as failures. But that is sometimes not the case; in fact, I would say that it is often not the case. When your evaluations uncover something out of whack, the true cause might not be resistance to process, which is usually the first assumption in immature PPQA programs. If you look closely, you might find that the process or work standard is poorly designed, that it's getting in the way of project activity. You might find that people have not been adequately trained. You might find that there's more variance in work cycles than you originally thought. In these cases, noncompliance can be a very good thing. It sheds light on improvement opportunities; it gives you and management insight into the effectiveness and efficiencies of operations. And that's the chief focus of PPQA.

Keep the Goal in Mind

In the same way that noncompliance can sometimes be a good thing and sometimes a bad thing, so can it also be a nothing. Here is where your sense of proportion and judgment becomes important. When you uncover a compliance issue, try to gauge its importance in relation to the goals of the project and the objectives of your process program. If the variance is obviously one that could impact the project or shift the shop away from its quality focus, certainly it should be addressed. But you may also find, especially if your program is new or if people are new to it, that noncompliance is not always a call for corrective action and follow-up. Small variances or variances that don't impact goals and objectives might be best handled as learning experiences, as bumps in the road. If you and your PQA analysts can keep this interpretation open, people will quickly begin to see that the spirit of process improvement is the important element at play and that the law is in place to help that spirit thrive.

Communicate the Value of Compliance

One way to resolve noncompliance issues in a positive way is as simple as communicating the value of compliance, reminding your teams that compliance promotes control and fosters success. It can be easy to spin this view the negative way by communicating the penalties of noncompliance. But that approach hides what is clearly a beneficial position. If you see your teams beginning to drift off process, the best way to get them back on might be such a reminder. And if you do this often enough and with a level of enthusiasm that carries your personal commitment, you'll probably find that your teams drift off course less often.

Follow Up with Support

Ensuring the resolution of noncompliance issues most often requires follow-up. The resolution may take the form of rework, or a commitment to work differently in the future, or additional training. Whatever form it takes, it's important for your PQA analysts to make sure that the resolution actions are carried out as recommended.

Resolution avenues typically follow three pathways.

1. The PQA analyst and the team agree that something really is out of compliance. The PQA analyst recommends (and documents) a corrective action, the team accepts it, and the PQA analyst follows up later to make sure the corrective action was taken.

2. The PQA analyst and the team agree that noncompliance did occur, but after a discussion they both agree that there was a valid reason for the noncompliance. In this case, there may be little need for follow-up (but the event and discussion should still be documented).

3. The PQA analyst sees noncompliance, but the team disagrees. Even after discussion there is still disagreement. Here it's helpful to have a documented escalation procedure, a pathway folks can take to appeal a noncompliance finding. This usually moves the issue up for an executive decision. These types of noncompliance events usually require the most follow-up because a mismatch in understanding genuinely exists.

SP 2.2: **Establish Records**

The second and final practice for the second goal recommended for Process & Product Quality Assurance calls for you to establish records of your PPQA activities. This is a simple recommendation but an important one. For all seven Process Areas we discuss in this book, there is always some form of record keeping. Records in this context serve two general purposes. First, they provide project management with a reference for determining the current degree of process and standards compliance. Second, they provide the organization with a set of data points it can use to consider and plan for process improvement in the future.

The unspoken term to apply here is *useful*. You want to establish useful records, that is, to shape the records you generate from PPQA audits and activities in such a way that they can contribute both to project success and to organizational success. If the aim is to simply generate reports, you'll quickly find that teams can put together an unending stream of records, most of it very accurate but perhaps not very useful. So, as you plan the kind of PPQA program you feel is right for your organization, think ahead to the need for establishing records of results and then reporting those results to their relevant audiences.

Here are four considerations you might wish to think through to help you establish useful records of your PPQA activities.

1. Reports to project management
2. Reports to the team
3. Reports to organizational management
4. Ways to shape the records

Reports to Project Management

The records you establish to reflect the results of PPQA audits and activities will hold a special interest for project management. These records will probably reflect to a large extent the smoothness of operations on a project. The audits that the PQA analysts conduct will reveal how well the team is staying on process and working within organizational standards. This should be of interest to project managers for two reasons.

First, it paints a picture of managerial effectiveness. If the teams are staying on process and working within standards, this confirms the assumption that the team is adhering to project management controls.

Second, it supports the commitment to quality. The records can be used by project management as a way to demonstrate that the right products are being produced by the team according to plan and that they are being constructed to meet predefined standards.

We mentioned earlier that PPQA practices can be seen as an adjunct service to project management. The records you establish here make that analogy real. They provide effective insight into project team work so that project management is better able to deliver on its commitments.

Reports to the Team

The PQA analysts who conduct audits, manage noncompliance, and then issue reports should do so always with the members of the project team in mind. In fact, many would support the idea that the team members may be the primary audience for PQA reports. The reasoning here is pretty clear. Auditing is not a tool to judge people's performance; it's a technique to gain insight into operational effectiveness. If a team is having a hard time staying on process, the PQA analyst is often the first-line source that can address this issue. PQA analysts can use audits and noncompliance records and reports as a springboard for recognizing solid performance and also as an opportunity to identify organizational needs for training, process refinement, enhanced project support, and so on.

When the PQA reports are shared with the team, this information has the opportunity to be properly and thoroughly vetted. That can lead to increased insight for both project management and executive management.

A final point here: The team members should always be among the primary audience members for PPQA records simply because they are the ones who execute your process program and the key project activities. Auditing should be set in place to support them, so they should be among the prime receivers of the reports.

Reports to Organizational Management

In the two cases just discussed, the use of PPQA records is intended to enhance project effectiveness. Here we see an added dimension: the use of PPQA records to enhance organizational effectiveness. People in project management might be responsible for what could be called local compliance to process and procedures. They manage projects—and the local activities—with a view toward compliance. The project team members are also concerned with local compliance. They deal with the here and now of project work and use process and procedures to shape that work.

But the people in organizational management—executive management, if you will—require another view. They own the process program, the procedures, and the methodologies. They have a responsibility to use PPQA records to gain insight into how the organization is operating as an organization. Audit results will inherently point out levels of harmonies, synchronicities, and consistencies across operating groups.

Management's job here is akin to a fiduciary responsibility. Management should use the PPQA records as a source for understanding cultural behaviors, for discerning improvement opportunities, and for shaping future strategic and tactical directions.

Ways to Shape the Records

The fourth consideration when planning useful PPQA reports involves ways to shape the data in the records. By *shape* I mean to give the data context, to present it in a way that captures the momentum of the organization, either as a snapshot in time or as a general trend. Here is where your PPQA records can truly provide insight and shed light into the organization.

Some IT shops turn their PPQA records into graphs that pictorially display compliance and performance data. They will then embed these visuals into reports presented to project management, the project team, or executive management. Each audience might receive a different visual report, each one emphasizing a graphical summary relevant to a particular business view.

Other shops might integrate a series of records to establish and communicate trends over time and then chart progress toward a predefined goal. Still others might create tables and scorecards that summarize how project teams are doing in relation to one another.

The shape you give to your PPQA records is entirely up to you and the needs of your organization. But keep shape in shape. The shape you give to your data—potentially mounds of data—turns it into information.

Some Other Ways to Achieve the Practices

In the domain of CMMI-DEV, the role of Process & Product Quality Assurance may be one of the model's more unique components. How you address the four Specific Practices recommended under this Process Area rests entirely in your domain. You are free to interpret these practices into any design that can provide the right level of objectivity and insight based on the size, structure, and culture of your group. That said, here are some valid interpretations you might consider.

- *Audit each other.* Organizations don't necessarily need a dedicated PPQA team in order to effectively conduct PPQA activities. You can always share the responsibility. Members from one project team can be charged with auditing members of another project team. As long as you establish objective evaluation tools (such as checklists and forms), there's no reason why people can't audit each other.

- *Make it part time.* Many small to medium-sized IT shops don't have the resources to dedicate to PPQA activities on a full-time basis. That's okay. The job of coach, mentor, or auditor can be a part-time role. For example, a person who functions as a business analyst on a project team might be asked to devote, say, eight hours a month to serving as a PQA analyst. The same approach could be used for other members of your project teams. In many cases and in many organizations, compliant PPQA activities do not require a commitment of forty hours per week. There is no reason why the function can't be well handled on a part-time basis.

- *Rotate the job.* If yours is a small shop, here's a handy idea: Rotate the job of the PQA analysts and their audit and reporting activities. This is similar to the part-time tactic just mentioned. In this case, you assign a person to the role for a set period of time (like a special tour of duty), and when that tour is up, you appoint someone else. This way the job rotates around your people. This approach often works well because it not only offloads the work on a temporary and equal basis but also spreads the PQA expertise throughout the organization, turning it into a commonly shared organizational capability.

- *Hire it out.* There's no reason why you can't outsource the functions of PPQA. I know of several companies that offer this kind of service. On a fixed schedule, they will send in their PQA analysts (trained of course in your methodology) and these independent analysts will conduct all scheduled audits and produce all requested forms of audit records and audit reports. In this way, outsourcing lets you focus more on core project management and development work while still maintaining compliance with PPQA recommendations, targets, and goals.

- *Combine audits in reviews.* If you feel you don't have the time or the resources to address PPQA activities as singular events, consider combining your audits and assessments with other team activities, such as peer reviews or status meetings. Whenever you bring team members together, this can be a good time to augment the event with some PPQA oversight activities. This way folks don't have to account for such oversight as a separate activity. You can blend it into the typical project review and status activities. The results should be just as valid as focusing on PPQA as an independent set of activities.

Don't Forget to Audit the PPQA Folks, Too

Here's an often-overlooked facet of effective PPQA programs: From time to time, you will want to audit your PQA analysts to ensure that they are following the processes and standards that shape their program. You'll also want to establish records and issue reports so that the PQA teams and organizational management will have the same insight needed for smooth operations and for the identification of potential improvement opportunities and targets within this realm.

The Benefits of Process & Product Quality Assurance

As noted at the start of this chapter, Process & Product Quality Assurance is a CMMI Process Area that many people might not associate with project management success. I hope some of the information here has made it clear that you can indeed use PPQA to further the reach of your project management activities and to help ensure that your project goals and objectives are being met.

PPQA complements your project management efforts in multiple ways. Its unique knowledge domain combined with its insight into project and team performance mean that it can provide you with new and additional facets of management information.

This section describes four of the chief benefits you can realize by implementing the practices recommended for this Process Area.

Support for Project Management Goals

Cost, schedule, resources, quality: that's the well-recognized project management *quartet du foci*. This intertwined and interrelated set of attributes impacts most definitions of project success. Each attribute represents a commitment between the customer and the project team, and between the project team and management. The ultimate goal of project management is to deliver—at the agreed-upon cost, at the agreed-upon time, and by using the stated resources—a product the customers recognize as that thing they wanted. The logical attitude is one that says, if process can't help you meet those goals, skip process. And in most cases, that's probably the right attitude to take.

The fact is that process has been proven to help you reach those goals. And PPQA can provide direct support in this mission. Working with project management, your PQA analysts can help ensure that work products are produced according to organizational standards, that appropriate work paths are being followed, and that noncompliance issues are resolved in an orderly fashion. These oversight services help keep the teams focused, help reduce rework, provide an avenue for online coaching, and extend the eyes and ears of project management. All of that supports the attainment of cost, schedule, resource, and quality goals.

Insight into Project and Organizational Movement

Many people see the benefits of Process & Product Quality Assurance, but they see it more as an after-the-fact contribution (see the next two benefit points). But your PPQA program can also provide you with an ongoing and complementary source of progress data, a source that project management can access to augment its view of things.

If your organization is following a process program (or if it plans to), you can easily see how the process can become the project, how implementing the steps in various linked processes can begin to shape the path of project execution. In the PMI world, we rely on variations of the IPEC model: Initiation, Planning, Execution/Control, and Closure. At the macro level, project management steers us through those phases. Process can easily live within that framework. In fact, they can make up the content of the framework. Therefore, with your PQA analysts' diligence in looking into process compliance, you get the added benefit of additional objective data on how the project is going, on what progress is being made at what rate, and on any process or performance issues that may be coming ahead. By working closely with project managers, PPQA can help you meet your project and organizational performance objectives.

An Open Window on Improvement

It's probably safe to assume that, most of the time, a project manager is pressed to focus on issues other than process performance and process compliance. Yet these issues deserve their own level of focus. Companies count on process. They rely on it to guide them through myriad activities and commitments. If the process doesn't work well, it's likely that teams won't be able to work well, and projects might falter.

A key responsibility of executive management is to keep an eye on its processes and to ensure that they are operating as best they can within given conditions. That's what makes PPQA an important Process Area surrounding project management. PPQA works at the front line of process implementation. Your PQA analysts will likely deal with process users all the time and so are in a unique position to learn about process performance, to observe it in action, and to discover improvement opportunities. PPQA serves as a great catalyst for an ongoing SWOT analysis: observing strengths and weaknesses, determining opportunities and threats.

A Source for Value Management

Project management is all about value management—bringing quality, profitability, and efficiencies to your project. Executive management is also all about value management—building an enterprise and a culture that operates successfully. In this light, Process & Product Quality Assurance can be seen as a contributor to value management. Through the objective insight provided by PPQA practices, project management and executive management can ascertain which processes are working well and which ones might need attention. They can measure the organization's progress toward compliance goals and position the organization for improvement and continued success in the future.

In fact, the fundamental assumption about process is that process works; following a tried and true path is a proven way of reaching your goals. Process—and especially process improvement—supports efficient design, effective use of resources, and the proper application of energies. The job of PPQA is to help keep an eye on these qualities across project teams. In this way, PPQA supports the direction and goal of value management.

Some Example Program Components

The way you implement Process & Product Quality Assurance highly depends on the size, culture, and focus of your organization. Maybe you'll use part-time analysts. Maybe your audits will focus on a small set of process components. PPQA, like most Process Areas within CMMI, is designed for flexible interpretation. The components you build to support the program can be, and indeed should be, a reflection of your style of project management and the particular organization goals established for your teams.

But however you work or however your organization is shaped, some elements of a PPQA program can be common across technology shops. This section mentions some typical components that almost every PPQA program can use in some form or another.

PPQA Policy

The consistency in reporting and insight you can expect to receive from a well-designed PPQA program needs to be backed up by an organizational policy that establishes its value to project management and organizational growth. This can be achieved through the adoption of an executive policy that promotes PPQA activities on all projects. Such a policy—usually a concise, one- or two-page document—promotes the use of quality assurance practices throughout the organization, endorses the support of PPQA resources across development groups, and recognizes the value PPQA activities can bring to the organization and its mission at large.

PPQA Plan Template

Earlier in this chapter, we looked at the value of preparing a PPQA plan for your technology projects. The plan lets your project team know up front when it will be audited, who will do the auditing, what elements will be assessed, and what qualities will be looked for. A plan template will help your PQA analysts plan in a consistent manner from project to project; it will give form and structure to the audit method. The template also makes a useful training tool, serving as a cue sheet about the essential considerations when working out an audit approach for any single project.

PPQA Audit Procedure

A documented audit procedure will help make your audit program objective. It will help ensure that your PQA analysts perform audits in largely the same way, regardless of different personalities. And it will help you communicate the strategy and method of auditing to different project teams. The audit procedure—just like any well-designed process—should describe such factors as the inputs needed to commence an audit, the activities or artifacts to be assessed, the criteria for evaluation, the manner in which results will be reported, the roles responsible for conducting these steps, and any measures that need to be collected from the process.

PPQA Audit Notification

It's handy to provide your PQA analysts with some form of standardized audit notification. This might be something as simple as sample e-mail text. The value here is to ensure that audits are not conducted willy-nilly. Teams should be notified a comfortable time in advance that an audit is upcoming. Such a notice typically informs the team about what will be audited, when the audit will take place, who needs to be available for the audit, and which artifacts will be requested. The idea is to prepare the team to properly prepare for the audit. A standard audit notice can help your PQA analysts work with your teams to maximize audit success.

Audit Form and Checklist

In addition to a PPQA plan and a documented audit procedure, it's a good idea to equip your PQA analysts with the forms and checklists they can use as they conduct audits. The forms and checklist really support two important aspects of any audit program. First, they establish the independent criteria that make an audit truly objective, that is, as removed from personal interpretation as is practical. Second, they give both the PQA analysts and the project team members a common reference they can use for planning and anticipating the audit, completing it, and reporting on audit results.

Audit Results Report Form

We noted earlier, when looking at SP 2.2 for this Process Area, the importance of designing useful audit reports for your PPQA program. Naturally, there are many ways you can report on and show audit results. The results will mean more when they are presented using an established format, one that can be used for all project teams and managers, and thus one that will be instantly recognizable across multiple efforts within the organization. Look at your organization, and then design a report form that you feel reflects the way the data will convey the most meaning and impact to the project team, project management, and executive management.

Look to the Web Site for . . .

- PPQA policy
- PPQA audit procedure
- PPQA noncompliance procedure
- PPQA plan contents
- PPQA audit checklist

Chapter 10

Supporting Success with the Generic Goals

Without a doubt process can be used as a competitive differentiator in a product-based company, and it's even more important for a services firm. Products and features are easily copied and so process excellence is one of the few differentiators a company can use to compete successfully over the long-term. How eTrials deploys, manages, and supports software to run clinical trials is one of our biggest competitive advantages, and is not easily duplicated.

John Cline, CEO, eTrials, Inc.
Data management for clinical drug trials

In the preface, I mentioned that the focus of this work is to forge a link between project management success and use of the SEI's CMMI-DEV. The idea is that, aside from being a very effective process improvement model, CMMI directly supports the fundamental needs of project management, particularly the seven Process Areas typically implemented at Maturity Level 2. I also want to demonstrate how, for those readers with a PMP focus, the Knowledge Areas contained in the PMI's PMBOK complement and augment the Level 2 goals and practices.

In Chapters 3 through 9, we looked at each of these seven Maturity Level 2 Process Areas: Project Planning, Project Monitoring & Control, Requirements Management, Configuration Management, Supplier Agreement Management, Measurement & Analysis, and Process & Product Quality Assurance. All of these bring to the table specific and practical activities that can help project managers control those areas they seek most to influence: scope, cost, schedule, resources, and quality. It's helpful here to remind you that the main intention of this book is not to guide you to achieve a Maturity Level rating recognized by the SEI. It's to help you use CMMI to achieve successful project outcomes. However, if you have followed along carefully with the recommendations in this book and have made plans to implement those Process Areas in the ways we've discussed, there's nothing that should prevent you from achieving that maturity target if it is indeed part of your game plan.

That's why this chapter is so important.

Here we come to a discussion of the Generic Goals within CMMI. If you do indeed wish to one day undergo a formal Maturity Level 2 appraisal, you'll need to account for the Generic Goals and Practices we discuss here. But there's another reason also, one directly tied to project management success: The Generic Goals and Practices provide your organization with the infrastructure needed to help project management work the ways it needs to.

Let's look at these Generic Goals now.

The Purpose of CMMI's Generic Goals

In our discussion of the CMMI Process Areas, we saw that each one was built on a series of Specific Goals that are typically achieved by following a set of recommended Specific Practices. The word *Specific* here is important; the Specific Goals and Practices of each Process Area are specific to its needs and purpose.

But CMMI also features Generic Goals and Generic Practices. This common set of goals and practices applies to all Process Areas. Here's a very quick example. One Generic Practice (GP 2.5) states, "Train the people performing or supporting the process as needed." If you created the kind of Project Planning process we discussed in Chapter 3, you would probably want to train your people in how that process works so they can follow it effectively. Likewise, if you created a Measurement & Analysis process similar to the one we discussed in Chapter 8, you would want to train your people in that flow as well. So, a single Generic Practice applies across your entire process program: Train people in how your processes work.

That brings us to the purpose of the Generic Goals (and their practices). When you look at them, you can see their design clearly. They are in place to help you cement your process program in place, to help it stick in the organization so that it can be used in a way that realizes its full potential. In this way, the Generic Goals support not just a process program but also a process *improvement* program.

CMMI contains five Generic Goals:

> GG 1: Achieve Specific Goals (through an institutionalized performed process)
>
> GG 2: Institutionalize a Managed Process
>
> GG 3: Institutionalize a Defined Process
>
> GG 4: Institutionalize a Quantitatively Managed Process
>
> GG 5: Institutionalize an Optimizing Process

The goals are sequential. They build on each other, adding a level of sophistication as you move up.

In the realm of CMMI, a *performed process* (GG 1) is one in which you perform the practices defined to help you achieve a Specific Goal for a Process Area. A *managed process* (GG 2) is one that you support further, through proper planning, training, resource assignments, management oversight, audits, and so on. A *defined process* moves a step further. It is a managed process that you establish as an organizational standard and for which you provide tailoring and use guidelines. A *quantitatively management process* is a defined process that you can control through sophisticated statistical and quantitative techniques. And an *optimizing process* moves the quantitative process into the highest realm, one of continuous and systematic innovation, improvement, and refinement.

Generic Goals 3, 4, and 5 are worthy and notable targets for any organization. But for the purposes of this book, they are out of scope. The focus we'll keep remains on project management, and the bulk of the benefits you'll get out of the Generic Goals relevant to project management comes with Generic Goals 1 and 2. In fact, Maturity Level 2 includes just these first two goals.

Maturity Level 2—A Recap

In Chapter 2, we presented an overview of CMMI and discussed the two official ways to implement the model: the Continuous Representation and the Staged Representation.

With the Continuous Representation, an organization is free to adopt and develop individual Process Areas in any order or sequence it chooses. Over time the idea is to increase a Process Area's capability by applying more Generic Goals and Generic Practices to it. For example, a Process Area rated at Capability Level 3 has achieved the Specific Goals and Specific Practices defined for that Process Area and has also implemented the practices defined for Generic Goals 1, 2, and 3.

With the Staged Representation, the approach is different. It's less about choice and more about structure. The Staged Representation describes a predefined approach to implementing CMMI. There are five levels defined, and the theme is maturity. The organization's process maturity increases as it moves up levels. Level 1, Initial, requires the implementation of no Process Areas. Level 2, Managed, calls for the organization to implement the seven Process Areas we discuss in this book. Level 3, Defined, requires the adoption of (about) eleven additional Process Areas. Level 4, Quantitatively Managed, adds two more; and Level 5, Optimizing, adds the final two. Twenty-two Process Areas in all. Because the Staged Representation requires the adoption of very specific Process Areas, use of all the Generic Goals is not required; there's enough overlap between the Specific Practices and the Generic Practices to support this limitation. So with the Staged Representation, Generic Goal 2 supports Maturity

Level 2 (with the assumption that Generic Goal 1 is accounted for). By adding Generic Goal 3, the organization can support Maturity Levels 3, 4, and 5.

That's why we're concerned here chiefly with Generic Goals 1 and 2. We discuss GG 2 because that's the heart of not only Maturity Level 2 but also of the Generic Goals in general. And we discuss GG 1 to set the foundation for GG 2.

The Concept of Institutionalization

The concept of *institutionalization* is essential to understanding the Generic Goals. The focus of the goals is to institutionalize use of the process program in an organization, to make use of the program the organization's way of doing business. That's the best way to ensure that the program will succeed in a company and will deliver the full range of potential benefits.

In its purest form, you can think of a company—any company—as a collection of institutionalized activities. This is the same thing we call corporate culture. It's the habits of the enterprise, those elements of business that the group insists on following, even without thinking about them. The culture always reflects what's valuable to the organization.

The purpose of the Generic Goals is to make the process program valuable to the organization, to make it an organizational habit. Without this integration into the business, even the best-designed process programs will likely fall short. The Generic Goals promote the full use and exercise of the program, across project teams and across time. This way the program becomes part of the way you do business and so can be realized as a guide and a management tool for conducting business.

Maturity Level 2 Generic Goals and Practices

There are two Generic Goals and a total of eleven Generic Practices that should be considered for implementation at Maturity Level 2 of the seven Process Areas we discuss in this book. Here is the official specification text for each of these elements.

GG 1   ACHIEVE SPECIFIC GOALS
The process supports and enables the achievement of the specific goals of the process area by transforming identifiable input work products to produce identifiable output work products.

GP 1.1   PERFORM SPECIFIC PRACTICES
Perform the specific practices of the process area to develop work products and provide services to achieve the specific goals of the process area.

GG 2   INSTITUTIONALIZE A MANAGED PROCESS
The process is institutionalized as a managed process.

GP 2.1   ESTABLISH AN ORGANIZATIONAL POLICY
Establish and maintain an organizational policy for planning and performing the process.

GP 2.2   PLAN THE PROCESS
Establish and maintain the plan for performing the process.

GP 2.3   PROVIDE RESOURCES
Provide adequate resources for performing the process, developing the work products, and providing the services of the process.

GP 2.4   ASSIGN RESPONSIBILITY
Assign responsibility and authority for performing the process, developing the work products, and providing the services of the process.

GP 2.5   TRAIN PEOPLE
Train the people performing or supporting the process as needed.

GP 2.6   MANAGE CONFIGURATIONS
Place designated work products of the process under appropriate levels of configuration management.

GP 2.7   IDENTIFY AND INVOLVE RELEVANT STAKEHOLDERS
Identify and involve the relevant stakeholders as planned.

GP 2.8   MONITOR AND CONTROL THE PROCESS
Monitor and control the process against the plan for performing the process and take appropriate corrective action.

GP 2.9   OBJECTIVELY EVALUATE ADHERENCE
Objectively evaluate adherence of the process against its process description, standards, and procedures, and address noncompliance.

GP 2.10   REVIEW STATUS WITH HIGHER LEVEL MANAGEMENT
Review the activities, status, and results of the process with higher level management and resolve issues.

GG 1: Achieve Specific Goals

The first Generic Goal is simple: Achieve Specific Goals. This makes good sense for a first Generic Goal. The idea is that if you are going to implement Process Areas, make the commitment up front to achieve the Specific Goals defined for those Process Areas. In the realm of CMMI, a team can't realize the promise of a Process Area unless it achieves the goals of that Process Area. That's the beginning premise for any organization implementing CMMI. It's also the definition of a performed process, one that realizes and supports performance to achieve the goals. In support of this, one Generic Practice is defined.

GP 1.1: Perform Specific Practices

The single practice defined for GG 1 is to perform the Specific Practices of the Process Area. That's the cleanest way to get to the Specific Goals. For each Specific Goal, CMMI defines a set of Specific Practices recommended to realize that goal and asks you to perform these practices. Take care of the practices, and the goals should take care of themselves.

A note: As you examine these practices, you might come across one or more that are not quite a fit for your organization. CMMI and the SEI anticipate this possibility, so they support the concept of Alternative Practices, those custom practices you develop in place of the defined ones to help you reach the goals. The important targets here, of course, are the goals. The practices are in place to support the goals. Whether Specific or Alternative Practices, if their shape directs the organization to the goals, the intention and spirit of CMMI have been met.

GG 2: Institutionalize a Managed Process

For GG 1, you establish a performed process; that's a process that works to achieve the Specific Goals of the selected Process Area. For GG 2, you institutionalize a managed process. A managed process is one that is built in your performed process; it can be seen as a more mature performed process. The word *managed* is an important reflection of the intention of this kind of process. A managed process is one that is consciously managed by the organization. It's a process that you make official within the organization, one that you plan for your projects, one that you train people to perform, one that you support with proper resources, and so on.

GG 2 carries with it ten Generic Practices, as described in the following subsections.

GP 2.1: Establish an Organizational Policy

It's important to understand that the true owner of an organization's process program is executive management. The program is management's accepted approach for running projects. Therefore, to endorse and promote this official position, management should create policies that endorse the program's official use. A policy is best shaped as a short document, one that summarizes the importance of, say, requirements management to the organization and then recognizes the preferred use of the requirements management processes you have developed. Because policies are issued by executive management, they carry the weight and authority to promote the use of the relevant processes across appropriate areas within the organization.

GP 2.2: Plan the Process

Because your process program is officially endorsed by organizational management, you want to make sure that process activities are properly exercised on projects. It's helpful to include the process steps in your schedules and work breakdown structures. This is the idea behind planning the process. A plan tells you who will do what and when they'll do it. Most project managers create a WBS for the jobs that will need to take place in order to create project deliverables. You should take the same approach with your process program. In fact, you can think of your process program as the project. When you bring the individual processes together, you end up with a generalized activity map of how the project will unfold. With that in place, you can add project specifics.

Planning the process will bring you two benefits. It will help create a framework that has been preapproved by executive management, and it will provide you with a sequential line of progression against which you can plan resources, measure progress, and monitor commitments.

GP 2.3: Provide Resources

"Provide Resources" is often read to mean "Provide People." And while that's a valid reading, it is not a complete one. You do need to provide people; you need to make sure that the right people are assigned to carry out the activities defined for your processes. Without people at the helm, even the best process will sit on the shelf collecting dust. But the organization needs to provide more than just people. Here resources include the right funding, tools, facilities, and supplies needed to implement your processes. This is an important practice to keep in mind because it's easy for many organizations to overlook. An effective process program is not simply a collection of effective processes. It represents a commitment by the company to support the program from project to project over time.

There are many ways you can show that you're providing the right resources. Your documented process program is a resource in itself. If you have a process program budget, that counts, too. Official staff assignments, office space, dedicated computer space—all this adds up to the set of resources the organization has set aside to give the program the support and structure it needs to work.

GP 2.4: Assign Responsibility

This practice is linked to GP 2.3 in that it specifically calls out people as a resource. Here you assign responsibility for executing process activities. In other words, you ensure that your processes will be used on projects by explicitly assigning team members to carry them out. Since your different processes are probably fairly task specific, you may end up assigning different jobs to different people. But nothing says that one person can't handle multiple roles or that jobs can't be shared—do whatever works best for your team. The idea is to treat process execution in the same way you would other project-related tasks.

You can account for this practice any number of ways. For example, you can create staff assignment forms on which you assign functional roles, including those related to process. You can send out e-mails to team members notifying them of their project duties. You can include a functional matrix in your project plan. The key to all of these options is that they are explicit actions. The responsibility is not implied, nor is it left to personal initiative. It's a direct and accountable role within the project team.

GP 2.5: **Train People**

In my opinion, training is one of the biggest success factors surrounding any process program. In fact, one of the biggest reasons that process programs fail to reach their potential is that the people weren't trained to use the program. So this Generic Practice is in place to position your teams to use the program properly and fully, in ways that will deliver the program's value to the project and to the organization.

You can take care of training in many different ways. On-the-job training is a valid approach, although it might not be the most effective one. You can employ new-employee orientations. You can conduct formal classroom-based training sessions. You can use coaching and mentoring, pairing inexperienced team members with more experienced ones. You can sponsor computer-based training, offsite training seminars, or quarterly reviews and refresher mini-classes.

A good training approach will go a long way toward ensuring that your process program is used properly across the organization. It will help you develop an informed and productive user base, and it will promote continuous improvement through intelligent and critical use.

GP 2.6: Manage Configurations

We discussed the Configuration Management Process Area in Chapter 6. The general purpose of Configuration Management is to protect the integrity of work products as they evolve over the life of a project. Evolving work products is a given on just about all projects: Plans change, requirements may change, resource levels and personnel are subject to change. One of the key jobs of project management is to keep the configuration of key project products current and up to date. The value of your status reports, progress reports, and management decisions relies on this kind of integrity.

The same approach should be taken with your process program. If you have built a Maturity Level 2 program using the seven Process Areas discussed in this book, you will have a process program made up in all likelihood of process descriptions, forms, templates, procedures, and other artifacts. To make sure that these tools all stay in sync with the current needs of the organization, you should apply a degree of configuration management discipline to them. This might be handled in a simple way, through some form of document version control, or you might elect to subject your whole program to formal configuration management, housing the assets in a configuration management system and then checking them in and out as needed. The rationale behind either approach is clear: You want to ensure that your project teams use the right versions of each process set. Configuration management is the cleanest way to meet this goal.

GP 2.7: Identify and Involve Relevant Stakeholders

Stakeholder involvement is an important part of successful project management. One of the main jobs of a project manager is to communicate with team members, customers, and internal management. These are the three most common groups of stakeholders, but your project may have others. Stakeholders are often viewed as being tied to certain project deliverables or work activities. Because their involvement is essential to project success, you should identify them early in the project lifecycle and then make sure you involve them when their key points arise.

Stakeholder involvement takes on an added dimension with a process program. The processes by which you will run the project define a series of activities that teams will undertake to produce project-specific deliverables and milestones. This being the case, you will find that certain people have a stake in making sure that certain processes are executed as planned. As an example, look at the Project Planning Process Area. Because this process set will produce cost estimates, schedules, and resource levels, you'll probably want to identify your customers and management as stakeholders here, and you will most likely want to involve them in planning assumptions and decisions. The same is true for the other major processes you'll exercise on the project. Take a look at each, then analyze who will execute the process activities and who may rely on the activities or may want to know about their progress. Identify these people as stakeholders, and ensure their involvement at relevant times during the project.

GP 2.8: **Monitor and Control the Process**

One of the real advantages of managing projects by using a formalized process program is that, over time, the process will become the project. What I mean by this is that the steps embedded in each part of your process program will link together to help shape overall project activity. Many companies that operate under CMMI, ISO 9001, or ITIL use their process activities as a foundation for building starting templates of work breakdown structures. And why not? If you're going to follow a process, you're going to follow a defined path to an established goal. To do this effectively, your project managers will want to monitor progress along the way and make any adjustments needed to ensure that the project stays on course. If you monitor and control your processes, you'll probably find that by default you are monitoring and controlling project progress as well.

This should not be seen as double duty: monitoring the process and the project. It's an integrated activity, and it works best as an integrated activity. The key is to build your project lifecycle on the structure of your process program, to wed your WBS to process activities. This will then set in place a fixed work direction for your project. Monitoring and controlling this direction takes care of both process activities and project progress.

GP 2.9: Objectively Evaluate Adherence

In Chapter 9, we looked at Process & Product Quality Assurance. This Process Area provides the oversight arm of your process program. It supports the use of auditing and compliance reporting. That's important for three reasons. First, the process program is an official program within the IT shop, so it's important to have the shop periodically check to make sure people are following the program as it has been defined. Second, project management should have built a good portion of the schedule and WBS around the process activities, so from a project management viewpoint, it's important to regularly check to make sure the team members are staying on process and thereby staying on plan. Third, you will not be able to establish a foundation for process improvement if your teams aren't using the program in a consistent and repeatable way. That's where PPQA and this Generic Practice come into play. Your PPQA program should probably include checkpoints for each of the Process Areas you have addressed in your program. Perhaps you'll elect a light audit approach and check up only on the major activities. Perhaps you'd prefer a deeper approach, in which case you'll look at a finer level of activities. However you approach it, objectively evaluating adherence to process activities provides a valuable level of insight into the use and value of your process program.

GP 2.10: Review Status with Higher Level Management

Here is the final Generic Practice for a Maturity Level 2 program. This practice recommends that you periodically review the status of your process efforts with senior management. I've already mentioned that the organization's executive managers are the true owners of the process program. That program holds the activities, regimens, and protocols that the organization wants to see executed for the various projects under way in the shop. Because senior management owns the program, it's important for project management to periodically report on how well the program is serving the organization. Is the program efficient and effective? Does it contribute in tangible ways to project success? Or is it cumbersome? Is it broken in places? Does it need some additional attention?

One theme I have tried to repeat now and again in this book is the value of process improvement as it relates to project management success. A good process program will go a long way toward ensuring that success, but it needs to be founded on a basis of continuous assessment and improvement. Management must be vigilant, always on the lookout for opportunities to make the program better, stronger, more able to meet organizational goals of performance, quality, and efficiency. This final practice, GP 2.10, helps make that a regular part of program use and management.

The Benefits of the Generic Goals

CMMI puts forth the Generic Goals as a method to help you institutionalize the elements of your process program. The Generic Goals (and the Generic Practices under them) establish the infrastructure that helps your program take hold in an organization. Everyone has heard stories of great process programs that sit on the shelf. These programs may have been thoroughly researched, carefully designed, and well documented. But when it came to rolling the programs out on a broad scale, the momentum stalled. These stories are common, and they tend to point out the importance of the Generic Goals. These goals, in effect, make it a point of policy to use the program; they set up the program as the way to do business. They ensure that you train your people to use the processes in your program, that you include process activities in overall project plans, that you monitor process use, that you involve relevant stakeholders, and so on. Through this infrastructure, you embed an organizational commitment to use the program. And that's the key to success for any process program.

That's the benefit from an organizational viewpoint. But the Generic Goals—and in particular for this discussion, Generic Goals 1 and 2—also play a direct part in the success of your individual projects. In short, you can use the goals to plan projects in a consistent way, to manage them in a consistent way, and to establish common expectations concerning communications, lifecycles, and progress tracking. Let's take a quick look at each of these benefits.

Project Planning Consistency

The strength of using Generic Goals 1 and 2 for project planning is that they recommend a series of targets and practices that greatly aid consistency in planning. One of the challenges of any IT shop is for project managers to take planning out of the realm of personal approach and supplant it with an organizational approach. That can be a tricky thing to pull off if the shop doesn't have an official alternative to the personal approach. But a well-designed process program can be that alternative. When the organization adopts its process program as the official way to do business, project management has access to what you could call a template for planning a project's future.

Through the Generic Goals, the organization establishes solid planning boundaries within which project management can operate. These boundaries spring from the Generic Practices. They state, among other things, that process activities will be planned and scheduled, that resources needed to execute the processes will be accounted for across the project teams, that relevant stakeholders will be involved in project activities, and so on. The value here is that the process program becomes the foundation for the project itself. And if all your project managers, working on different and diverse projects, settle on this as a common foundation, planning will be conducted in a consistent and predictable manner. That's the basis for making your planning activities more effective and efficient over time, thus contributing not only to project success but also to organizational success.

Project Management Consistency

Another benefit to be derived from implementing the Generic Goals is project management consistency. Here's another area where the personal approach often takes precedence. In organizations that lack formalized processes, you'll often find a heavy reliance on the individual talents of your project managers. Individual initiative, judgment, experience, and energy are required to carry the day. To be sure, talented project managers are needed for project success in any organization. But the lack of an organizational approach to project management means there is little organizational capability here; if the talented folks move on, the organization is left in the cold.

Adopting the Generic Goals is a way to embed a project management capability within the organization. When your project managers begin to account for these goals in project management activities, you'll find that projects begin to be managed within a similar framework and a common set of base targets. You'll see that progress is monitored and controlled with process activities in mind. Communication with stakeholders and management is a regular occurrence. Work products are properly managed. Accountability and responsibilities are clear, and reporting and status management are regularly assured. Through all of these elements, you will begin to establish an organizational approach to project management that sets a common bar for performance that everyone in your shop can work toward.

Standardized Expectations

Finally, using the Generic Goals delivers a common set of project management expectations that will need to be endorsed and promoted by organizational management, and this will boost the ability of you and your project teams to meet their business objectives. For example, the Generic Goals make use of the process program a matter of organizational policy. Executive management mandates its use, so executive management therefore takes on the obligation of supporting its use. The Generic Practices under the Generic Goals promote the provision of adequate resources to project teams, helping to reduce reliance on unrealistic expectations and squeeze-and-puff team assignments. The practices also support the use of training to ensure that your team members are indeed ready to contribute in positive ways. The practices help ensure that project management will always have the ear of executive management. And they set in place a common base of elements that, taken together, can make up a definition of project success. This definition can then serve as a basis for standardized expectations of how a project is to be planned, how it is to be managed, and what success factors will be evaluated to determine its ultimate level of performance.

Chapter 11

An Integrated Approach to Project Management Success

The foundation of our approach to project management rests in a blend of disciplines. We utilize recommendations found in ISO 9001, CMMI, and the PMBOK to shape and direct our project management efforts. Our aim is not to conform to the bounds of one or all programs as much as it is to borrow what's best for us from each.

Rod Parnell, Director/PMO, WellWorth USA
Banking and finance management systems

As a discipline, project management has been around since before the time of the Roman Empire. The aqueducts, public theaters, highways and so on are all great examples of advanced project management at work. Tax dollars funding these projects had to be accounted for. Workers had to be paid, fed, and in many cases transported. Plans had to be copied, maintained, and distributed. In fact, today, with all its history, project management in the field of construction may be the most mature form of the discipline. In the realm of technology development, however, the field is not as mature.

There are many kinds of technology organizations—system shops, software shops, integrators. In many of these you'll discover that project managers are little more than transmogrified administrators, forever chasing after status and reporting from behind the curve. In others you'll find that project managers are linebackers, charged with plowing through obstacles and setbacks, authorized to push toward the goal with little else than brute force. The two approaches are quite different, but the atmosphere that generates each is the same. Shops that rely on administrators or linebackers most often do so in environments pretty much free of project management process. And in the absence of process, they have no real alternative but to rely on individuals. The better the individual (or the luckier), the better the chance for success.

Of course, that's not a professional way to run a business—not when millions and millions of dollars might easily be banked on any one technology project. So more and more shops these days are recognizing the value in project management and operating with an approach that embraces the kinds of practices Caesar Tiberius endorsed: planning, oversight, control, and communications. Today the *discipline* of project management is making itself known in technology shops, and with that comes the introduction of process—in one form or another. Here, in the final chapter of this book, we now revisit the advantages of process and the advantages that the SEI's CMMI can deliver for project management success.

Project Management Disciplines

Many well-known associations and professional organizations promote professional project management practices. For example, the International Association of Project and Program Managers offers a Certified Project Manager (CPM) certification. The American Academy of Project Managers offers the Master Project Manager (MPM) certification. Perhaps the best-known, at least in technology circles, is the Project Management Institute (PMI) and its Project Management Professional (PMP) certification.

Each of these associations publishes its own body of knowledge; the PMI's is the PMBOK. These tomes contain considerations and practices deemed to fall within the responsibility domains of project managers. The idea behind all these is management through reliable and predictable practices. If you hire a PMP or a CPM or an MPM, you should be able to count on that person to apply this knowledge in ways beneficial to your projects (administrating and linebacking aside). In theory at least, a project manager wielding a PMP should have the ability to deliver on the discipline of project management for your organization. That's a definite plus, especially if your shop respects the scope and content of the corresponding body of knowledge. But that turns out to be only half of the equation. If you drop a PMP into an administrating culture, you will end up with a highly qualified administrator. If you drop a PMP into an off-the-bench-and-charge culture, you may end up with a very elegant linebacker. But if you take the theory and practices that should be found under the hood of a PMP and place him or her in a process-driven environment—say, one based on CMMI—you will have an environment that promotes, supports, and enhances the mission of formalized project management.

And that has been the message running through the threads of this book.

CMMI without PMP (or CPM or MPM)

Another message I introduced at the start of this book should probably be revisited now. That is the pure view that CMMI, and specifically those Process Areas described for Maturity Level 2, can be used to promote and manage project success even in the absence of PMI programs or PMPs. The project management organizations and associations that exist today are no doubt viable and valuable contributors to the industry. But not every technology shop is going to operate using their philosophies. In the same vein, I recognize that not all shops are going to embrace CMMI—or ISO 9001, or Six Sigma, or any of the other popular process management programs. So the message I want to stress and then flavor with the strength of CMMI is that the single, unfettered key to project management success probably is process, process in some form, whether proprietary or borrowed. You don't *have* to have PMPs in place in order to run successful projects, and you don't *have* to have CMMI in place to run successful projects. But I would argue that you do have to have a *way* to achieve success, and that way—whatever it is—will need to be built on process.

The characteristic I like about the SEI's Capability Maturity Model Integration is that many of the goals and practices it promotes have direct bearing on effective project management. They establish mechanisms that not only enhance general operational efficiencies but also establish direct and tangible project governance guidelines.

Am I saying that CMMI is a clear-cut substitute for the PMI's PMBOK? No. But I am saying something related to that. I'm saying that in the absence of an organizational way—a process program based on, say, CMMI—the seeds of wisdom contained in the PMBOK will find little ground to take root in. So if you were to establish an order or priority as to how you might build up your own project management capability, I would advise using the structure shown in Figure 11–1.

At the first level is a decision to seek effective management not through sole reliance on individual performance but on the design and implementation of a process program geared to the organization's project management needs. Project management success needs to be based on a foundation of process management.

At the next level—built on and enhancing the first—is the adoption of the seven Process Areas described for CMMI Maturity Level 2. Here the organization takes the recommendations concerning the goals and practices described under CMMI and shapes a customized and

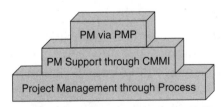

Figure 11–1: *A potential view of how process, CMMI, and PMP practices can build on each other*

tactical set of tools, procedures, and artifacts to support the specific needs of the shop.

With this in place, the capstone (so to speak) can be added. This is the integration of PMBOK techniques and the acquisition of trained PMP professionals who will operate in the universe of the process program, bringing two things together to work toward project success: their experience as disciples of disciplined project management and their abilities to harness the organization's process program to the greater good of the various development groups.

So, commitment to process first, then the adoption of CMMI, and finally the integration of select PMBOK philosophies.

As an added benefit, let's revisit the concept that CMMI and the PMBOK have a high degree of correlation and can be used to greatly complement one another.

CMMI Maturity Level 2 and the PMBOK

There are all kinds of technology projects, so there are all kinds of ways to define successful projects. The PMI's PMBOK promotes a vision that includes full-cycle control of scope, costs, schedule, resources, and quality. If you can deliver within the parameters established and agreed upon for each, you can say that you have a successful project.

That's the view of the PMI's PMBOK and, in my experience, that's the view of CMMI Maturity Level 2. As a process improvement framework, CMMI sets in place goals and practices that add cumulative degrees of consistency, predictability, and capability to any technology shop. At Maturity Level 2, the model recommends that the organization adopt seven Process Areas: Project Planning, Project Monitoring & Control, Requirements Management, Configuration Management, Supplier Agreement Management, Measurement & Analysis, and Process & Product Quality Assurance. The goals and practices found in these Process Areas directly support the needs and structure of formalized project management. They also directly complement implementation of the PMBOK across technology projects.

The PMBOK features nine Knowledge Areas. These nine Knowledge Areas map very cleanly to the seven CMMI Process Areas. And the PMBOK promotes five Process Groups that also map to CMMI's goals and practices.

Let's do a quick mapping ourselves.

Process Groups

The PMBOK Process Groups represent five areas where project management processes can come into play during a development effort. In a way, these five groups establish a project lifecycle, moving from Initiation through Closure. Table 11–1 shows the relationships between these five PMBOK Process Groups and the related CMMI Process Areas.

Table 11–1: *A Generalized Relationship Map between CMMI and PMBOK Structures*

CMMI Process Area	PMBOK Process Group
Project Planning	Initiation, Planning
Project Monitoring & Control	Execution, Control
Requirements Management	Initiation, Planning, Execution
Configuration Management	Initiation, Control
Supplier Agreement Management	Planning, Execution, Control
Measurement & Analysis	Execution, Control, Closure
Process & Product Quality Assurance	Execution, Closure
Generic Practices	Initiation, Planning, Execution, Closure

Initiation

During Initiation, the scope of the project is established. This typically includes the development or analysis of requirements, which can then be baselined. A project charter is also usually set in place here, along with project resources, facilities, and so on. Three CMMI Process Areas can be used to support the focus of Initiation. Requirements Management helps you establish and maintain scope. Configuration Management helps you establish and maintain baselines. Project Planning helps you set a project charter in place. Also, the Generic Practices help establish the resources and infrastructure needs of the project.

Planning

Once Initiation is complete (and the scope of the project is well defined), full planning can begin. Work breakdown structures, budgets, and schedules are established, reviewed, and approved. The CMMI Process Area of Project Planning directly supports the focus of Planning, and the Generic Practices lend to this focus by providing for planning of the process activities the project will employ, including those related to the other Process Areas, such as Supplier Agreement Management and Process and Product Quality Assurance.

Execution and Control

These two groups typically operate in parallel. Planned activities are executed and controlled to achieve the project objectives. All seven of the Level 2 Process Areas can contribute to one or both of these groups. Project Planning can be used when you need to revisit plans and schedules. Project Monitoring & Control provides for appropriate project oversight, reporting, and communication. Requirements Management provides degrees of scope control. Configuration Management protects the integrity of evolving work products. Supplier Agreement Management controls suppliers external to the project team. Measurement & Analysis provides the raw and calculated data to manage by. And Process & Product Quality Assurance adds an extra layer of internal oversight to ensure project success. As in Initiation and Planning, the Generic Goals provide the infrastructure to institutionalize these different activities.

Closure

At Closure, final work products are delivered, lessons learned are discussed, and resources are released. Two of the CMMI Process Areas can contribute here. Measurement & Analysis can provide the information that reveals true project performance. Process & Product Quality Assurance can be used to measure the effectiveness of process performance for the project as a whole. And the Generic Practices once again help make sure these points of emphasis remain in focus.

Knowledge Areas

In addition to the five Process Groups, the PMBOK also features nine Knowledge Areas. Similar to Process Areas, the Knowledge Areas contain techniques and considerations for managing the attributes of project work. The CMMI Level 2 Process Areas can be seen as complementing these Knowledge Areas in a cross-matrix fashion. Table 11–2 shows their relationships.

Table 11–2: *Relationships between Process Areas and Knowledge Areas*

CMMI Process Area	*PMBOK Knowledge Area*
Project Planning	All nine Knowledge Areas
Project Monitoring & Control	All nine Knowledge Areas
Requirements Management	Scope
Configuration Management	Scope and Quality
Supplier Agreement Management	Procurement
Measurement & Analysis	All nine Knowledge Areas
Process & Product Quality Assurance	Integration, Quality
Generic Goals	Integration

Integration

This first Knowledge Area addresses issues that impact the operation of the project team as a cohesive unit: integration of expectations, of resources and tools, of goals and objectives, and so on. Integration can be seen as the wrapper that enfolds the other eight Knowledge Areas and brings an added collective value from them. CMMI takes a similar view with the Level 2 Generic Goal and its Practices. These practices institutionalize activities across the life of the project, integrating separate elements of process and product management into a single, cohesive program.

Scope

Scope deals with constraining the degree of work to be performed on the project while providing for required change. This is a classic consideration of project management and is usually expressed as a form of requirements management and change control. CMMI addresses this through Requirements Management, Configuration Management, and Project Monitoring & Control, and to a lesser extent portions of the other four Maturity Level 2 Process Areas.

Time

Time deals with the creation of the WBS and schedule management, a second classic consideration of project management. Maintaining the project schedule not only ensures the timeline but also protects issues of scope, cost, and quality. CMMI addresses this through Project Planning (where the schedule and WBS are established) and Project Monitoring & Control (where schedule parameters are continually monitored).

Cost

Cost is budget management and represents a third classic consideration of project management. Keeping the project running on budget is almost always viewed as a critical success factor. CMMI addresses this through Project Planning (where the budget is established) and Project Monitoring & Control (where budget parameters are continually monitored).

Quality

Quality deals with performance expectations in line with organizational standards and customer requirements. CMMI's Process & Product Quality Assurance sets in place practices to help you monitor project performance from a quality standpoint. In fact, CMMI as a process improvement framework is strategically focused to help you define, manage, and improve production steps that influence quality.

Human Resources

Human Resources deals with the proper and appropriate assignment of project personnel, including analysis of technical skills, performance requirements, and training needs. Resource provisions, responsibility domains, and training likewise are addressed by the Level 2 Generic Practices.

Communications

Communications deals with providing the right flow of information to the various stakeholder groups connected to a project. This typically includes project team members, customers, and executive management. Project Planning and CMMI's Generic Practices for Level 2 provide similar communications practices, such as ensuring stakeholder involvement and communicating with senior management on a periodic basis.

Risk

As an independent Process Area in CMMI, Risk Management is usually not introduced in full form until Maturity Level 3 (although when using the Continuous Representation you can bring it in whenever you want). This PMBOK Knowledge Area deals with the identification, management, and mitigation of risk across the life of the project. At Level 2, Project Planning and Project Monitoring & Control provide for the tracking and management of risks and ongoing issues.

Procurement

Procurement deals with the coordinated integration of suppliers into the project mix. Supplier Agreement Management has direct bearing here. SAM provides for definition of acquisition types, establishment of balanced contracts and agreements, periodic in-process inspections, product acceptance, and product component integration.

Conclusion

CMMI is a process improvement framework that directly supports project management success. Process programs based on CMMI, particularly those that adopt the seven Process Areas recommended at Maturity Level 2, can be designed to promote project success across any technology development shop, either alone or in conjunction with such well-known project management philosophies as the PMI's PMBOK.

The term *project management success* can mean many different things to different organizations. But when you seek to pursue, foster, and achieve success, you invariably distill this objective to its essence. If I were to describe project management success based on my own experiences with technology shops, based on my work with project management professionals, and based on input from executive management, I would define it as an outcome of predictability best achieved through the conscious pursuit of four objectives:

1. A sustained common understanding of what the organization wants to achieve

2. Application of control techniques to keep that understanding intact

3. A willingness among stakeholders to be flexible with the give-and-take of project evolution

4. A dedication to open and constructive communications across the life of the project

CMMI Maturity Level 2 promotes all four of these goals across its Process Areas. In this concluding section, let's take a quick look at each.

Understanding

Perhaps the most visible sign of success-in-peril is a noticeable lack of understanding among project members as to what the objectives, mission, and goals of the project really are. Weak, conflicting, shifting, or misdirected understandings can threaten the chances of success for even the most straightforward of projects. CMMI realizes this and at Level 2 seeks to set in place practices to establish and maintain common understandings among team members, management, customers, and other relevant stakeholders.

The specification spells out practices to plan upcoming work, to review those plans with the people impacted by them, and to seek from these parties common commitment to the plans. The specification also calls for project management to revise plans, requirements, and other scope documents as they change over time and to keep the project base informed about these changes. CMMI also promotes the regular involvement of both internal and external stakeholders as well as regular communications with senior management concerning project status. Taken together, these focal points maintain a common understanding of project essentials across different project parties who need to rely on their successful realization.

Control

Next is control. Call it management, oversight, or mission support, the idea is the same: You control the outcome of the project by regularly monitoring project activity and work products. By keeping an eye on the small things, the large things (success being the largest of those) should not require an inordinate amount of attention. Naturally, as a process improvement framework, CMMI features plenty of practices that promote project control. There are recommendations for monitoring and oversight, for effective version control and configuration management of work products, for the collection of progress metrics, for the regular reporting of status, for risk management, and for open feedback from relevant parties. Process Areas such as Project Monitoring &

Control, Configuration Management, and Supplier Agreement Management are structured around these elements of control.

Flexibility

Flexibility can be seen as both an operational and a cultural trait of a development project. Good project management (actually, good management in general) promotes an atmosphere of flexibility, of give-and-take during the life of a project. No project will ever go exactly as planned. Business needs change, resources may fluctuate, other priorities might make themselves known. And so adjustments will have to be made. A project has a stronger chance of being successful—of everyone arriving at the same destination—when exactitude and rigidity take a back seat to cooperation and intelligent compromise. This degree of flexibility will help your project endure the winds of change and the pressures of evolving business objectives. CMMI, being a process improvement framework, appreciates and supports the need for flexibility, emphasizing this through practices that promote documentation, reviews, collection of data, regular reporting, and communication.

Communication

A major reason why projects drift off course or expectations waver is lack of communication. Failure to communicate will inevitably place a project at risk. As noted earlier, communication deals with providing the right flow of information to the various stakeholder groups connected to a project: project team members, customers, and executive management. For a project manager, communicating is a priority job, and it's the job of the project manager to establish a project environment that promotes free, full, and open communications. CMMI takes this same view and sets in place Generic Practices that promote stakeholder involvement and communicating with senior management on a regular basis.

Each of these four attributes, when securely in place, will help push your project to a conclusion everyone can embrace. And CMMI supports each of these success attributes. CMMI also provides for a high degree of organizational interpretation, so you can shape your process program to the exact needs of your technology shop. When you take these factors in mind and then apply proven project management disciplines, you'll end up with a management formula that can better ensure success for all your technology projects.

Index

A

307

M

V

W

BOOKS ONLINE
ENABLED

THIS BOOK IS SAFARI ENABLED

INCLUDES FREE 45-DAY ACCESS TO THE ONLINE EDITION

The Safari® Enabled icon on the cover of your favorite technology book means the book is available through Safari Bookshelf. When you buy this book, you get free access to the online edition for 45 days.

Safari Bookshelf is an electronic reference library that lets you easily search thousands of technical books, find code samples, download chapters, and access technical information whenever and wherever you need it.

TO GAIN 45-DAY SAFARI ENABLED ACCESS TO THIS BOOK:

● Go to **http://www.prenhallprofessional.com/safarienabled**

● Complete the brief registration form

● Enter the coupon code found in the front of this book on the "Copyright" page

If you have difficulty registering on Safari Bookshelf or accessing the online edition, please e-mail customer-service@safaribooksonline.com.

PRENTICE
HALL